GRAPHIC ARTISTS GUILD

Graphic Artists Guild's Directory of Illustration

Madison Square Press, New York

ISBN 0-8230-2112-2
ISSN 81-80062

Distributors to the trade in the United States and Canada:
Watson-Guptill Publications
1515 Broadway, New York, N.Y. 10036

Distributed throughout the rest of the world by:
Hearst Publications International
105 Madison Avenue, New York, N.Y. 10016

Publisher:
Madison Square Press
10 East 23rd Street, New York, N.Y. 10010

Printed in Japan

Thanks to Paul Basista and the Board of Directors of The Graphic Artists Guild, with special thanks to Jeff Seaver for his efforts on behalf of this project and to Michael Doret for the use of his Graphic Artists Guild logo.

Edited by Jill Bossert
Designed by Walter Bernard and
Milton Glaser, WBMG, Inc.
Assistant Designer, Shelley R. Fisher
Cover Design by Mirko Ilić
Production Coordinator, Jason Taback

The Book

It was the most natural thing in the world for the Graphic Artists Guild and Madison Square Press to join forces. Illustrators, and anything that concerns them, concerns Madison Square Press. As publishers of the *Society of Illustrators Annuals of American Illustration, The New Illustration, The Illustrator in America,* and *Legal Guide for the Visual Artist,* it's clear that illustration is a discipline close to our hearts. That one of us was an illustrator for over 30 years and an ex-president of the Guild doesn't hurt, not to mention the other was counsel for the Guild and is author of *Legal Guide for the Visual Artist.*

To be an illustrator can be a wonderful thing, making art and being rewarded for it is the stuff of dreams for many. But to imagine that it is a glamorous business is a notion from the past. That it is a business is unquestionable. *Directory 5* is a tool of the marketplace, for both buyer and seller. The days of the four-martini lunch are gone and time is always fleeting, so the *Directory* serves as an instant introduction between artist and client.

We know the kind of quality illustrators demand, we know the marketplace that will best serve them and will be best served by them. And though one need not be a member of the Graphic Artists Guild to be included in *Directory 5*, we believe in the Guild's principles – we helped to formulate some of them. Everyone in the business benefits from fair practices and high standards.

It's a funny business, illustration. The vagaries of taste, timing, fashion, client idiosyncrasies ("My wife hates yellow...change the background."), and financial considerations are all part of the equation that brings illustrator and art buyer together. *Directory 5* provides choices for the buyer in this complex market.

Tad Crawford and Gerald McConnell

Publishers

List Of Artists

List Of Artists

List Of Artists

List Of Artists

The Guild

The Graphic Artists Guild celebrated its twentieth birthday last year. Two decades, in this frenetic age, is a long time – long enough, you might think, for the Guild to have defined itself, if not to have settled into a nice comfortable groove. But the Guild resists easy categorization, just as its members do.

Are we a labor organization? Today, we wear that label with a little discomfort, but that's clearly what the Guild's founders had in mind. They were a group of specialized illustrators, employed by ad agencies in Detroit. Maybe they saw unionized assembly-line workers getting paid more to bolt together motown iron than they were for creating polished illustrations of the finished product. Their efforts, culminating in the Guild's one and only strike (against Campbell Ewald in 1971) were not notably successful, but they did organize a branch in New York, which grew and prospered while the Detroit parent declined. It was the New York chapter that became the nucleus of the present Graphic Artists Guild.

Today there are also active chapters in Boston, Buffalo, Vermont, Atlanta, Central Florida, Indianapolis, Denver, Los Angeles – and a substantial "at-large" chapter for members unserved by the geographical chapters. New chapters appear to be coalescing in several cities. We've become the largest artist's advocacy organization in the history of the United States.

The Guild has hung on to its "union" status because it affords us the freedom to engage in a powerful and wide-ranging advocacy for our members' interests, beyond the "educational" and "philanthropic" purposes of other kinds of associations. And of course we do, from time to time, engage in true collective bargaining, most recently in the case of Children's Television Workshop, where our members won freedom from "work-for-hire" contracts as well as other concessions.

Since the majority of our members are employed on a free-lance basis, a form of employment that's old hat for artists but which seems to be a wave of the future for other kinds of workers, the Guild is in a sense at the vanguard of the labor movement. If we can figure out how to represent "self-employed" free-lance workers effectively, we'll provide a valuable model for other organizations concerned with the loss of traditional manufacturing jobs and the growth of service-sector, high-tech, cottage industry. The CTW negotiations show that it's possible to establish a sort of umbrella which protects free-lancers from the worst abuses they've endured, while leaving them free to negotiate individual contracts with their clients.

The Guild's constitution spells out the organization's purposes and objectives. We are mandated "to advance and extend the economic and social interests of (our) members" and to "promote and maintain high professional standards of ethics and practice and to secure the conformance of all buyers, users, sellers and employers to established standards." The Constitution explicitly endorses the articles of the *Code of Fair Practice* formulated by the Joint Ethics Committee as the expression of such professional standards of business relations. You'll find a copy of the Code on page xiii of this book. The pursuit of those objectives has led us to act, by turns, like an educational institution, a professional association, a social club and a political lobby.

A major portion of our energy goes into the ongoing effort to educate members and nonmembers alike about the *business* of being a graphic artist. Both nationally and at the chapter level, we run regular programs on negotiation and pricing strategies, tax issues, self-promotion, time management, and all the other essential business skills that are not, by and large, taught in the art schools. The Guild provides a means for experienced artists to share their understanding of the advertising and publishing markets with young artists, and a way for artists of every level of attainment to share concerns and information. Many artists initially join the Guild for the information and "networking" it offers, and find themselves drawn into other activities as well.

We publish the Graphic Artists Guild Handbook, *Pricing and Ethical Guidelines*, perhaps the most important industry reference of the graphic arts profession. Now in its sixth edition, P.E.G.s has grown from a small pamphlet to a large-format 200-page book, with the result of careful surveys of pricing levels in every corner of the graphic arts, as well as extensive information on professional practices, business management, and sample contracts. The publication of P.E.G.s is a massive project, requiring the volunteer cooperation of hundreds of Guild members.

Some Guild chapters directly assist their members in the marketing of their work. In New York, the Guild's referral service "Placement Center" helps to bring artist and client together. In Boston, annual "See Parties" place work of many illustrators before a steady stream of buyers who come to survey the talent available. Indianapolis and Vermont run graphics-industry trade shows which bring all kinds of illustrators and designers, as well as color separators, typesetters, printers, and other members of the graphic arts community together at one time. The response of artists and buyers to these shows has been very enthusiastic.

But it's not enough to help artist-members to cope with the market as it is. When the market stacks the deck unfairly against artists, we're determined to do something about it. The recent exponential growth of the use of "work-for-hire" contracts by publishers and other buyers is a case in point. There's an innocuous-sounding provision in the copyright law, originally intended to vest ownership of copyright in employers when artists are conventionally employed. Salary, benefits and vacations are perhaps a fair trade for copyright ownership. Somehow this "work-made-for-hire" provision has engulfed many artists who receive none of the benefits of traditional employment. "Work-for-hire" contracts are often presented on a take-it-or-leave-it basis, sometimes even after work is done. "You want to get paid? Sign." An individual artist, faced with such an ultimatum from a corporate client, has little choice.

While we make every effort to help clients understand why the surrendering of authorship is offensive to artists, the Guild realizes that the real remedies are legislative. Clearly, the "work-for-hire" provision should be made applicable only to artists who receive a regular paycheck and other employee benefits as compensation.

The Guild was instrumental in forming the Copyright Justice Coalition, which brings 43 separate arts organizations together in one voice of protest. We helped to write a bill, the Copyright Justice Act (S. 1223), which was introduced last year by Senator Thad Cochran of Mississippi. Guild members have barraged their congresspeople with letters and telegrams, testified in hearings, and financially supported the Coalition's lobbyist. We've published an extensive collection of artists' testimonies about the copyright issue in the form of a *Special Edition* of the Guild Newsletter. It's the most vivid presentation of artists' feelings about "work-for-hire;" copies are available from the national office.

Legislative struggles require patience and determination, but these qualities abound in the Guild. We're not new to the process; we've successfully promoted artists-rights legislation in four states, and we've made our voice heard in Washington before. We'll eventually win, because what we want is truly in the nation's best interest. As was strongly acknowledged in the U.S. Constitution, creativity itself is encouraged when creators profit from their own inventions.

Today artists are faced with an even more urgent legislative priority: the new tax law. "Uniform Tax Capitalization," intended to put an end to the sham tax shelters of movies never made and books never written, was established with legislation so broadly and imprecisely written that it appears to forbid artists and other creators to deduct the expenses of creating artwork *until it is sold* and then only in proportion to the percentage of the work's total value received. Artists, when not saddled with "work-for-hire" contracts, sell limited reproduction rights, not the work itself; the total value of the work will not be known for years. And artists spend time and money working out ideas in pieces which are never sold – surely legitimate business expense, but apparently not deductible under the new tax law. If allowed to stand, these rules will drive many artists and other creators out of business. Creative works are not manufactured products, with fixed and easily calculated value. To tax them as if they were so many wingnuts or shoelaces is wrong.

The Guild has once more applied its coalition-building skills to this issue, spearheading the formation of Artists for Tax Equity. We have hired a lobbyist in the coalition's behalf and members of both houses of Congress are getting a lot of mail from artists and designers across the country. We know that we have some allies in the Congress; we hope that in this age of deficit-consciousness, they'll help us convince their colleagues to tax artists fairly.

The Graphic Artists Guild appears to be poised for major growth in the months and years ahead. Artists in several cities have expressed strong interest in forming new chapters. We're planning a first-ever national members' convention. New ideas abound, and new energy is welling up. Whether you label the Guild as "union" or "professional association" or "artists advocacy organization" doesn't matter, ultimately. It's what we *do* that matters, and we're doing a lot.

Michael Patterson
Vice President for Publications
Graphic Artists Guild

Code of Fair Practice

for the Graphics Communications Industry

In 1945 a group of artists and art directors in the City of New York, concerned with the growing abuses, misunderstandings, and disregard of uniform standards of conduct in their field, met to consider possibilities for improvement. They reached the conclusion that any effort, to be successful, must start with the most widespread backing, and further that it must be a continuing, not a temporary, activity. On their recommendation, three leading New York art organizations together established and financed a committee known as the Joint Ethics Committee.

In 1978 the expanded committee representing six organizations revised the code to include the new communications industries. This code has been published in response to the many requests for information concerning the operation and scope of the Committee.

Personnel The Joint Ethics Committee is composed of four members with three votes from each of the following organizations: Society of Illustrators, Inc., The Art Directors Club, Inc., American Society of Magazine Photographers, Inc., Society of Photographers and Artist Representatives, Inc., and The Graphic Artists Guild, Inc. appointed by the directing bodies of each organization, but serving jointly in furtherance of the purposes for which the Committee was founded.

Members of the Joint Ethics Committee are selected with great care by their respective organizations. Their selection is based upon their experience in the profession, their proven mature thinking and temperament, and their reputation for impartiality.

Code of Fair Practice The Code of Fair Practice, as established by the Joint Ethics Committee, was conceived with the idea of equity for those engaged in the various aspects of creating, selling, buying and using graphic arts.

The Code is reproduced later in this book. The Committee zealously upholds the ethical standards set forth in the Code and invites with equal readiness any and all reports of violations.

Action The Committee meets one or more times a month to read and act upon complaints, requests for guidance, and reports of Code violations. The proceedings and records of the Committee are held in strict confidence. In the interest of the profession typical cases are published periodically without identification of the parties involved.

All communications to the Committee must be made in writing. When complaint justifies

The Joint Ethics Committee
Formulated in 1948,
revised in 1978

Sponsored by:
Society of Illustrators, Inc.

The American Society of
Magazine Photographers, Inc.

Society of Photographers and
Artists Representatives, Inc.

The Graphic Artists Guild, Inc.

action, a copy of the complainant's letter may be sent, with the plaintiff's permission, to the alleged offender. In the exchange of correspondence which follows, matters are frequently settled by a mere clarification of the issues. Further action by the Committee becomes unnecessary, and in many instances both sides resume friendly and profitable relationships. When, however, a continued exchange of correspondence indicates that a ready adjustment of differences is improbable, the Committee may suggest mediation or offer its facilities for arbitration.

In the case of flagrant violation, the Committee may, at its discretion, cite the alleged offender to the governing bodies of the parent organizations and recommend that they publicize the fact of these citations when (a) the Committee after a reasonable length of time and adequate notice receives no response from the alleged offender or (b) when the Committee receives a response which it deems unacceptable.

Mediation Both parties meet informally under the auspices of a panel of mediators composed of three members of the Committee. If the dispute requires guidance in a field not represented in the Committee's membership, a specially qualified mediator with the required experience may be included. The names of members of the panel are submitted to both parties for their acceptance.

The conduct of a panel of mediators is friendly and informal. The function of the panel members is to guide; not to render any verdict. The panel's purpose is to direct the discussion along such lines and in such a manner as to bring about a meeting of minds on the questions involved. If mediation fails, or seems unlikely to bring about satisfactory settlement, arbitration may be suggested.

Arbitration A panel of five arbitrators is appointed. One or more is selected from the Committee, and the remainder are chosen by virtue of their particular experience and understanding of the problems presented by the dispute. Names of the panel members are submitted to both parties for their approval. Both parties involved sign an agreement and take an oath to abide by the decision of the panel. The panel itself is sworn in and the proceedings are held in compliance with Arbitration Law of the State of New York. After both sides are heard, the panel deliberates in private and renders its decision, opinion, and award. These are duly formulated by the Committee's counsel for service on the parties and, if the losing side should balk, for entry of judgment according to law.

So far, every award has been fully honored. The decisions and opinions of this Committee are rapidly becoming precedent for guidance in similar situations. The Committee's Code has been cited as legal-precedent.

Committee Scope The Committee acts upon matters which can be defined by them as involving a violation of the Code or a need for its enforcement.

Upon occasion, the Committee has been asked to aid in settling questions not specifically covered by the Code of Fair Practice. The Committee gladly renders such aid, providing it does not exceed the limitations of its authority.

Committee Limitations The Committee offers no legal advice on contracts, copyrights, bill collecting, or similar matters. But its judgment and decisions as to what is fair and ethical in any given situation, are backed by the support of the entire profession represented by the Committee.

The Committee's influence is derived from widespread moral support, and while it has neither judicial nor police powers, and cannot punish offenders, nor summon alleged violators to its presence, still, its growing prestige and dignity of operation have made it a highly respected tribunal to which few have ever failed to respond when invited to settle their differences.

Committee Maintenance The Committee's facilities are not limited to members of its supporting groups. They are available to any individual, business, or professional organization in the field of communications.

The operating expenses of the Committee are defrayed by the sponsoring organizations represented. The time and services of the members are voluntarily contributed without any form of personal gain.

Articles of the Code of Fair Practice

Relations Between Artist and Buyer

Article 1
Dealings between an artist* or the artist's agent and a client should be conducted only through an authorized buyer.

Article 2
Orders to an artist or agent should be in writing and should include the specific rights which are being transferred, the price, delivery date, and a summarized description of the work. In the case of publications, the acceptance of a manuscript by the artist constitutes an order.

Article 3
All changes or additions not due to the fault of the artist or agent should be billed to the purchaser as an additional and separate charge.

Article 4
There should be no charges to the purchaser, other than those authorized expenses, for revisions or retakes made necessary by errors on the part of the artist or the artist's agent.

Article 5
Alterations should not be made without consulting the artist. Where alterations or retakes are necessary and time permits and where the artist's usual standard of quality has been maintained, the artist should be given the opportunity of making such changes.

Article 6
The artist should notify the buyer of an anticipated delay in delivery. Should the artist fail to keep his contract through unreasonable delay in delivery, or nonconformance with agreed specifications, it should be considered a breach of contract by the artist and should release the buyer from responsibility.

Article 7
Work stopped by a buyer after it has been started should be delivered immediately and billed on the basis of the time and effort expended and expenses incurred.

Article 8
An artist should not be asked to work on speculation. However, work originating with the artist may be marketed on its merit. Such work remains the property of the artist unless purchased and paid for.

Article 9
Art contests for commercial purposes are not approved because of their speculative and exploitative character.

Article 10
There should be no secret rebates, discounts, gifts, or bonuses requested by or given to buyers by the artist or the artist's agent.

Article 11
Artwork ownership and copyright ownership is initially vested in the hands of the artist.

Article 12
Original artwork remains the property of the artist unless it is specifically purchased and paid for as distinct from the purchase of any reproduction rights.**

Article 13
In cases of copyright transfers, only specified rights are transferred in any transaction, all unspecified rights remaining vested in the artist.**

Article 14
If the purchase price of artwork is based specifically upon limited use and later this material is used more extensively than originally planned, the artist is to receive adequate additional remuneration.

Article 15
Commissioned artwork is not to be considered as "done for hire."**

Article 16
If comprehensives, preliminary work, exploratory work, or additional photographs from an assignment are subsequently published as finished art the price should be increased to the satisfaction of artist and buyer.

Article 17
If exploratory work, comprehensives, or photographs are bought from an artist with the intention or possibility that another artist will be assigned to do the finished work, this should be made clear at the time of placing the order.

Article 18
The publisher of any reproduction of artwork shall publish the artist's copyright notice if the artist so requests and has not executed a written and signed transfer of copyright ownership.**

Article 19
The right to place the artist's signature upon artwork is subject to agreement between artist and buyer.

Article 20
There should be no plagiarism of any creative artwork.

Article 21
If an artist is specifically requested to produce any artwork during unreasonable working hours, fair additional remuneration should be allowed.

Article 22
An artist entering into an agreement with an agent or studio for exclusive representation should not accept an order from, nor permit his work to be shown by any other agent or studio. Any agreement which is not intended to be exclusive should set forth in writing the exact restrictions agreed upon between the two parties.

Article 23
All artwork or photography submitted as samples to a buyer by artist's agents or studio representatives should bear the name of the artist or artists responsible for the creation.

Article 24
No agent, studio, or production company should continue to show the work of an artist as samples after the termination of the association.

Article 25
After termination of an association between artist and agent, the agent should be entitled to a commission on accounts which the agent has secured, for a period of time not exceeding six months (unless otherwise specified by contract).

Article 26
Examples of an artist's work furnished to an agent or submitted to a prospective purchaser shall remain the property of the artist, should not be duplicated without the artist's consent, and should be returned to the artist promptly in good condition.

Article 27
Interpretation of the Code shall be in the hands of the Joint Ethics Committee and is subject to changes and additions at the discretion of the parent organizations through their appointed representatives on the Committee.

Sponsored by Society of Illustrators, Inc., The Art Directors Club, Inc., American Society of Magazine Photographers, Inc., Society of Photographers and Artist Representatives, Inc., The Graphic Artists Guild, Inc.

*The word artist should be understood to include creative people in the field of visual communications such as graphics, photography, film, and television.

**Artwork ownership, copyright ownership, and ownership and rights transfers after January 1, 1978 are to be in compliance with the Federal Copyright Revision Act of 1976.

The Illustrators

Andrea Baruffi
341 Hudson Terrace
Piermont, NY 10968
(914) 359-9542

Marc Yankus

Marc Yankus
400 West 25th Street, 1G
New York, NY 10001
(212) 242-6334

Clients include:
Adweek, Arbitron Rating Company, AT&T, *Business Week,* CBS, Chemical Bank, Doubleday & Company, Dun & Bradstreet, E.F. Hutton, *Life,* Macmillan Publishing Company, McGraw-Hill, *Newsweek, New York Magazine, New York Times,* Ogilvy & Mather, Parke-Davis, *Psychology Today,* Random House, Squibb Corporation, Sudler & Hennessey, Ted Bates Advertising, *Time, Vogue,* Whittle Communications.

Medium: Collage
Exhibitions include:
Brooklyn Museum, New York Art Directors Club, Society of Illustrators.

To View More Work:
Adweek Portfolio 1987; American Showcase #8, 10, 11; Art Direction, August 1986; *Contemporary Graphic Artist,* 1988; *Print's Regional Design Annuals,* 1984-1987.

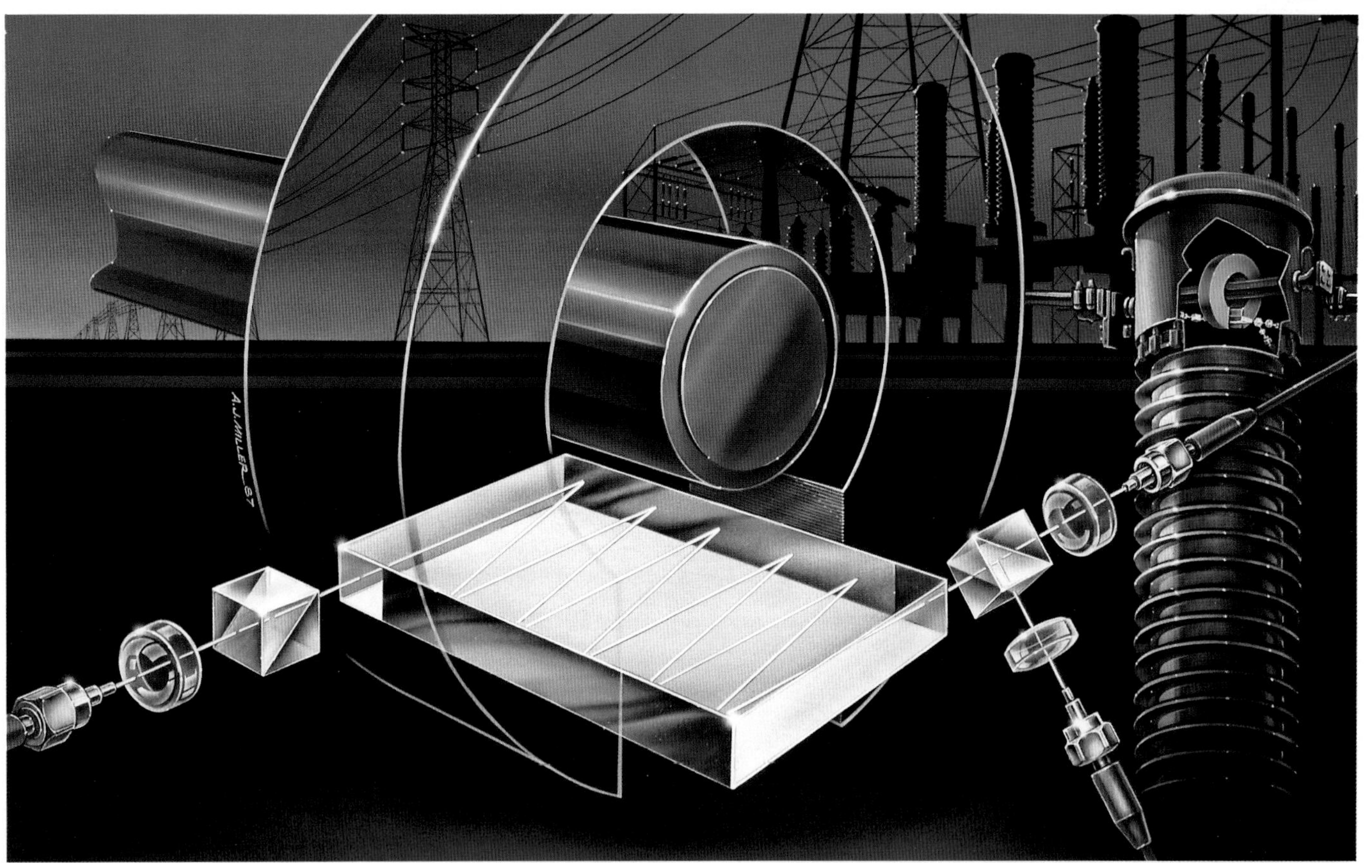

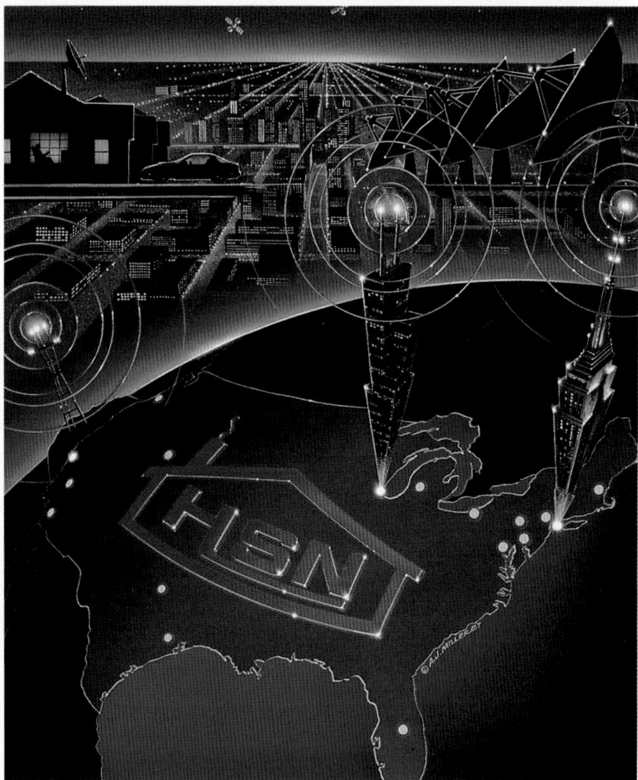

A.J. Miller
(813) 596-6384

I specialize in tight air-brush illustration with a decorative flair. A wide range of projects makes me happy, whether it's the latest breaking technology or challenging solutions which tell my clients' stories.

I am Florida born, Detroit trained, and accepting work from all over the country. I honor all dead-lines with precision work. I'm happily living and painting in Indian Rocks Beach, Florida.

Plato Taleporos

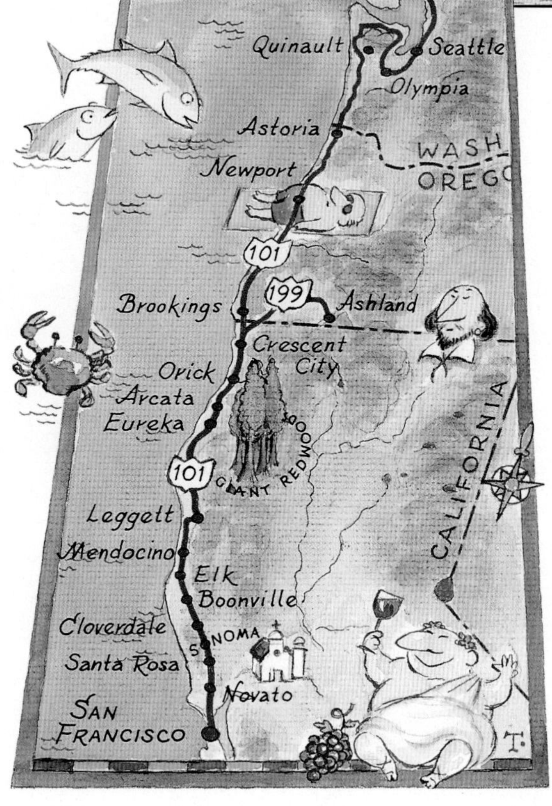

Plato Taleporos
333 East 23rd Street
New York, NY 10010
(212) 689-3138

Clients shown:
U.S. Air, Financial World, Diversion, Personal Computing, Travel Weekly.

Member Graphic Artists Guild

Kenneth Spengler

Kenneth Spengler
43-17 55th Street
Woodside, NY 11377
(718) 898-8591

Illustrations in gouache and conté

Clients include:

ABC, Fairchild Publications, Workman Publications, American Kennel Club, *ASTA Travel News*, Michael Friedman Group, Crain Communications, Macmillan Publishing.

Member of the Graphic Artists Guild

Peter Scanlan

Peter Scanlan
60 Oak Street
Closter, NJ 07624
(201) 767-7342

Janet Street
Represented by Ward Turner
7 Berkshire Avenue
Florence, MA 01060
(413) 543-6796
Telefax:
(413) 543-6816

Portfolio available on request.

10

Peter de Sève
461 West 21st Street, 3rd floor
New York, NY 10011
(212) 627-5533

Clients include: Dancer Fitzgerald Sample; Hill, Holliday; Klemtner Advertising; Lalley, McFarland & Pantello; Mojo M.D.A.; McCann-Erickson; Wells, Rich, Greene; *Forbes; Newsweek; New York Times Magazine; Rollingstone; Sports Illustrated; Time*. To view more work: *Graphis #243* (a profile); *Communication Arts Annuals 85, 86, 87; American Showcase 10, 11; Adweek Portfolio 1988; Society of Illustrators 29th Annual* and *Humor*. Awards: Society of Illustrators Silver Medal, 1987.

ANIMATION REEL AND TRAVELING PORTFOLIO AVAILABLE UPON REQUEST!

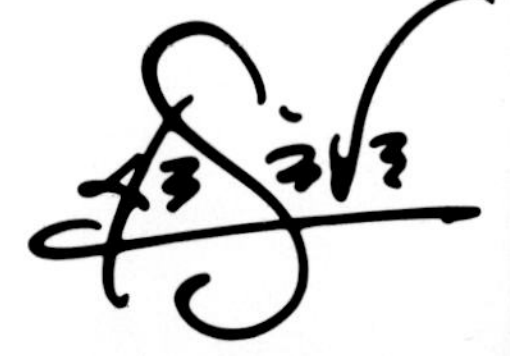

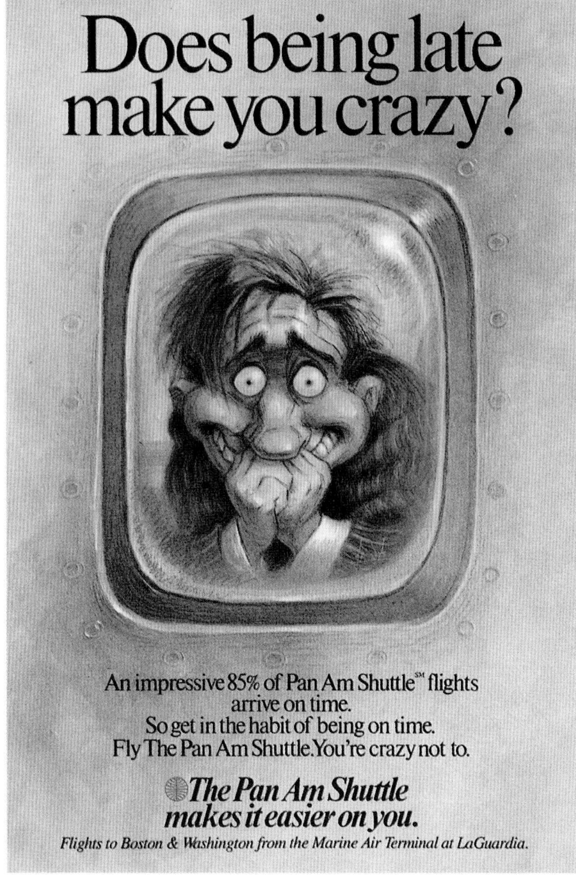
Does being late
make you crazy?
An impressive 85% of Pan Am Shuttle℠ flights
arrive on time.
So get in the habit of being on time.
Fly The Pan Am Shuttle. You're crazy not to.
The Pan Am Shuttle
makes it easier on you.
Flights to Boston & Washington from the Marine Air Terminal at LaGuardia.

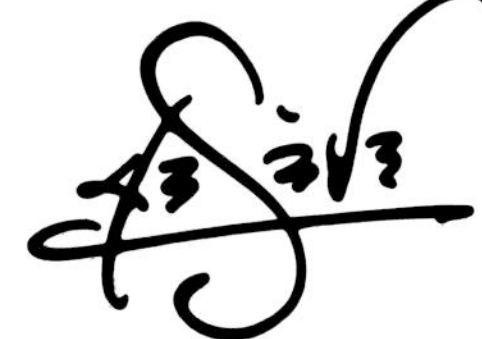

Linda Winchester

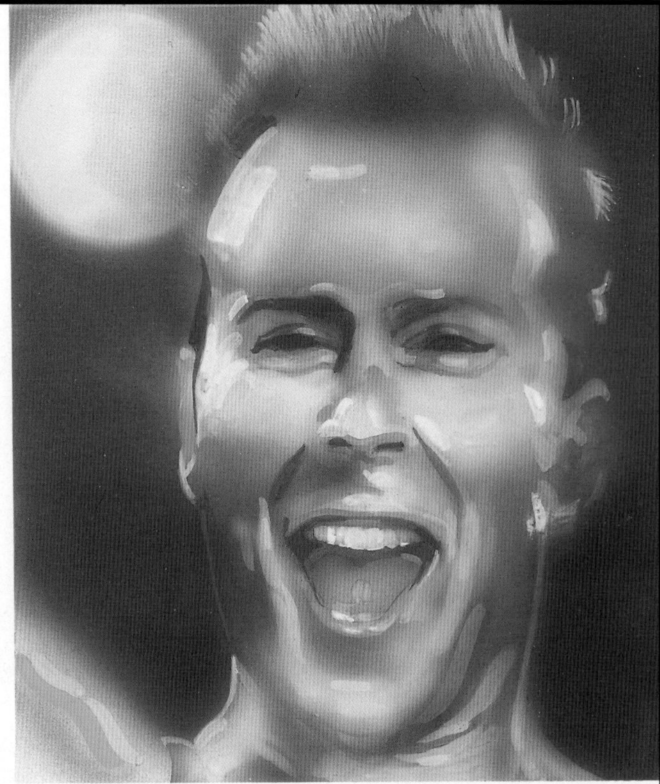

Linda Winchester
228 Clinton Street
Brooklyn Heights, NY 11201
(718) 625-1930

Clients include:
Berol Corporation
CBS
Coleco
Dodd, Mead & Company
Doubleday
General Foods
Hallmark
Warner Bros./7 Arts
Western Publishing

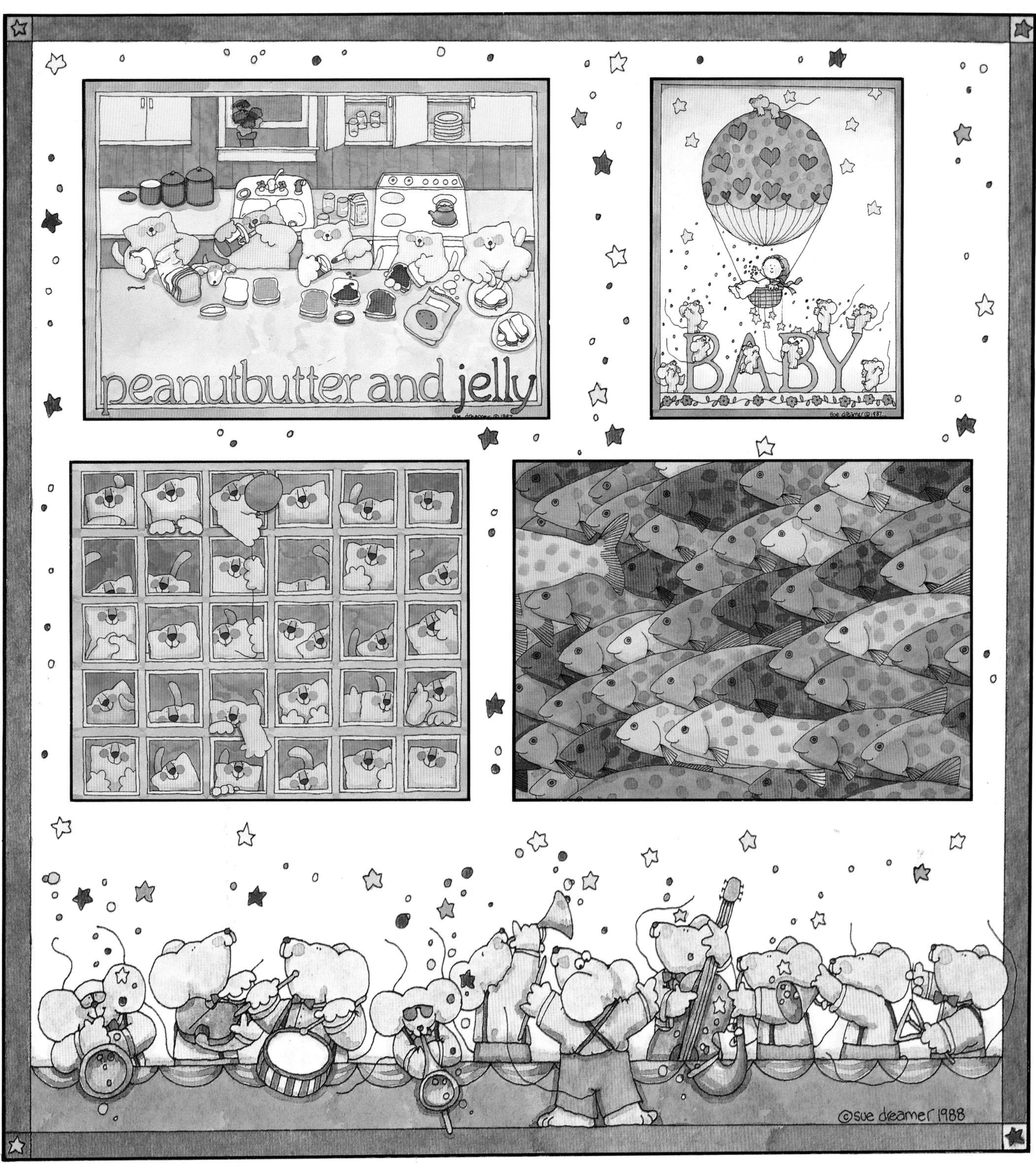

Sue Dreamer
345 Cross Street
Hanson, MA 02341
(617) 294-4508

...children's books, greeting cards, stickers, advertising, infant bedding, infant clothing, wallpaper, balloons, paper products...

clients...
...Little, Brown & Company; Ringling Bros. and Barnum and Bailey Circus; Intervisual Communications Inc.; Price/Stern/Sloan; *Highlight Magazine;* Artfaire; Current Inc.; Country House; Rainbow Arts; Springs Industries, Inc.; Desart Wallcoverings; Classic Balloon; Brownstone Group; Bright of America; Inkadinkado; Piccolo; Carter, Hawley, Hale Stores...

Bryn Barnard

© Hughes Aircraft Company 1988

Baron H. S. Strouth *The Cities of the Break of Dawn* book cover illustration

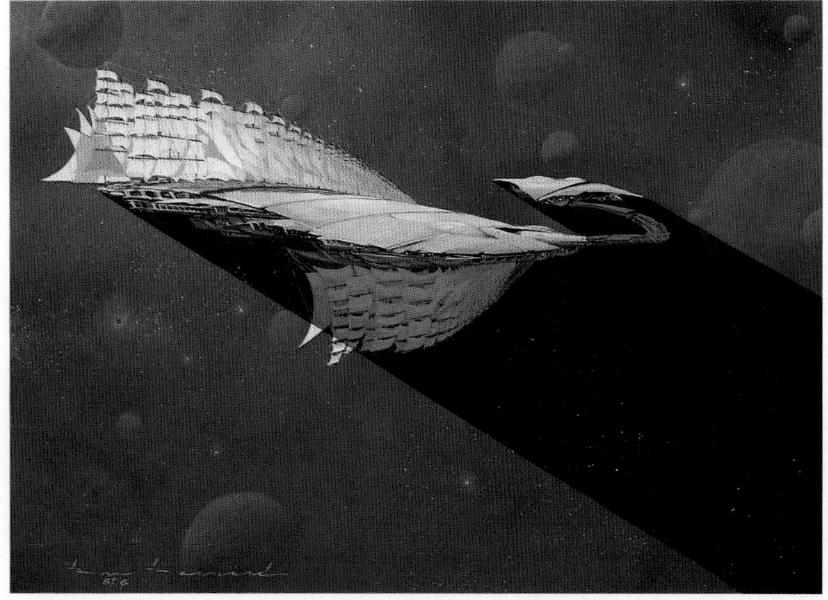

Doubleday and Company *Urth of the New Sun* story illustration

The Magazine of Fantasy and Science Fiction cover illustration August 1987

Bryn Barnard
P.O. Box 285
Woodbury, NJ 08096
(609) 853-4252

Clients include:
Arbor House Books
Avis Rent A Car
Berkley Publishing
Davis Publications
Doubleday & Company
Fluor Corporation
Harcourt Brace Jovanovich
HR Textron
Hughes Aircraft Company
International Robotics
Llewellyn Publishing
The Magazine of Fantasy and Science Fiction
NASA
National Geographic Society
Pocketbooks
Popular Mechanics
Tor Books
Unilever

Additional work may be seen in *American Showcase 10*

Member Graphic Artists Guild

Robin Brickman
32 Fort Hoosac Place
Williamstown, MA 01267
(413) 458-9853

Illustrations from the academic to the fantastic.

Clients include:

The New Yorker: Little, Brown & Co.; *New York Times; Horticulture,* Houghton Mifflin Co., *Science '85;* Rodale Press; National Wildlife Federation; Harper & Row; D.R. Godine; Princeton University Press; *Cricket.*

Eduardo Reyes

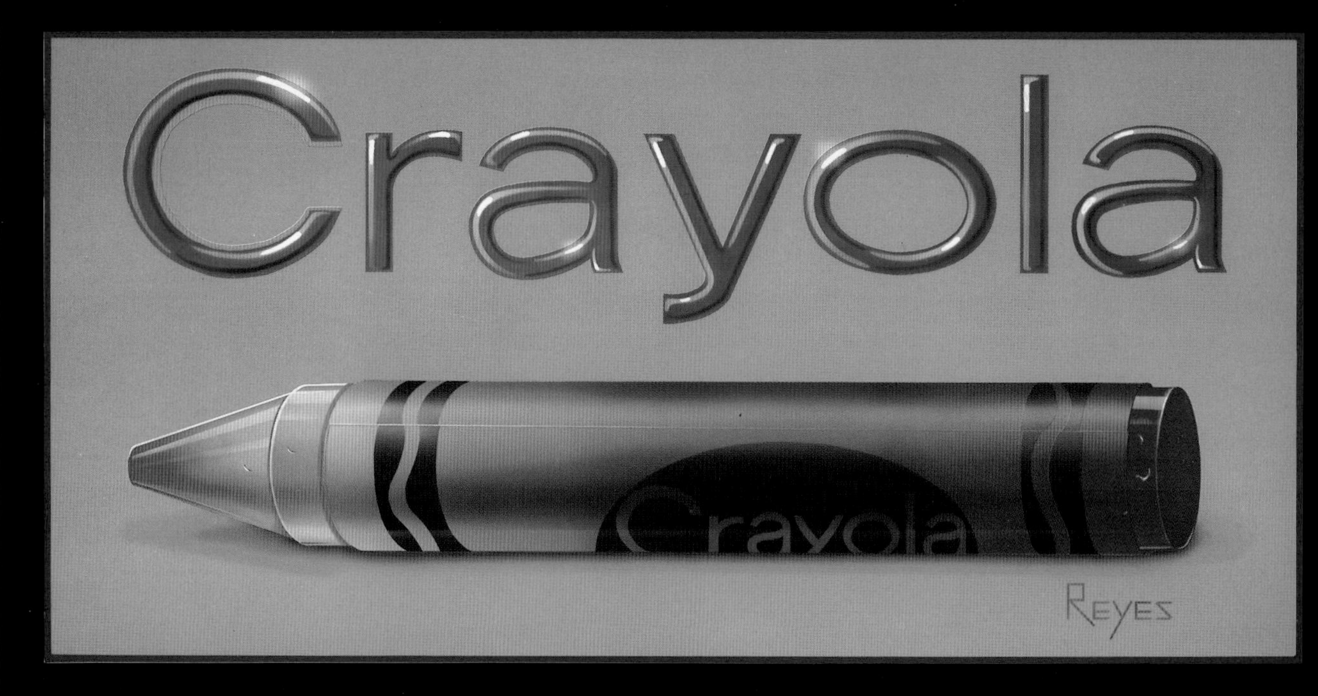

Eduardo Reyes
300 W. Raymond Street
Philadelphia, PA 19140
(215) 455-9176

A contemporary Studio/Office offering complete illustration and creative services. Clean, bold, conceptual visuals created within your demanding deadlines! Advertising, Editorial, Promotional.

Feel free to call or write for a complete portfolio presentation.

Member Graphic Artists Guild

Al Hughes
242 East 38th Street, #2D
New York, NY 10016
(212) 972-2074

Clients include:
Biotherm
Lancome
L'Oreal
Revlon
Chetta B.
Liz Claiborne Shoes
Andrew Fezza
Henry Grethel
Alexander Julian
J. Mendel Furs
Bon Jour Jeans
Rigolletto Jeans
Willi Smith
Diane Von Furstenberg
Loehman's
Russell Fabrics
Ballantine's Scotch
Daily News Record
Men's Fashion Association
National Association of
Men's Sportswear Buyers
Vogue Magazine

Patricia Doktor

Patricia Doktor
95 Horatio Street, #9A
New York, NY 10014
(212) 645-4452

Clients include:
- Security Pacific Bank
- Fairchild Publication
- DIC Enterprises
- Westar Production
- Hamilton Avnet
- *Atlantic Monthly Press*
- *Watch Magazine*
- *Sports Car Magazine*
- *50 Plus Magazine*

Education:
- Art Center College

Awards:
- Two awards from Society of Illustrators Annual Scholarship Competition.

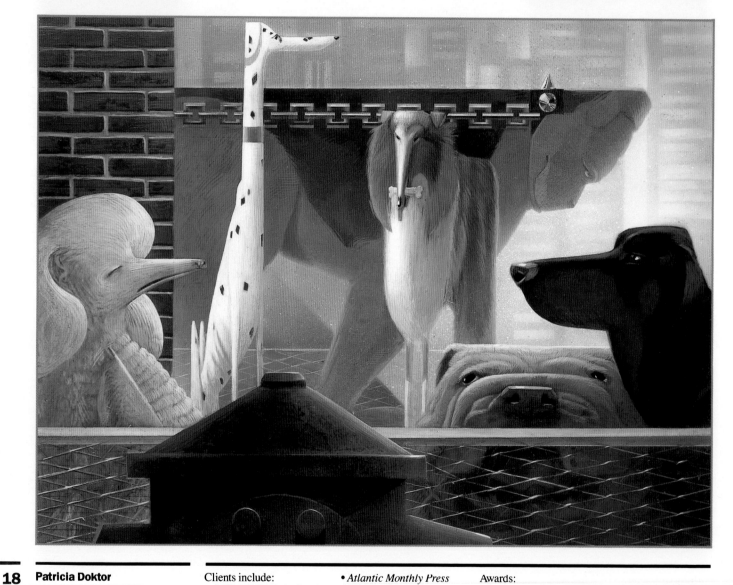

Barry E. Jackson

Barry E. Jackson
95 Horatio Street, #9A
New York, NY 10014
(212) 645-4452

Clients include:

- Warner Bros. Records
- MCA Records
- CBS Records
- Universal Studios
- 20th Century Fox
- Chiat Day Advertising
- Dailey Advertising
- N.W. Ayer
- *New York Times*
- *L.A. Times*
- *Watch Magazine*

Awards:

- six awards of excellence from *CA Magazine*
- two awards of recognition from the Society of Illustrators

Instructor:

- Art Center College
- Otis Parson (L.A.)

Cathy Hull

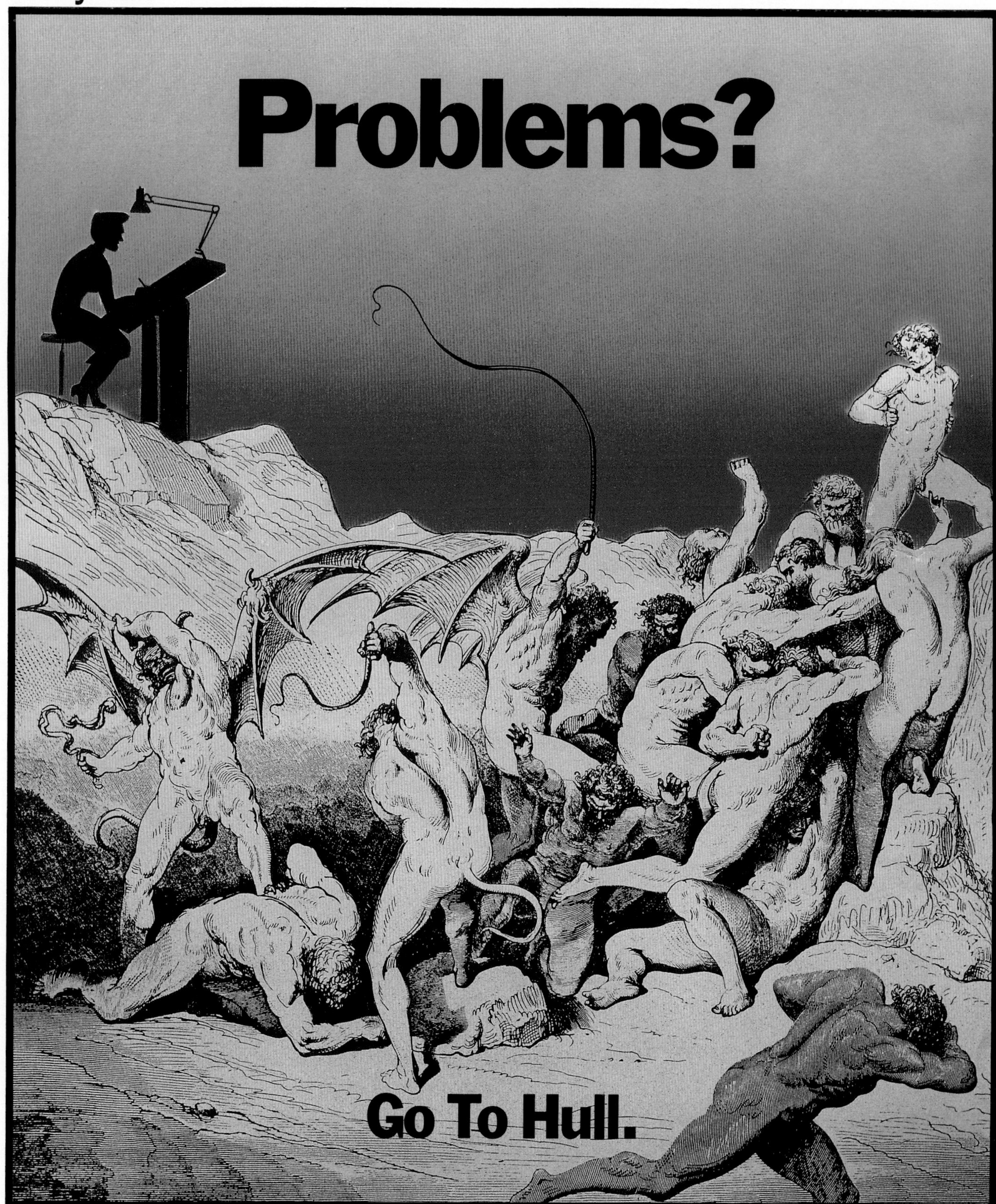

Cathy Hull
165 East 66th Street
New York, N.Y. 10021
(212) 772-7743

Conceptual illustration for advertising, editorial, and corporate communications.

Clients include:
ABC, CBS, Mobil Oil, Pan American, Eastern, *Playboy, Business Week,* Time Inc., *The New York Times,* E.F. Hutton, Paine Webber, and Marsh & McLennan.

Instructor:
The School of Visual Arts, New York.

Miriam Larsson
410 Riverside Drive, Apt 92
New York, NY 10025
(212) 713-5765
(212) 222-1150

Member of Graphic Artists Guild

Clockwise from top:
The nightsets.
Still life with Beaujolais wine.
Portrait of Albert Einstein.

Jim Carson

Jim Carson
11 Foch Street
Cambridge, MA 02140
(617) 661-3321

Clients include:

Digital
Polaroid
NYNEX
Honeywell
Prime Computer
John Hancock
Bank of Boston
Stride Rite
Baltimore Sun
Boston Globe
Chicago Tribune
Philadelphia Inquirer
Adweek
Houghton Mifflin
Rodale Press
Whittle Communications
Ziff-Davis

Awards include:

Society of Illustrators
Art Directors Club
Ad Club
Print Magazine

Linda Y. Miyamoto
P.O. Box 022310
Brooklyn, NY 11202-0049
(718) 596-4787

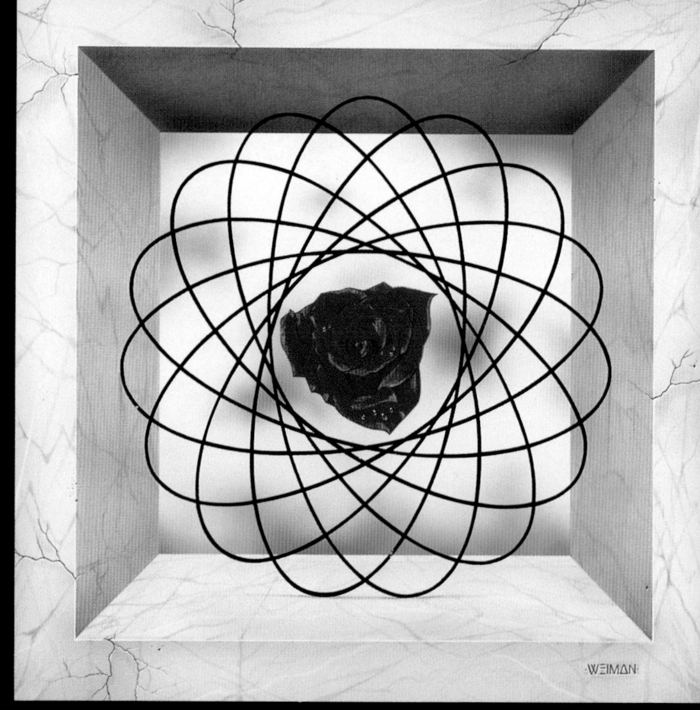

Jon Weiman
2255 Broadway (306)
New York, NY 10024
(212) 787-3184

Clients include: Bradbury Press; *Business Week;* Davis Publishing; Ensign Bank; Harper & Row; Holt, Rinehart & Winston; Lowe's Companies, Inc.; Klemtner Advertising; Murdoch Magazines; Macmillan; McGraw-Hill; NBC; The New York Times Syndication Sales Corporation; Nutri-Systems; Ogilvy & Mather Merchandising; PBS; Scribner's/Atheneum; Shaller Rubin, Inc.; Sudler & Hennessey;Suffolk Downs Race Track; WDAS; William Morrow & Company.

Works exhibited in *Print's Regional Design Annual 1984, '85, '86;* Master Eagle Gallery 1985, '86, '87.

Member: Graphic Artists Guild, Society of Illustrators

Jon Weiman
2255 Broadway (306)
New York, NY 10024
(212) 787-3184

Clients include: Bradbury Press; *Business Week;* Davis Publishing; Ensign Bank; Harper & Row; Holt, Rinehart & Winston; Lowe's Companies, Inc.; Klemtner Advertising; Murdoch Magazines; Macmillan; McGraw-Hill; NBC; The New York Times Syndication Sales Corporation; Nutri-Systems; Ogilvy & Mather Merchandising; PBS; Scribner's/Atheneum; Shaller Rubin, Inc.; Sudler & Hennessey;Suffolk Downs Race Track; WDAS; William Morrow & Company.

Works exhibited in *Print's Regional Design Annual 1984, '85, '86;* Master Eagle Gallery 1985, '86, '87.

Member: Graphic Artists Guild, Society of Illustrators

John Winter Hale

John Winter Hale
329 East 13th Street, Apt. A
New York, N.Y. 10003
(212) 254-6665

Clients include:
American Health
Barron's
Davis Publications
Forbes
50 Plus
Parents
The New York Times
The Wilkerson Group
Ziff-Davis Publications

Page design:
Patty Richards

Member Graphic Artists Guild

John P. Courtney

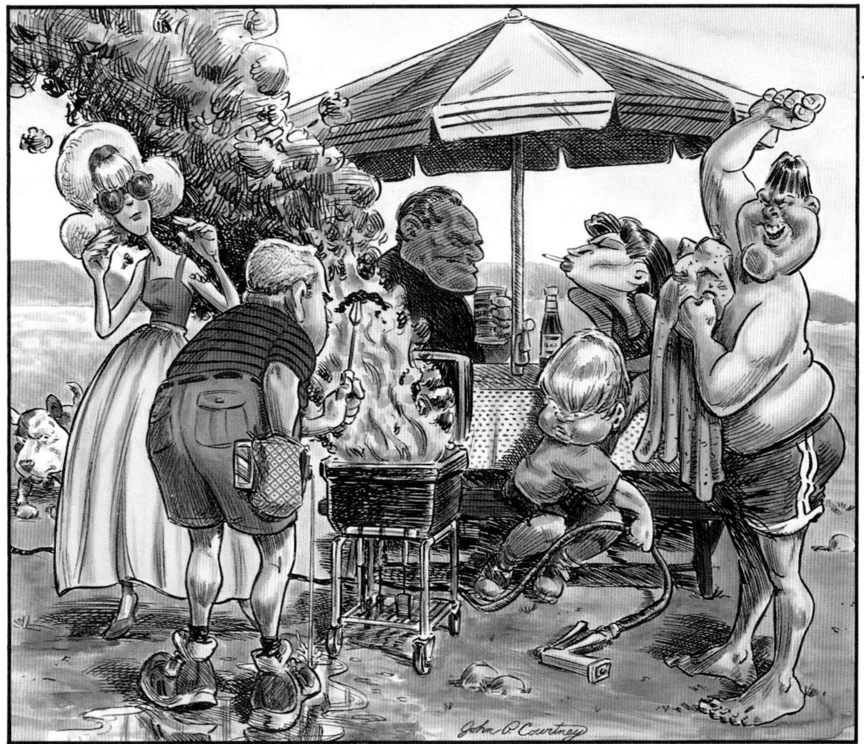

John P. Courtney
137 Center Street, Apt. 7
Clifton, NJ 07011
(201) 546-6133

Clients include:
Toys "R" Us
The New York Times
Simon and Schuster
New Jersey Monthly
Scholastic Publications
Latin Percussion Inc.
Video Review
Ziff-Davis

Member Graphic Artists Guild

John Gampert

John Gampert
P.O. Box 219
Kew Gardens, NY 11415
(718) 441-2321

Member: Graphic Artists Guild

Illustration and design from comp to finish for major publishers and advertising agencies.

Clients include:
CBS Records, Grey Advertising, Beaumont/Bennett, Houghton Mifflin, Macmillan, Viking/Penguin, Random House, Dell, Berkley/Jove, Scribner's, Mobil, Grove, Scholastic.

Private collections

Simms Taback
15 West 20th Street
New York, NY 10011
(212) 627-5220

Represented by
Milton Newborn
135 East 54th Street
New York, NY 10022
(212) 421-0050

Credits:

Mercantile Bank Outdoor Campaign/The Richards Group

Deb Hoeffner

Deb Hoeffner
538 Cherry Tree Lane
Kinnelon, NJ 07405
(201) 838-5490

Portfolio available for viewing in NYC
(212) 989-8588

Member Graphic Artists Guild

Amanda Wilson

Amanda Wilson
346 East 20th Street
New York, NY 10003
(212) 260-7567

Melanie Reim

Melanie Reim
214 Riverside Drive
New York, NY 10025
(212) 749-0177

Clients include:
Newsweek, Inc.
Newsweek International, Inc.
Food & Wine Magazine
Travel & Leisure Magazine
The Wall Street Journal
The Daily News
Woman's Day Magazine
Inside Sports

Skip Morrow
Box One Two Three
Ware Road
Wilmington, Vermont 05363
(802) 464-5523 TEL
(802) 464-2555 FAX

National bestselling
author/illustrator

Jody A. Lee

Jody A. Lee
175 Ninth Avenue
New York, NY 10011
(212) 741-5192

Janice Belove
211A 20th Street
Union City, NJ 07087
(201) 392-8258

Member Graphic Artists Guild

Robert
Gunn

Robert
Gunn

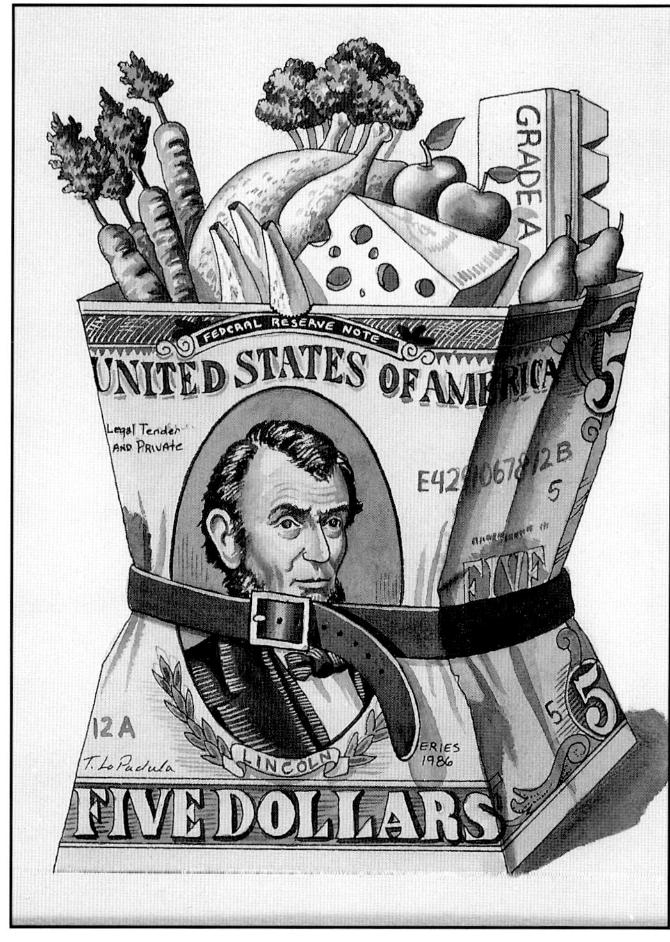

Tom LaPadula

represented by

Bud and Evelyne Johnson

ARTIST REPRESENTATIVES

EVELYNE JOHNSON ASSOCIATES

201 E. 28th ST., N.Y. , N.Y. 10016/212-532-0928/FAX 212-696-0958

Larry Daste

represented by

Bud and Evelyne Johnson
ARTIST REPRESENTATIVES

EJA

EVELYNE JOHNSON ASSOCIATES
201 E. 28th ST., N.Y. , N.Y. 10016/212-532-0928/FAX 212-696-0

Frank Daniel

represented by

Bud and Evelyne Johnson

ARTIST REPRESENTATIVES

EVELYNE JOHNSON ASSOCIATES

201 E. 28th ST., N.Y., N.Y. 10016/212-532-0928/FAX 212-696-0958

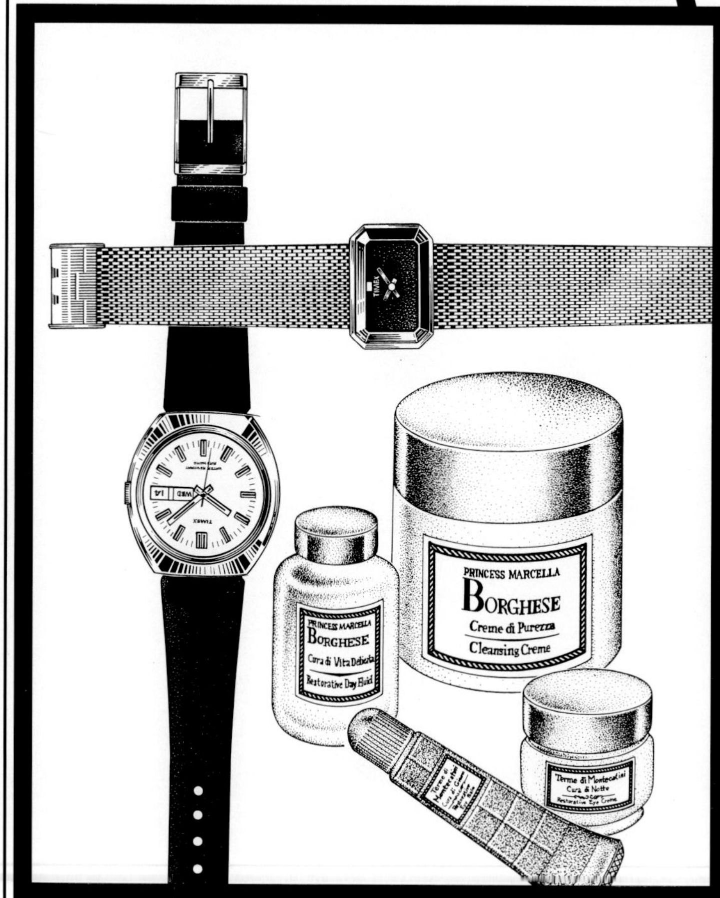

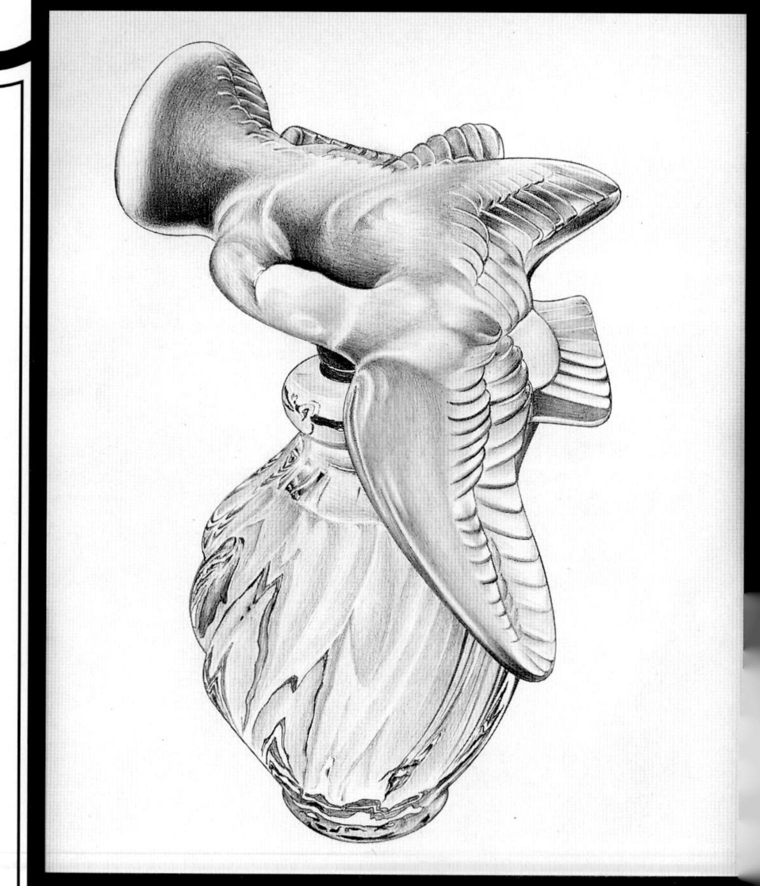

Yukio Kondo

represented by

Bud and Evelyne Johnson

ARTIST REPRESENTATIVES

E/A

EVELYNE JOHNSON ASSOCIATES

201 E. 28th ST., N.Y. , N.Y. 10016/212-532-0928/FAX 212-696-0

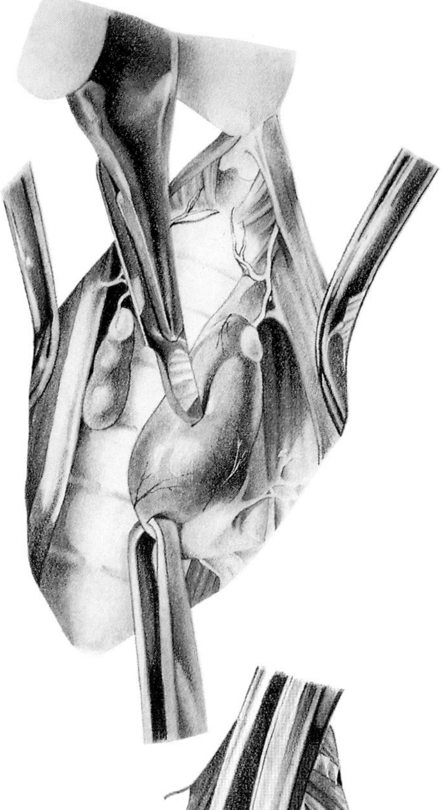

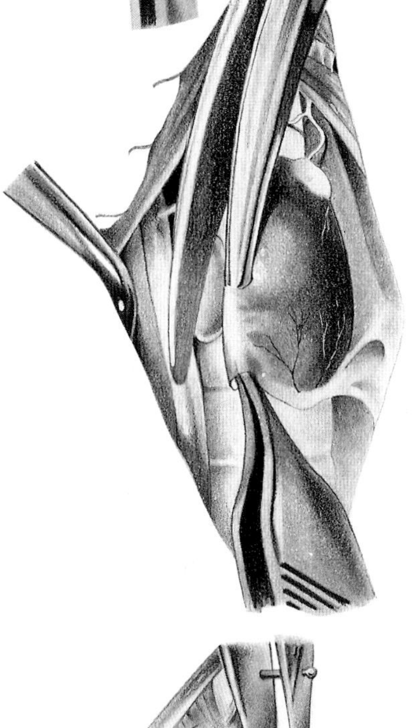

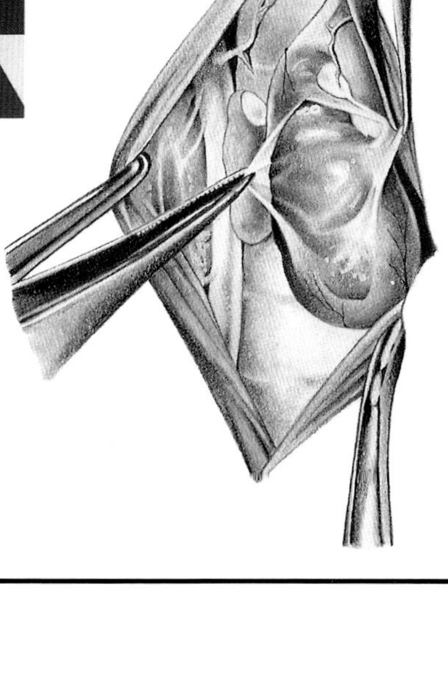

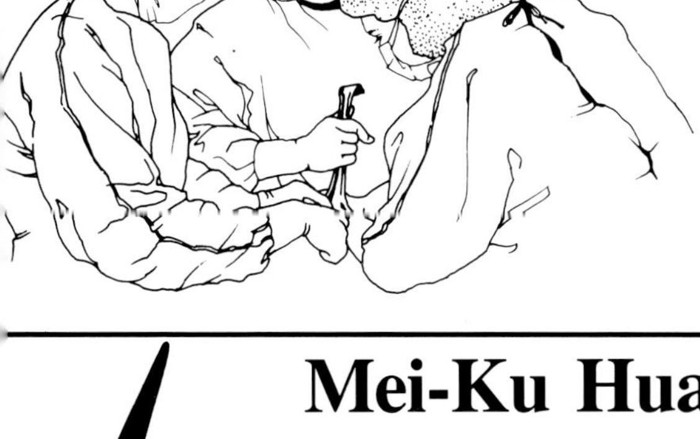

Mei-Ku Huang, MD Medical Illustration

represented by

Bud and Evelyne Johnson
ARTIST REPRESENTATIVES

EVELYNE JOHNSON ASSOCIATES
201 E. 28th ST., N.Y. , N.Y. 10016/212-532-0928/FAX 212-696-0958

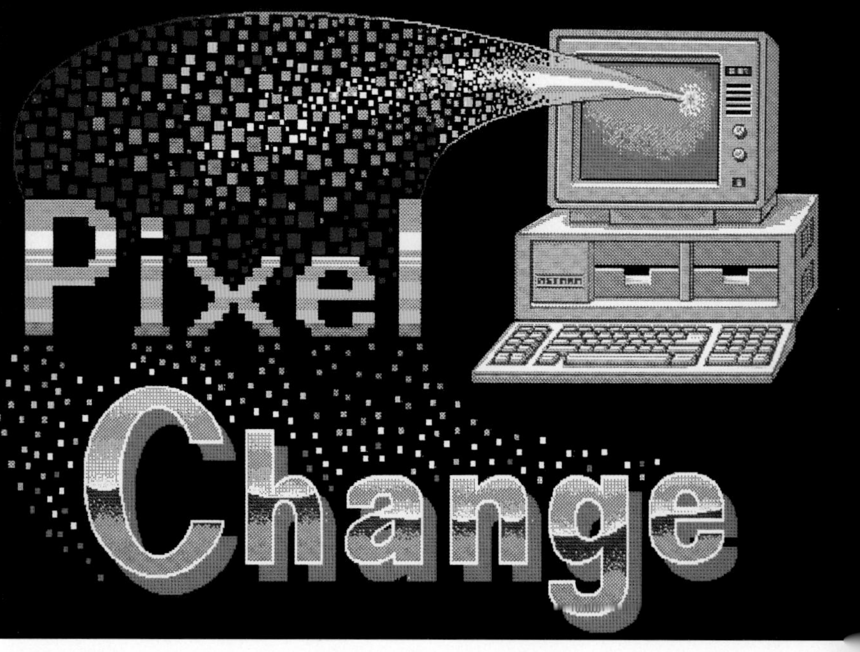

Ilene Astrahan **Computer Graphics/Air Brush Illustration**

represented by

EJA

Bud and Evelyne Johnson

ARTIST REPRESENTATIVES

EVELYNE JOHNSON ASSOCIATES

201 E. 28th ST., N.Y. , N.Y. 10016/212-532-0928/FAX 212-696-09

I have a dream that one day this nation will rise up and live out the true meaning of its creed: "We hold these truths to be self-evident: that all men are created equal." I have a dream that one day on the red hills of Georgia the sons of former slaves and the sons of former slaveowners will be able to sit down together at the table of brotherhood. I have a dream that my four little children will one day live in a nation where they will not be judged by the color of their skin but by the content of their character. I have a dream today. This is our hope. With this faith we will be able to work together, to pray together, to struggle together, to go to jail together, to stand up for freedom together, knowing that we will be free one day. When we let freedom ring from every village & every hamlet, from every state & every city, we will be able to speed up that day when all of God's children, black men & white men, Jews & Gentiles, Protestants & Catholics, will be able to join hands & sing in the words of the old Negro spiritual, "Free at last! free at last! thank God Almighty, we are free at last!"

Lanie Johnson

Word Images through Calligraphy

LANIE JOHNSON

represented by

Bud and Evelyne Johnson

ARTIST REPRESENTATIVES

E/A

EVELYNE JOHNSON ASSOCIATES

201 E. 28th ST., N.Y., N.Y. 10016/212-532-0928/FAX 212-696-0958

E/A

Turi MacCombie

represented by

Bud and Evelyne Johnson
ARTIST REPRESENTATIVES

EVELYNE JOHNSON ASSOCIATES
201 E. 28th ST., N.Y. , N.Y. 10016/212-532-0928/FAX 212-696-0

Pat Stewart

represented by

Bud and Evelyne Johnson

ARTIST REPRESENTATIVES

EVELYNE JOHNSON ASSOCIATES

201 E. 28th ST., N.Y. , N.Y. 10016/212-532-0928/FAX 212-696-0958

Barbara Steadman

represented by

Bud and Evelyne Johnson

ARTIST REPRESENTATIVES

EVELYNE JOHNSON ASSOCIATE

201 E. 28th ST., N.Y. , N.Y. 10016/212-532-0928/FAX 212-696-

John O'Brien

represented by

Bud and Evelyne Johnson

ARTIST REPRESENTATIVES

EVELYNE JOHNSON ASSOCIATES

201 E. 28th ST., N.Y., N.Y. 10016/212-532-0928/FAX 212-696-0958

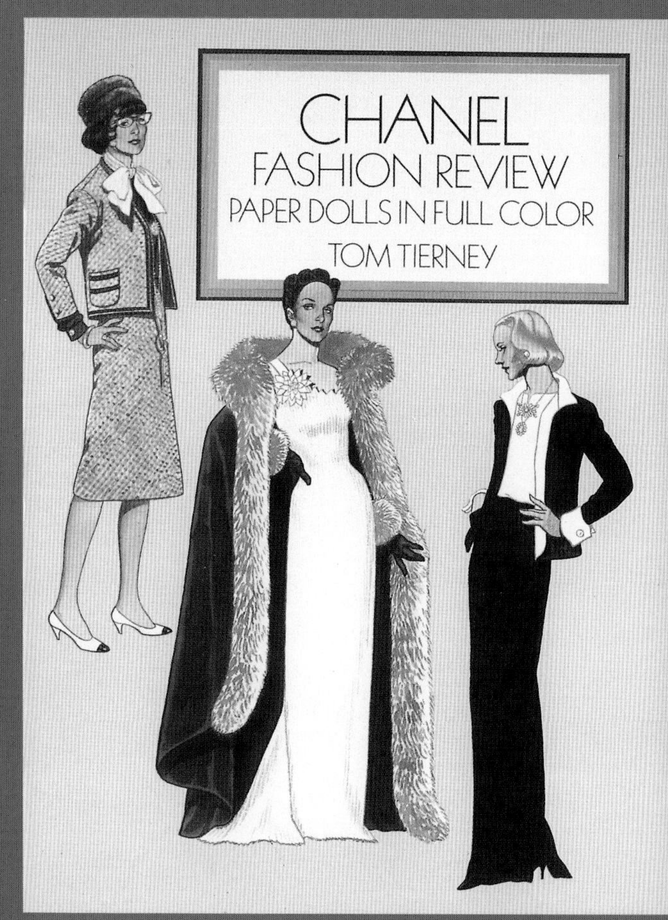

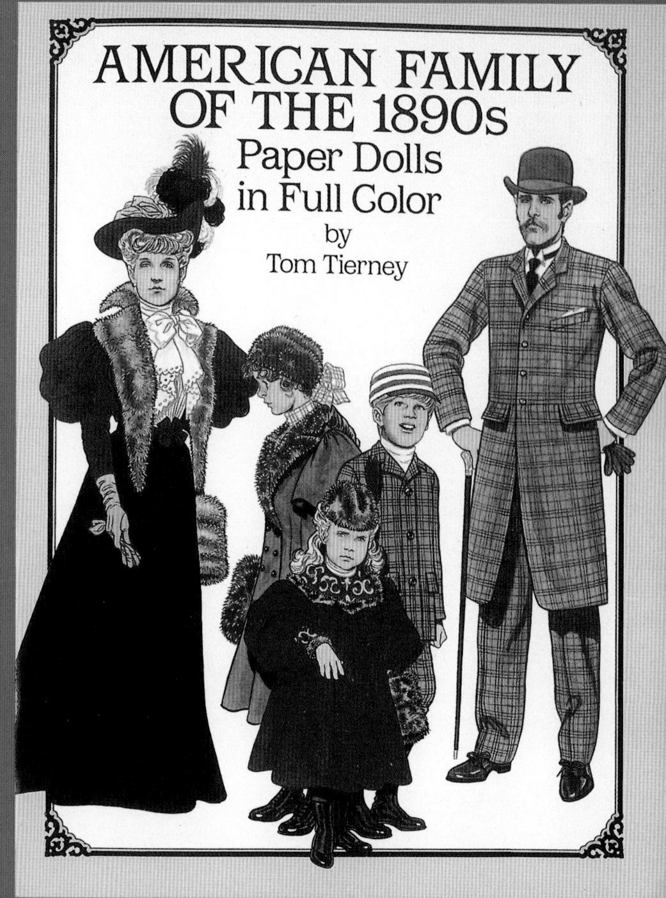

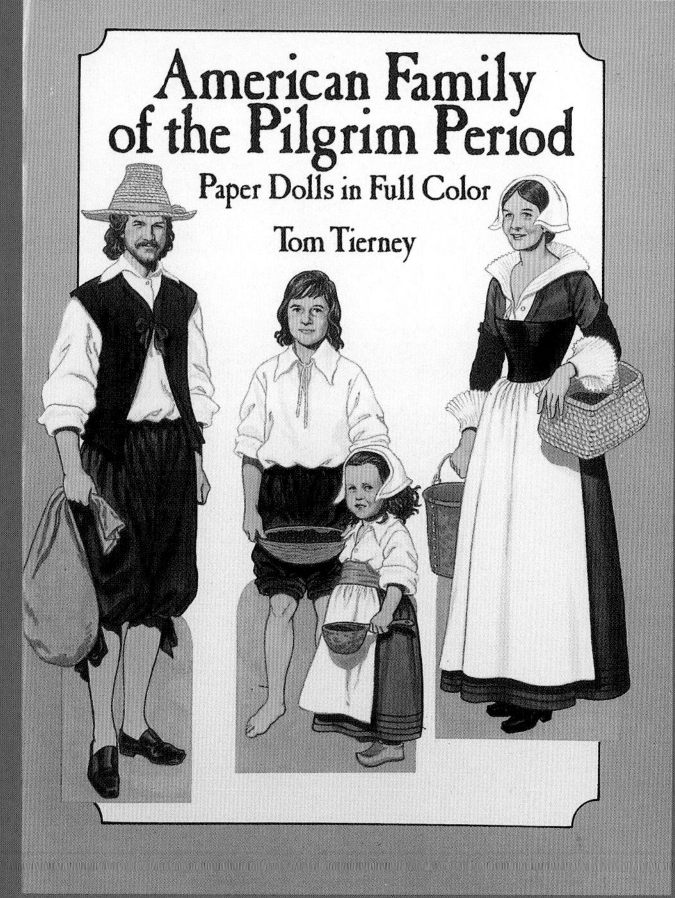

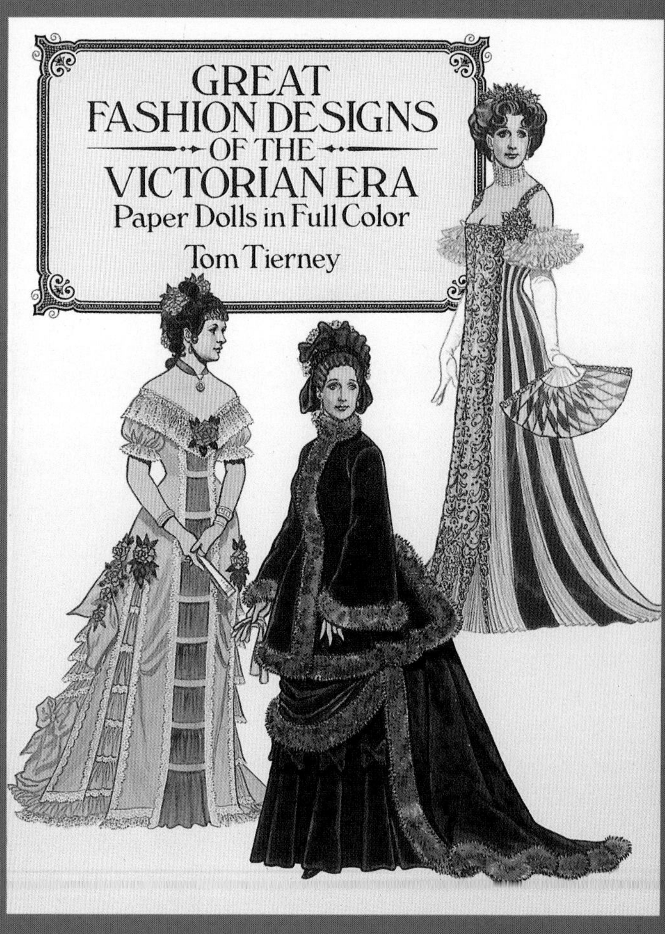

Tom Tierney

represented by

Bud and Evelyne Johnson

ARTIST REPRESENTATIVES

EVELYNE JOHNSON ASSOCIATE

201 E. 28th ST., N.Y. , N.Y. 10016/212-532-0928/FAX 212-696-0

Rowan Barnes-Murphy

represented by

Bud and Evelyne Johnson

ARTIST REPRESENTATIVES

EVELYNE JOHNSON ASSOCIATES

201 E. 28th ST., N.Y. , N.Y. 10016/212-532-0928/FAX 212-696-0958

Steven Petruccio

represented by

Bud and Evelyne Johnson

ARTIST REPRESENTATIVES

E/A
EVELYNE JOHNSON ASSOCIATES
201 E. 28th ST., N.Y., N.Y. 10016/212-532-0928/FAX 212-696-0

George Ford

represented by

Bud and Evelyne Johnson

ARTIST REPRESENTATIVES

EVELYNE JOHNSON ASSOCIATES

201 E. 28th ST., N.Y. , N.Y. 10016/212-532-0928/FAX 212-696-0958

Ted Enik

represented by

E/A

Bud and Evelyne Johnson

ARTIST REPRESENTATIVES

EVELYNE JOHNSON ASSOCIATES

201 E. 28th ST., N.Y. , N.Y. 10016/212-532-0928/FAX 212-696-0

Kathy Allert

represented by

Bud and Evelyne Johnson

ARTIST REPRESENTATIVES

EVELYNE JOHNSON ASSOCIATES

201 E. 28th ST., N.Y. , N.Y. 10016/212-532-0928/FAX 212-696-0958

Carolyn Bracken

LITTLE JACK HORNER

SIMPLE SIMON AND THE PIEMAN

JACK, BE NIMBLE

LITTLE BO-PEEP

MOTHER GOOSE

KNA OF HEAR

OLD WOMAN TOSSED UP IN A BASKET

THE OLD WO AN'S SHOE

THREE BLIND MICE

JACK AND JILL

Carolyn Bracken
represented by
Bud and Evelyne Johnson
ARTIST REPRESENTATIVES

EVELYNE JOHNSON ASSOCIATES
201 E. 28th ST., N.Y. , N.Y. 10016/212-532-0928/FAX 212-696-0

Cathy Beylon

represented by

Bud and Evelyne Johnson

ARTIST REPRESENTATIVES

EVELYNE JOHNSON ASSOCIATES

201 E. 28th ST., N.Y. , N.Y. 10016/212-532-0928/FAX 212-696-0958

E/A

Darcy May

represented by

Bud and Evelyne Johnson

ARTIST REPRESENTATIVES

EVELYNE JOHNSON ASSOCIATE

201 E. 28th ST., N.Y. , N.Y. 10016/212-532-0928/FAX 212-696-

Carolyn Ewing

represented by

Bud and Evelyne Johnson

ARTIST REPRESENTATIVES

EVELYNE JOHNSON ASSOCIATES

201 E. 28th ST., N.Y. , N.Y. 10016/212-532-0928/FAX 212-696-0958

EJA

Roberta Collier

represented by

Bud and Evelyne Johnson

ARTIST REPRESENTATIVES

EVELYNE JOHNSON ASSOCIATE

201 E. 28th ST., N.Y., N.Y. 10016/212-532-0928/FAX 212-696-

Roberta Remy

represented by

Bud and Evelyne Johnson

ARTIST REPRESENTATIVES

EVELYNE JOHNSON ASSOCIATES

201 E. 28th ST., N.Y., N.Y. 10016/212-532-0928/FAX 212-696-0958

Jonathan Annand

Jonathan Annand
345 Hudson Street
New York, NY 10014
(212) 924-7228

Clients include:
Backer Spielvogel & Bates (Prudential ad)
Business Week
Bowne Inc.
The Café Zealot
Discover
Lotus Magazine
Money
Sports Illustrated
SSC&B Lintas Worldwide (Johnson & Johnson Ad)

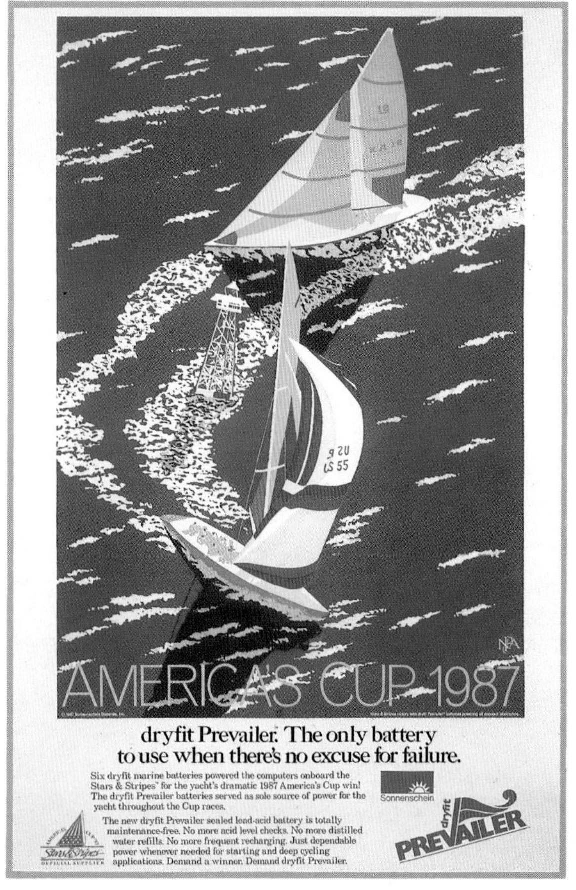

Nan Parson
13 Smoke Hill Drive
New Fairfield, CT 06812
(203) 746-9784

Al Romano

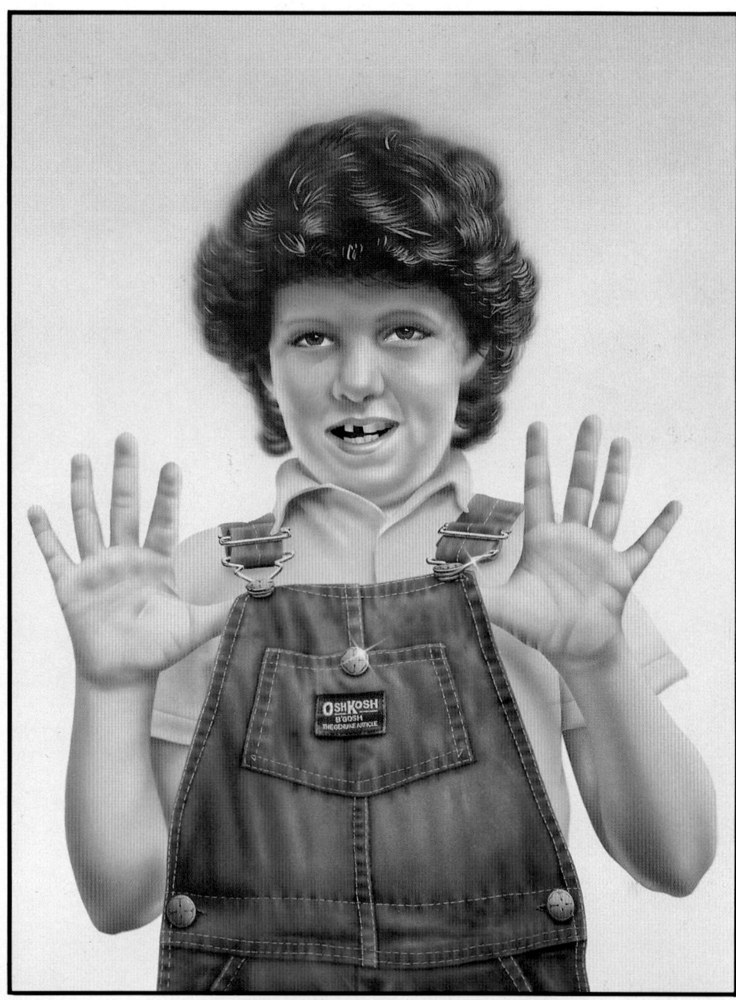

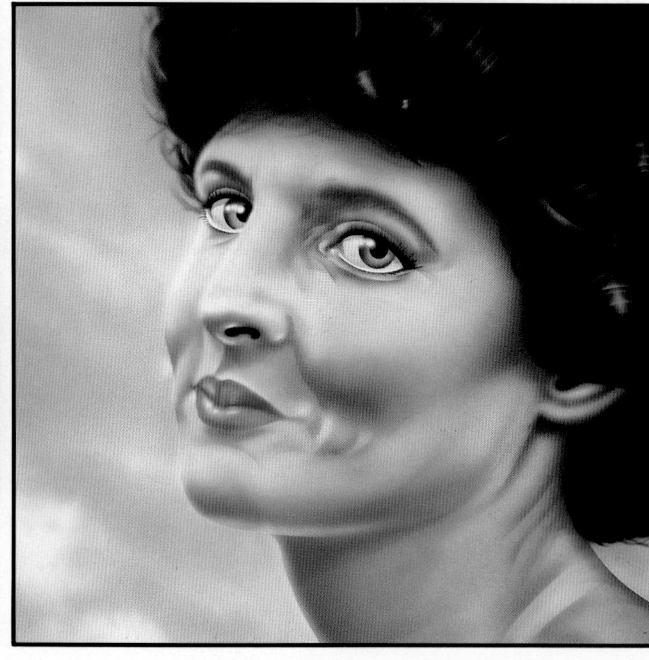

Al Romano
62 Kelsey Place
Madison, CT 06443
(203) 245-3006

Distinctive airbrush illustration for advertising, editorial, and corporate assignments.

Partial list of clients includes:

American Telephone & Telegraph BIC Hamilton Beach/Scovil Smith Corona Corporation Southern New England Telephone Stanley Tools

Telecopier in studio.

8 x 10 portfolio on request.

Member Graphic Artists Guild

Ken Condon
47 Garage Road
Sunderland, MA 01375
(413) 665-2747

Some clients I've worked with:

California Business
GK Hall
Hanover Insurance
Inc.
Lotus Development
McCormack and Dodge
Raytheon
Symbolics
Ziff-Davis

Additional samples appear in *American Showcase 10*

Call for Travelling Portfolio

Member Graphic Artists Guild

Carol Schweigert

Carol Schweigert
791 Tremont Street, E-406
Boston, MA 02118
(617) 262-8909

Clients include:
Fidelity Investments
Ziff-Davis (*PC Week* & *Digital Review*)
General Foods (Maxwell House)
Filene's Department Stores
Hawthorne Hotel
Brigham & Women's Hospital
Northern Isles (Goodman Knitting, Co.)
Pine Manor College
March of Dimes
International Racquet Sports Association

Member of Graphic Artists Guild

Valerie Costantino
2037 New Hyde Park Road
New Hyde Park, NY 11040
(516) 358-9121

Michael McGurl

Michael McGurl
83 Eighth Avenue, Apt 2B
Brooklyn, NY 11215
(718) 857-1866

Clients:
Atlantic Records, Bank of California, Brigham Young University, CBS, *Chicago Tribune*, Cooper Vision, *Detroit News*, *East West Magazine*, *Florida Magazine*, *Newsday Magazine*, Ralston Purina, Scholastic Software, Southwestern Bell, *Sport Detroit Magazine*, Unisys, Wheaton College.

Awards:
Society of Publication Designers, Creativity '87/*Art Direction Magazine*, New York Art Directors Club, Desi Award/*Graphic Design: USA*.

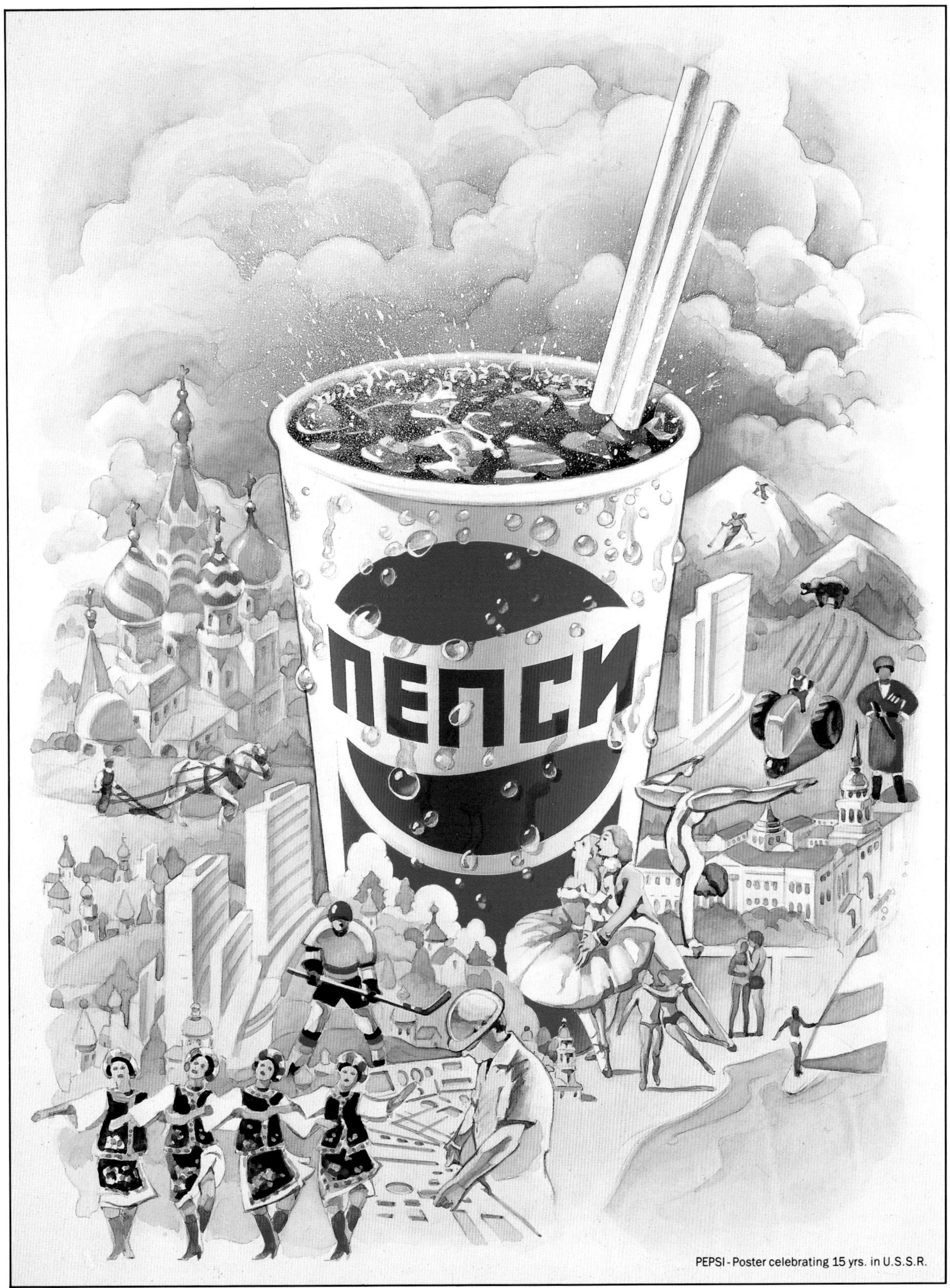

PEPSI - Poster celebrating 15 yrs. in U.S.S.R.

Tom Daly
47 East Edsel Avenue
Palisades Park, NJ 07650
(201) 943-1837

Over 20 years experience working for the top advertisers. He has won many awards including the New York Art Directors Club Gold Medal and the Award of Excellence from the Society of Illustrators.

He brings a light, airy look to products and services and is known for delivering "quality work on deadline."

Jeffrey Smith
255 East Prospect Avenue,
Apt. 1B
Mt. Vernon, NY 10550
(914) 667-6397

"BANK LINES"
Illustration for *Forbes Magazine* about the "Great Depression."

"AFFIRMED AND ALYDAR"
Black and white illustration for the "Views of Sport" section of the *New York Times.*

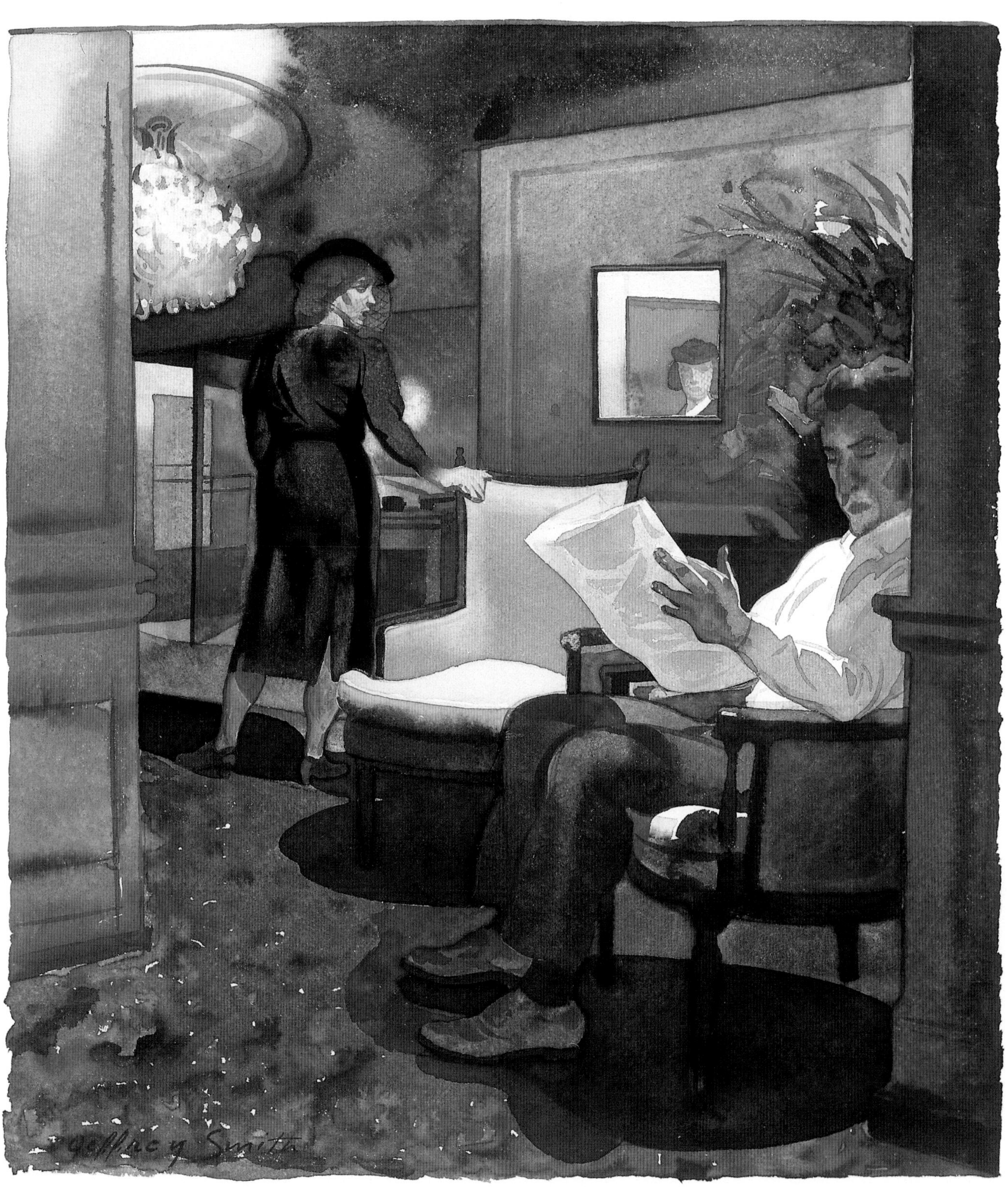

Jeffrey Smith
255 East Prospect Avenue,
Apt. 1B
Mt. Vernon, NY 10550
(914) 667-6397

"KISS IN THE HOTEL
JOSEPH CONRAD"
Illustration for the *Boston Globe*, a short story by Howard Norman.

Richard Giedd

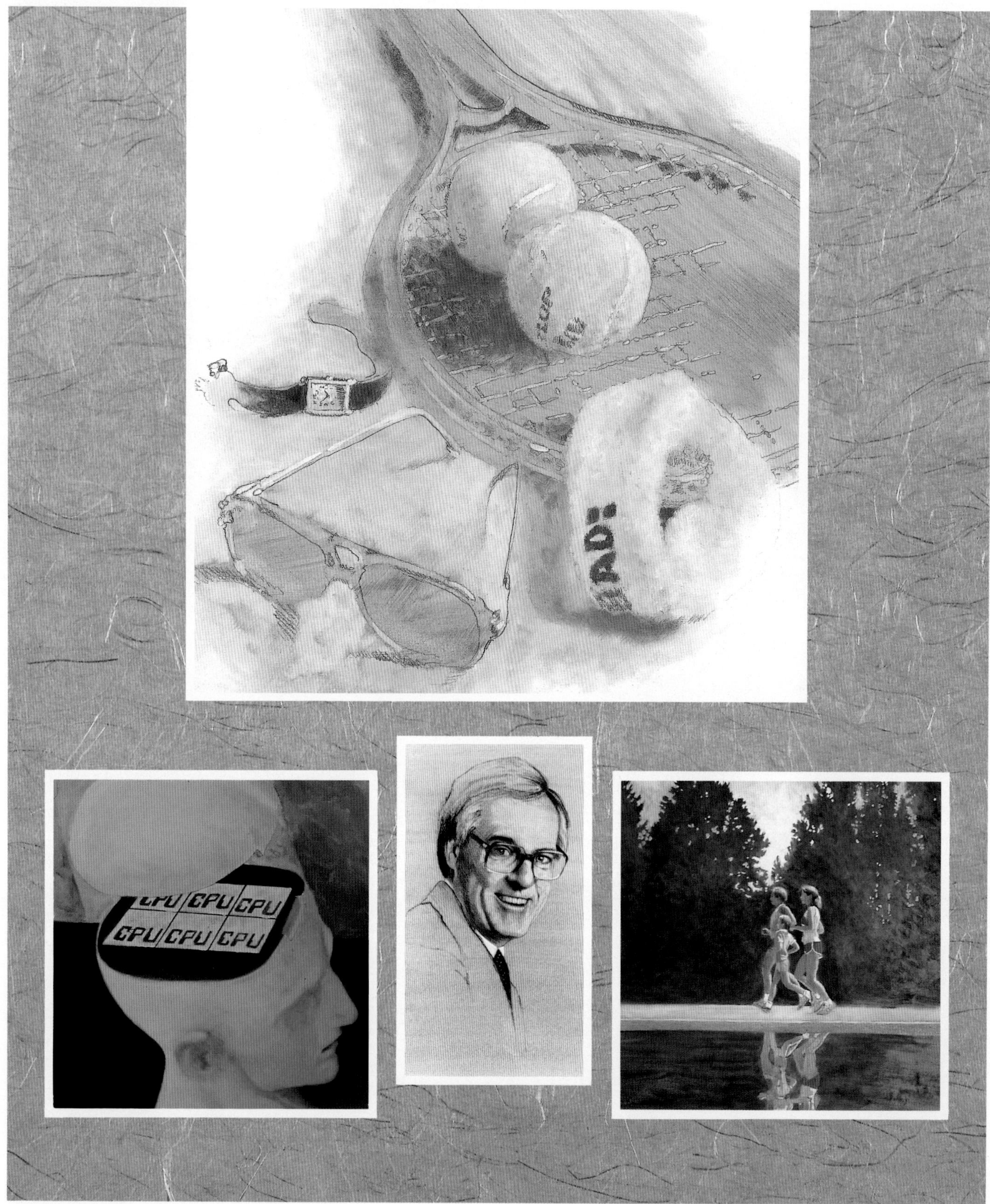

Richard Giedd
101 Pierce Road
Watertown, MA 02172
(617) 924-4350

Corporate, Advertising & Editorial Illustration

Clients include:
WBZ-TV, Affiliated Pub., Cabot, Cabot & Forbs; Apple Computer; Analysis & Technology Inc.; *The Boston Globe;* Cahners Publishing, *High Technology Magazine;* The Interface Group; John Hancock Insurance Co.; M/A-COM Inc.; McDonald's Corp.; *New England Business Magazine; PC Week;* Stride-Rite; Worcester Polytechnic; The N.R.A.; Adams-Russell Co. Inc.; Ziff-Davis Publishing.

To view more work:
Design Source (Boston) 1986, 87, 88
Adweek Portfolio 1987

Member:
Graphic Artists Guild

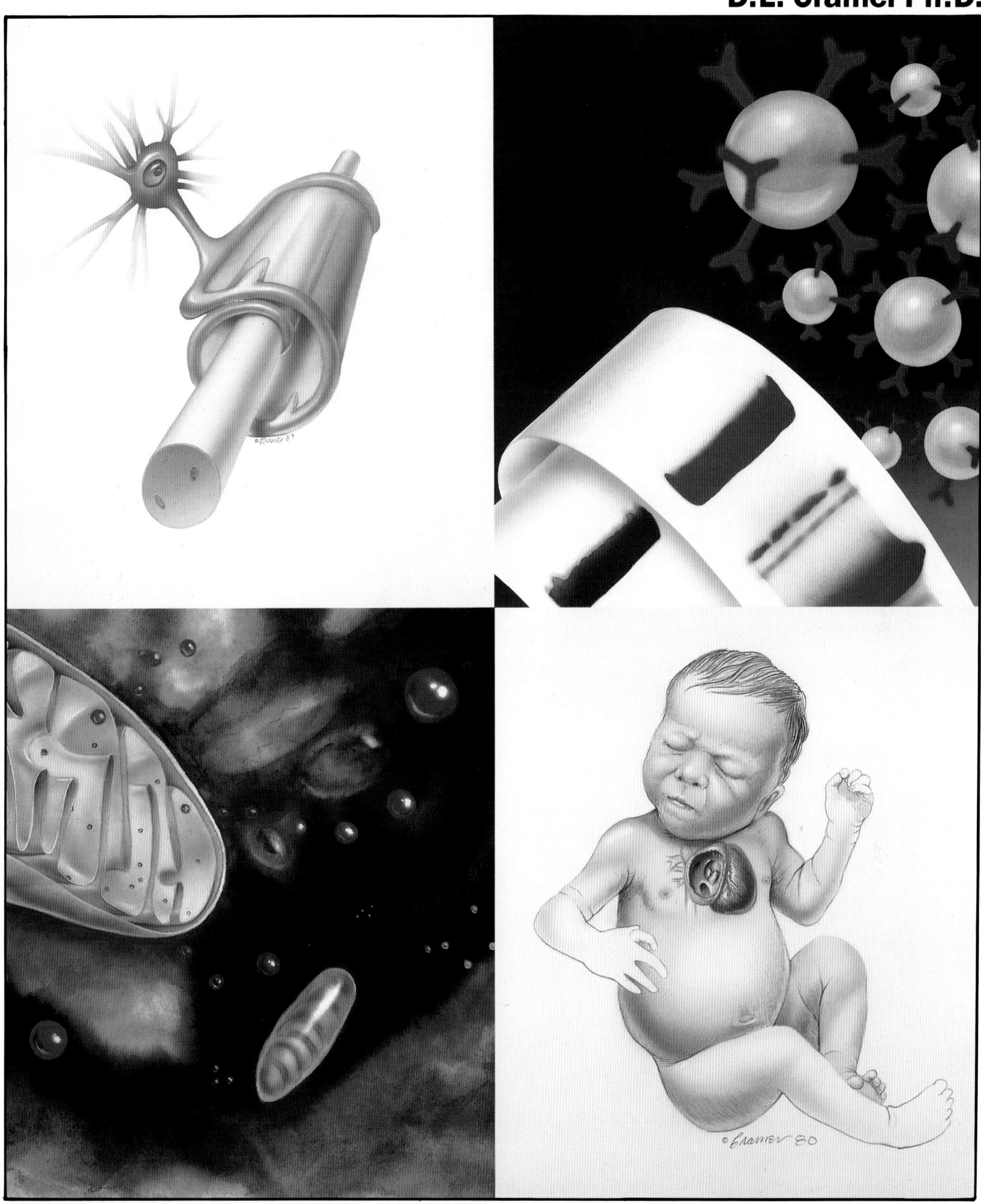

D. L. Cramer Ph.D.
10 Beechwood Drive
Wayne, NJ 07470
(201) 628-8793

Medical/Biological Illustration

Illustrations for: *Time, Sports Illustrated, Reader's Digest, Natural History, Runner, Science Digest, Med. Publishing, Modern Medicine, Hospital Medicine, RN, Cardiovascular Medicine, Drug Therapy, The Journal of Respiratory Diseases,* Crown Publishing, McGraw-Hill, S. Karger, Grolier, CIBA, Hoffman-LaRoche, Searle, Bristol-Myers, Winthrop Labs, Pfizer, Schering, Burroughs Wellcome, Mead Johnson, William Douglas McAdams, Lawrence Charles and Free, Chiat Day, Chedd Angier, Benton and Bowles.

Teaching: Currently Director of the Human Anatony Labs NYU School of Medicine.

Exhibitions: Society of Illustrators Invitational, AIGA.

Affiliations: Society of Illustrators (Past President), Graphic Artists Guild, AAAS.

Tom Ickert

A little song, *a little dance,*

A little seltzer *down your pants.*

Tom Ickert
354 East 83rd Street, #5A
New York, NY 10028
(212) 794-9723

Clients:
NBC, American Express, Finnair, Harcourt Brace Jovanovich, Cambridge University Press, Macmillan Publishing, Clairol, Maxell, Pepsi, *Newsweek, Inside Sports,* Ricoh, Computerland, Consumer Electronics, General Foods, Bristol-Myers.

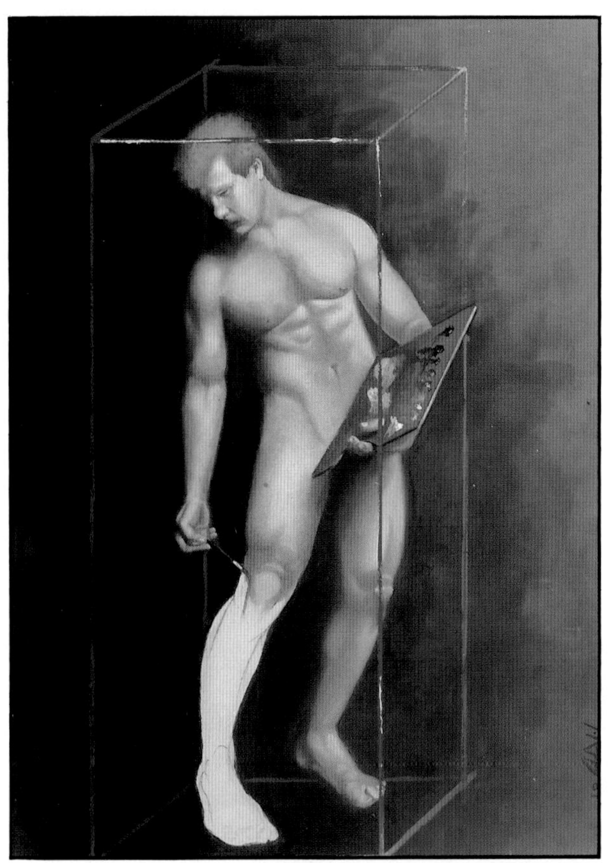

Floyd M. Rappy
Illustrator/Designer
(718) 241-2039

Clients include:
Pan Am
Manhattan Epicure
HBO
Hair Anew Inc.
Intrepid Communications

Exhibited in Society of Illustrators 28th Annual of American Illustration

Published in *Illustrators 28*

Master Eagle Gallery Annual Exhibition, Honorable Mention

Member Graphic Artists Guild

Instructor of drawing and oil painting

Alfred Ramage

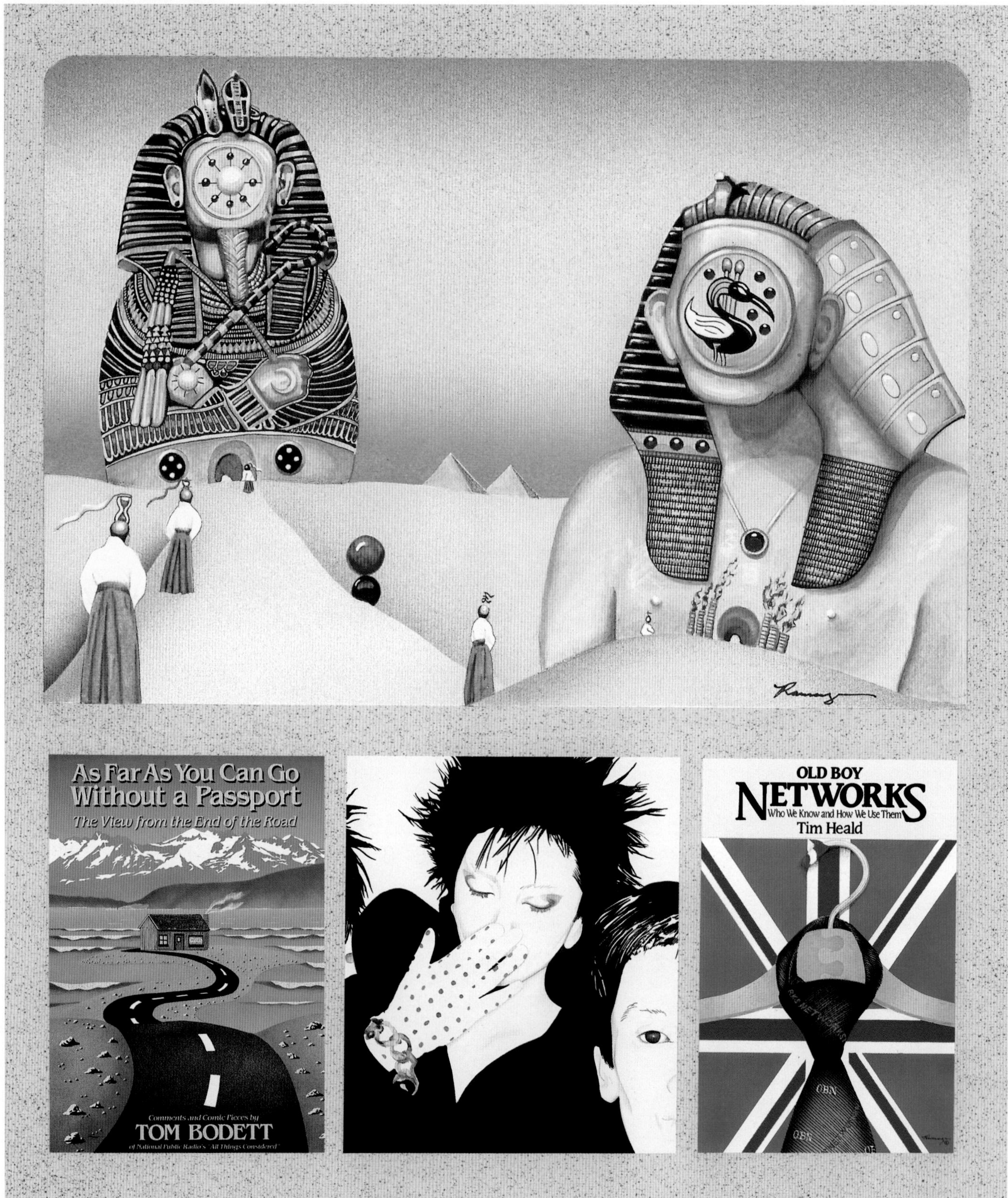

Alfred Ramage
Silent Sounds Studio
5 Irwin Street
Winthrop, MA 02152
(617) 846-5955

"Conceptual imagination, will travel."

Media: Oil, ink, watercolor, collage, colored pencil, whatever–

Area of expertise: Editorial, book cover, advertising, 3D action premiums, graphics, animation, exhibit design.

Clients:

Digital, Honeywell, Delta Airlines, American Red Cross, Boston Garden, New England Deaconess Hospital, University of Massachusetts Media Center, Pro Corporation, American Premium, Allyn & Bacon, Addison-Wesley Publishing, Houghton Mifflin, *Inc. Magazine, Boston Globe, Boston Monthly, Boston Phoenix, East West Journal,* C.W. Communications.

Awards:

Boston Society of Illustrators Certificate of Excellence, Boston Art Directors Club Distinctive Merit.

Anna Veltfort
16 West 86th Street, #B
New York, NY 10024
(212) 877-0430

David Tamura

David Tamura
153 East 26th Street
New York, NY 10010
(212) 686-4559

Clients:

Random House, Macmillan Publishing, Houghton Mifflin, Harper & Row, Warner Books, Amtrak, and Holiday Inns.

Awards:

Society of Illustrators, American Illustration, Communication Arts, New York Art Director's Club, and Creativity.

Jacqui Morgan

Jacqui Morgan
692 Greenwich Street
New York, NY 10014
(212) 463-8488

Watercolor

Clients include:

Architectural Digest, AT&T, Booz-Allen & Hamilton, Champion Papers, Citibank, Colgate Palmolive, *Communications Week*, General Electric, Hilton International, IBM, ITC, Irving Trust, Johnson Wax, *Lear's Magazine*, *New Woman Magazine*, *New York Magazine*, *New York Times*, Pfizer, Scott Paper Company.

Also seen in:

Graphis, *Idea Magazine*, *Gebrauchs Graphik*, *Print Magazine*, *American Artist*, Society of Illustrators Annuals, and Art Directors Annuals.

Listed in *Who's Who in Graphic Art*. Author of *Watercolor for Illustration*, Watson-Guptill.

Member Graphic Artists Guild

Alan Nahigian

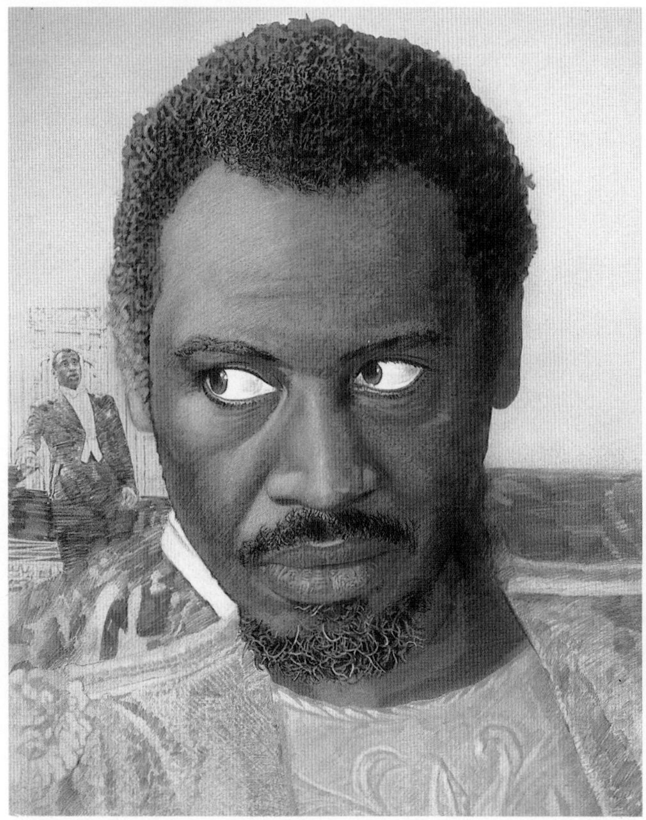

Alan Nahigian
33-08 31st Avenue, Apt. 2R
Long Island City, NY 11106
(718) 274-4042

Clients:
Canon, Chelsea House Publishers, *The Daily News*, DCA Advertising, *Institutional Investor*, McGraw-Hill, New York Telephone, *The New York Times*, *The Ring Magazine*, Soul Note Records, *Success! Magazine*, Twice Publishing Corp., *Video Magazine*, Walker and Company, Young & Rubicam.

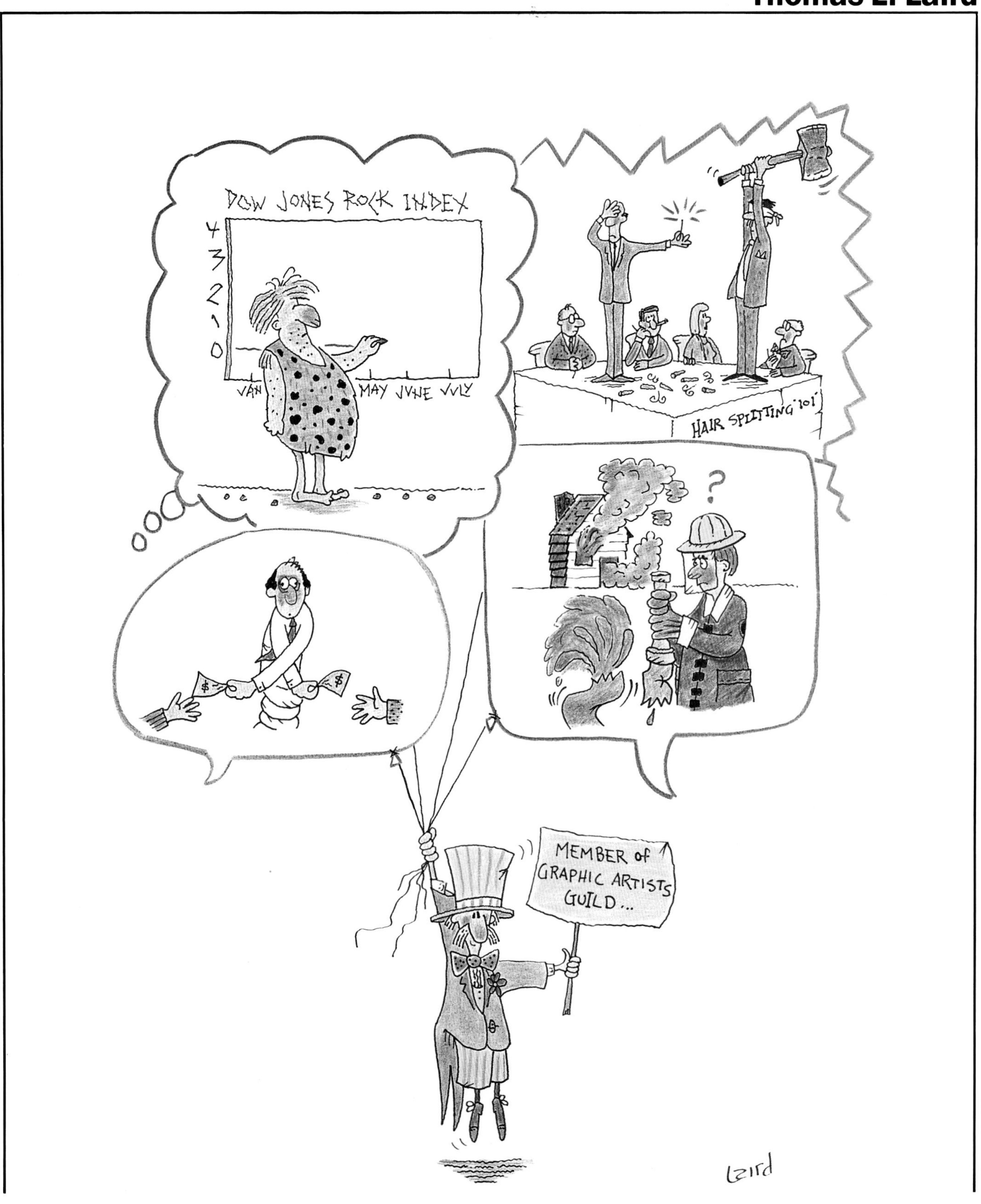

Thomas L. Laird
Philipsburg, PA 16866
(814) 342-2935

Cartooning/Humorous Concepts & Illustration

Specializing in–but not limited to–Advertising, Corporate, Editorial, Book, and Magazine Illustration.

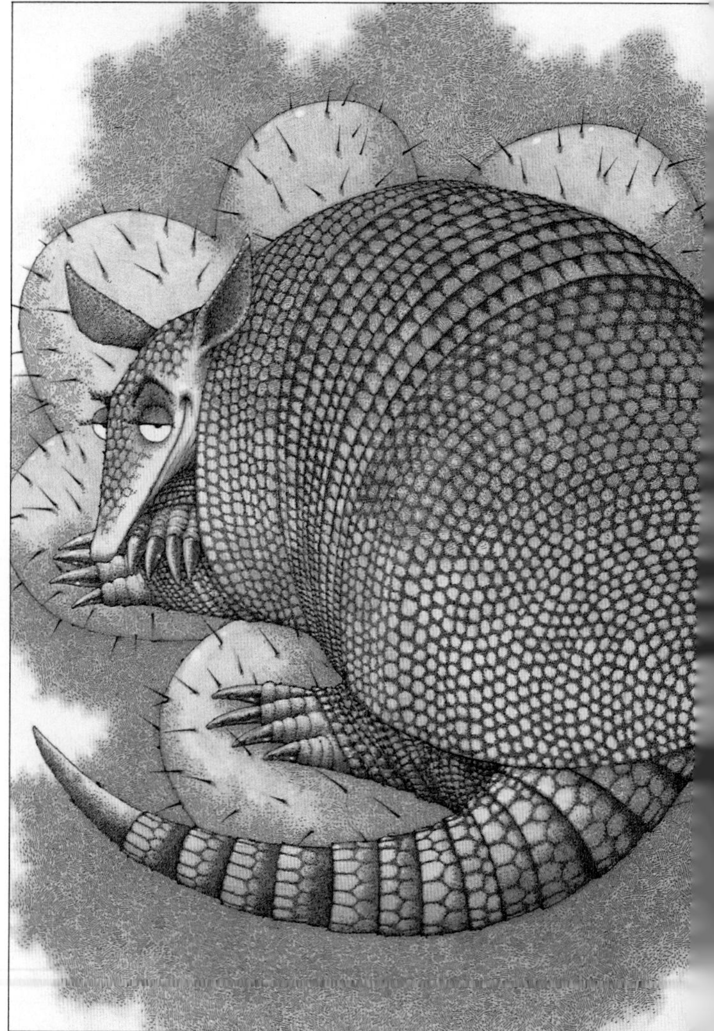

SEAVER

JEFF SEAVER 130 WEST 24TH STREET 4B
NEW YORK NY 10011 212/741-2279

JEFF SEAVER 130 WEST 24TH STREET 4B
NEW YORK NY 10011 212/741-2279

Joe Ciardiello

Joe Ciardiello
2182 Clove Road
Staten Island, NY 10305
(718) 727-4757

Clients include:

Anthony Russell Inc., Bell South, *Changing Times*, Citibank, *Creative Living*, *Emergency Medicine*, *Financial Executive*, Franklin Library, *Inc.*, *The Progressive*, Reader's Digest Books, Sony, *Sports Illustrated*, Texaco, *The Washington Post*.

Work has also been featured in *U&lc*, *How*, *Print*, *Idea* (Japan), and *Gráfica* (Brazil).

Member Society of Illustrators, Graphic Artists Guild.

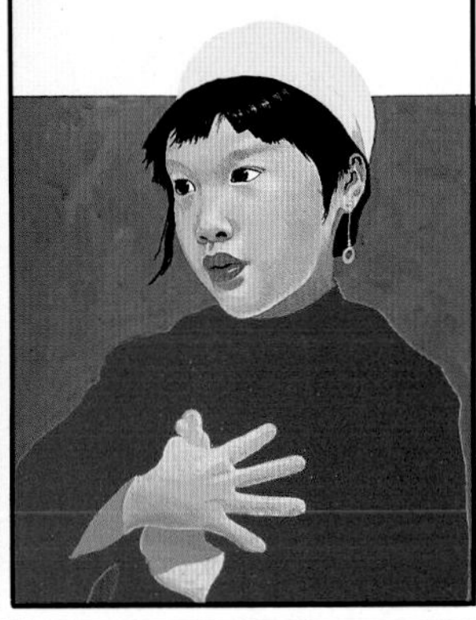

Christopher Graham
1028 Elberon Avenue
Long Branch, NJ 07740
(201) 870-0373

Glenn Gustafson

GUSTAFSON

Glenn Gustafson
307 North Michigan Avenue
Suite 2016
Chicago, IL 60601
(312) 368-4536

Clients include:
American Academy of Pediatrics, Milton Bradley, Turtle Wax, Kraft Foods, Deltak, *Illinois Business Magazine,* Sears, Rust-O-Leum, Citicorp, Kimberly-Clarke, Container Corporation of America, Miller Breweries, American Dental Association, Jockey International, *Consumer Digest Magazine, Logic Magazine,* Standard Oil, Kaiser Aluminum.

Member Graphic Artists Guild

Sam Viviano
25 West 13th Street
New York, NY 10011
(212) 242-1471

Cartoon, caricature, and humorous illustration

Exhibitions:
Illustrators 23, Humor '87

Member Graphic Artists Guild

Clients include:

ABC, BBDO, Cahners Publishing, CBS, Citibank, Colgate-Palmolive, Compton Advertising, *Consumer Reports*, *Crain's New York Business*, CTW, Cunningham & Walsh, DFS Dorland, Diener/Hauser/Bates, Doyle Dane Bernbach, *Dynamite*, *Family Circle*, FCB/Leber Katz Partners, *Field & Stream*, *Golf Digest*, IBM, *Institutional Investor*, J. Walter Thompson, Lowe Marschalk, *Mad Magazine*, McCaffrey and McCall, McCann-Erickson, McNeil/Lehrer Report, Metromedia, *Money*, MONY, N W Ayer, NBC, New American Library, New Line Cinema, New York Life, Ogilvy & Mather, *People*, RCA, *Reader's Digest*, *Redbook*, *Rolling Stone*, Scholastic, Showtime, Smirnoff, *Tennis*, United Artists, Ziff-Davis.

Alan Bortman

Alan Bortman
33 Brainerd Road
Brighton, MA 02135
(617) 277-0676

Danny Crouse

Danny Crouse
24 Appleton Road
Glen Ridge, NJ 07028
(201) 748-1650

Society of Illustrators
Graphic Artists Guild

Susan Swan

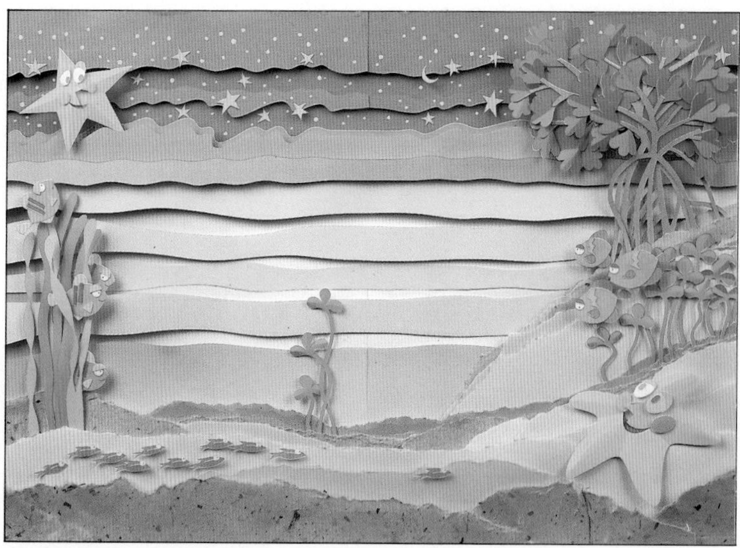

Susan Swan
83 Saugatuck Avenue
Westport, CT 06880
(203) 226-9104

Member Graphic Artists Guild

John R. Gould
300 West 107th Street, St. 1-D
New York, NY 10025
(212) 662-7854

Illustration and Design

Member Graphic Artists Guild

Tom Huffman

Tom Huffman
130 West 47th Street, 6A
New York, NY 10036
(212) 819-0211

Whether you are looking for a clever idea or just the birth of a notion, think witty, think smart, think Tom Huffman. Choose punchy black and white or dazzling color—add zest, speed, and inimitable style. It all adds up to a winning formula for a job that delivers.

It's a joy! Pampered and satisfied clients include: ABC Television; AC&R/DHB & Bess; AT&T; Backer, Spielvogel & Bates; Bozell, Jacobs, Kenyon & Eckhardt; Burson Marstellar; *Cosmopolitan;* Greenwillow; Houghton Mifflin; Macy's; McGraw-Hill; Mobil; Ogilvy & Mather; Pfizer; Saatchi & Saatchi DFS Compton; Sudler & Hennessey, Inc.; *Travel & Leisure; Woman's Day.*

Chris Spollen

1

2

4

1. BOOK OF THE MONTH CLUB
2. AMERICAN EXPRESS COMPANY
3. CONSUMER REPORT MAGAZINE
4. MEDICAL ECONOMICS COMPANY

3

Chris Spollen
Moonlight Press Studio
(718) 979-9695
Telex in studio
(718) 979-8919

High Contrast Illustration

Client List:

Graphic illustraion for major corporations and agencies worldwide.

To View More Work:

American Showcase 8, 9, 10, 11, 12; Corporate Showcase 5, 6; Art Directors Index 12, 13, 14; Blackbook 1988.

Awards:

Society of Illustrators 1984, Print Regional 1985, Art Directors Club of New Jersey bronze and gold 1987.

Professional Associations:

Graphic Artists Guild, Society of Illustrators, New Jersey Art Directors Club

Areas of Expertise:

Design illustration b & w and 4-C; a mini-portfolio of samples sent upon request.

Karen Leon

Villa Mosconi
"That night at Villa Mosconi, we enjoyed fresh pasta and a perfect evening, until Janice decided the setting was appropriate for an aria from Rigoletto."
AMERICAN EXPRESS
Don't leave home without it.

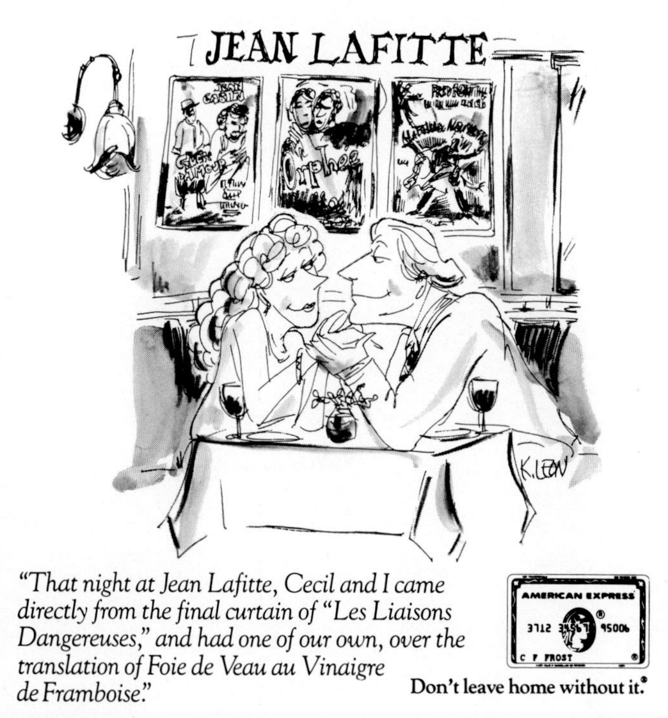

JEAN LAFITTE
"That night at Jean Lafitte, Cecil and I came directly from the final curtain of "Les Liaisons Dangereuses," and had one of our own, over the translation of Foie de Veau au Vinaigre de Framboise."
AMERICAN EXPRESS
Don't leave home without it.

Karen Leon
134-01 Barclay Avenue
Flushing, NY 11355
(718) 461-2050
(718) 463-3159

Cartoon Illustration, Humor and Editorial Cartoons, Caricatures.

Clients include:
American Express, Kellogg's, Seagram's, *Crain's New York Business, Woman's World,* Thomas Publishing Co.,
Public Relations Society of America.

Member of the Graphic Artists Guild

Nancy L. Hoffmann

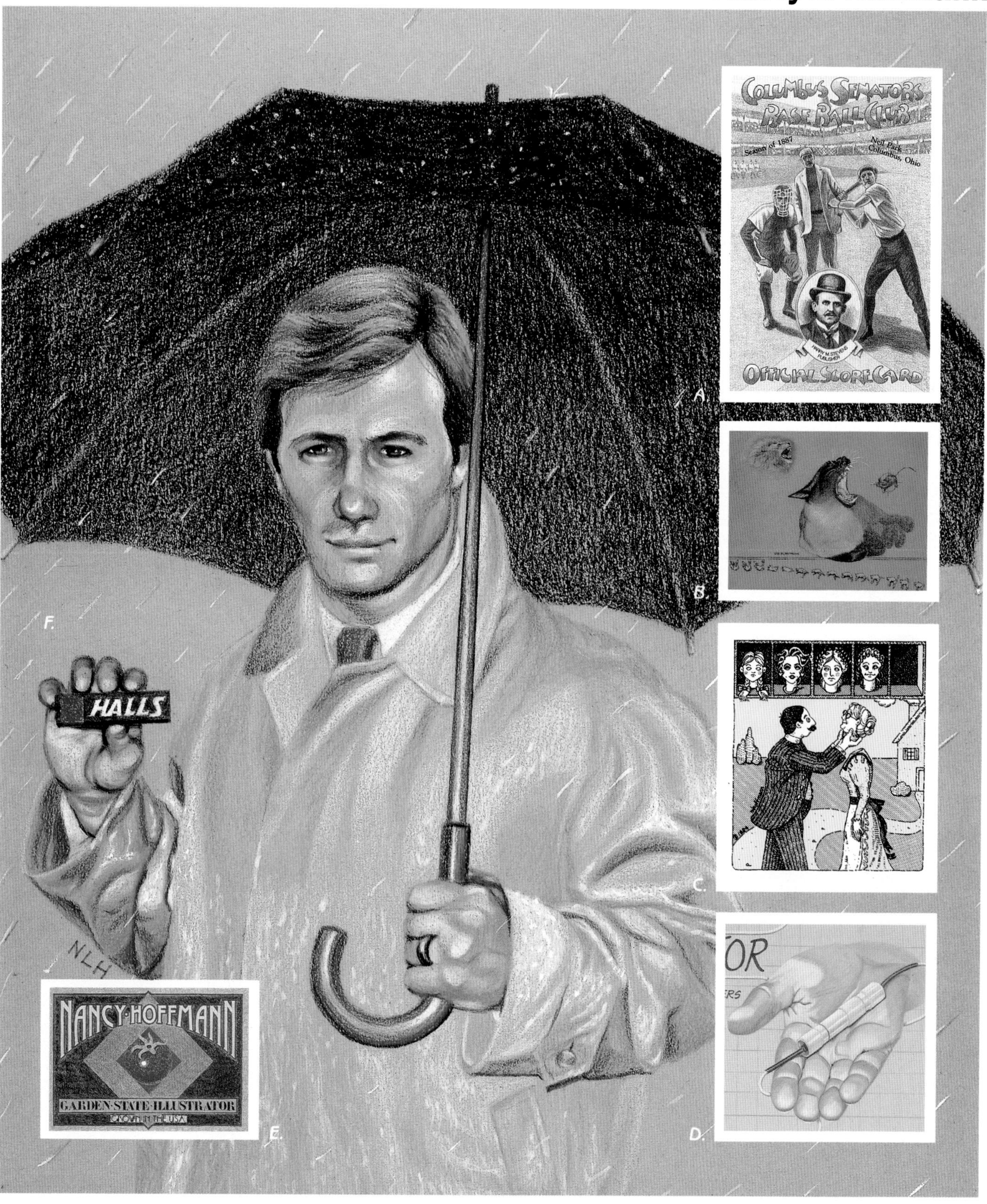

Nancy L. Hoffmann
16 Ridge Drive
Berkeley Heights, NJ 07922
(201) 665-2177

A. Harry M. Stevens, Inc.
B. Self Promotion
C. Illustration, "Jung's Dream Theory"
D. Bell Communications Research (Bellcore)
E. Corporate Identity
F. Warner Lambert

Affiliations:
Partner, AD Communications
VP, Board of Directors, NY Graphic Artists Guild
Member, Art Directors Club of NJ
Member, Society of Illustrators

1987 Awards:
Certificate of Excellence, ADC/NJ
Silver Medal, ADC/NJ
Print's Regional Annual, p. 251 (Certificate of Design Excellence)

Doug Cushman

Doug Cushman
31 West Prospect Street
New Haven, CT 06515
(203) 387-6327

Clients include:
Harper & Row Junior Books, E.P. Dutton, Little Brown, Grosset and Dunlap.

Jonathan Rosenbaum

Jonathan Rosenbaum
4 Carroll Street
Stamford, CT 06907
(203) 324-4558

Clients include:
A.C. Nielsen
All Brand Importers
American Express
Cadbury Schweppes
Consumer Reports
DFS Dorland
Family Circle
Frito-Lay
General Foods
Golf Digest
Hanes Hosiery
Home Box Office
Institutional Investor
Maclean Hunter Media, Inc.
Macmillan Publishing
Nabisco Brands
National Hockey League
Reader's Digest
R.J. Reynolds Tobacco Company
Smucker's
Stroh Brewing Company
Tennis Magazine
Time-Life
United Parcel Service
Waldenbooks
Wrangler
Young & Rubicam

Member Graphic Artists Guild

Harry R. Davis

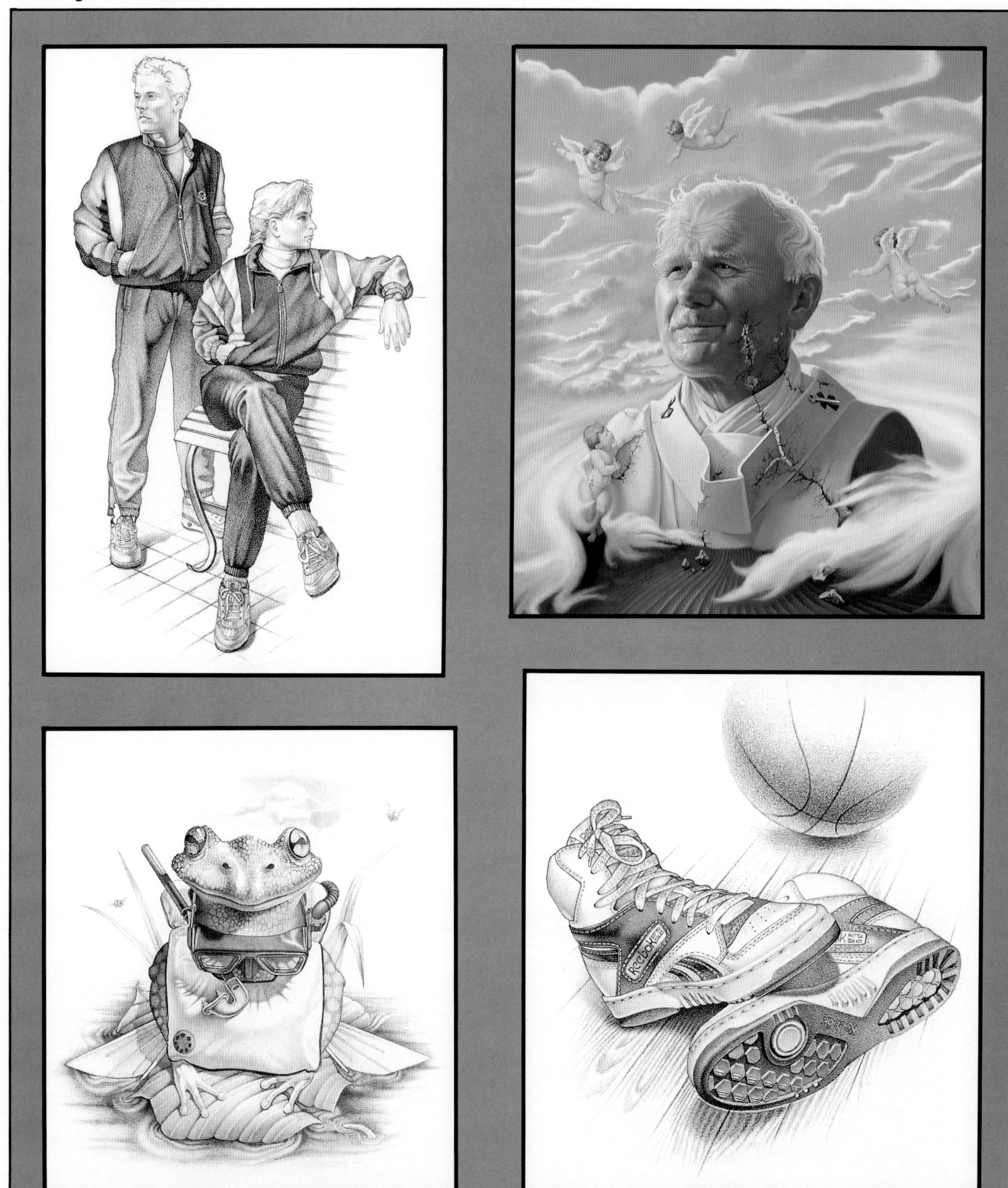

Harry R. Davis
189 East 3rd Street, Apt. #15
New York, NY 10009
(212) 674-5832

Partial client list:
AT&T
Eastern Telephone Systems
Pizza Hut
Paragon Sporting Goods
Walker Press
Spring House Corporation
Nike
Boyds
Speedo
Henri Lloyd
Bally's Casino
Reebok
After Six Tuxedo
Ellesse

Richard Anderson
7916 Winston Road
Philadelphia, PA 19118
(215) 247-9155

Illustrations

Sean Farrell

Commerce Street: *The taunting and gibing is all in good spirits Friday night, when the friendly states of Oklahoma and Texas meet for their annual Cotton Bowl Classic. Drawing from memory, 14 x 14, markers, airbrush, colored pencils.*

Sean Farrell
245 East 44th Street
New York, NY 10017
(212) 949-6081

Storyboard and comp. illustrator

Thomas Payne
11 Colonial Avenue
Albany, NY 12203
(518) 482-1756

Clients include:

National Geographic Society
Yankee Publishing Inc.
Cape Cod Compass
Cosmopolitan
Home Mechanix
PC Week
Mature Outlook
GTE
MCI
Philip Morris
Citibank
Prentice Hall
Blue Cross and Blue Shield
New York State Department of Environmental Conservation
National Trade Publications
National Public Radio

Mitchell Hooks

(212) 986-5680

Mendola LTD.

GRAYBAR BLDG. • 420 LEXINGTON AVE. • PENTHOUSE • NEW YORK, N.Y. 10170

(212) 986-5680

Mendola LTD.

GRAYBAR BLDG. • 420 LEXINGTON AVE. • PENTHOUSE • NEW YORK, N.Y. 10170

DENNIS LYALL

© 1987 Unicover Corporation

© 1987 Unicover Corporation

CHUCK GILLIES

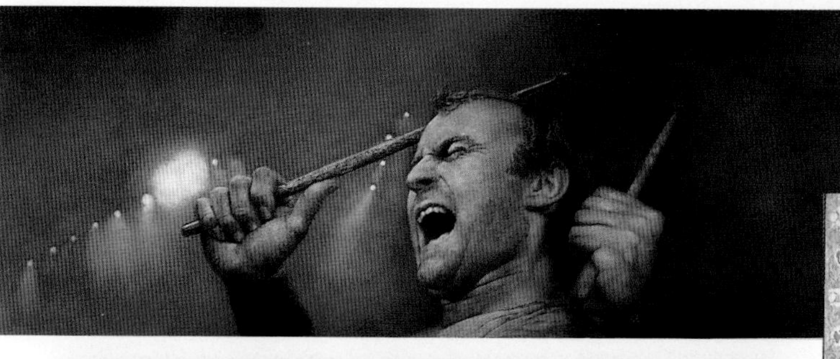

ANN MEISEL

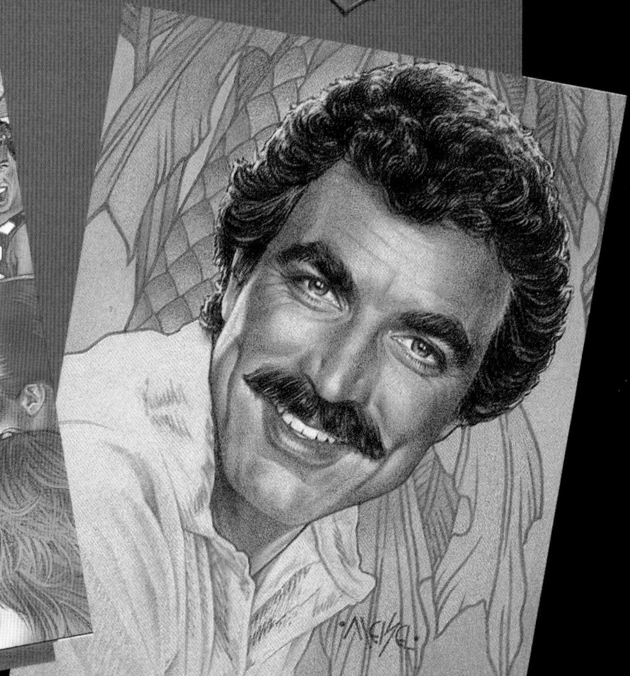

(212) 986-5680

GRAYBAR BLDG. • 420 LEXINGTON AVE. • PENTHOUSE • NEW YORK, N.Y. 10170

BRIAN SAURIOL

ALFONS KIEFER

(212) 986-5680

Mendola

GRAYBAR BLDG. • 420 LEXINGTON AVE. • PENTHOUSE • NEW YORK, NY 10170

DALE GUSTAFSON

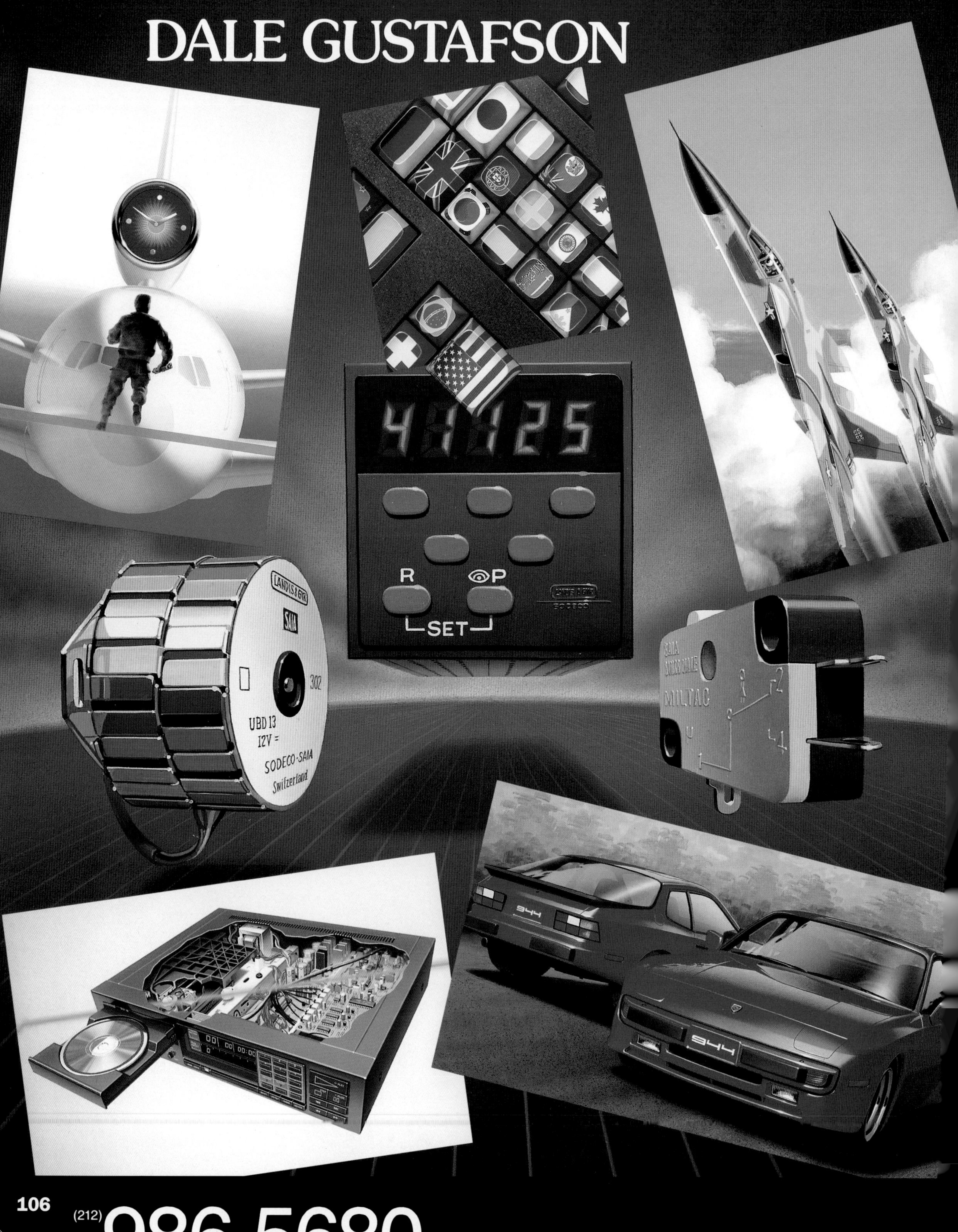

(212) 986-5680

Mendola LTD.

GRAYBAR BLDG. • 420 LEXINGTON AVE. • PENTHOUSE • NEW YORK, N.Y. 10170

CHRIS NOTARILE

Marilyn Monroe
Limited Edition
Collector Plates

(212) 986-5680

Mendola LTD.

GRAYBAR BLDG. • 420 LEXINGTON AVE. • PENTHOUSE • NEW YORK, N.Y. 10170

JOHN F. EGGERT

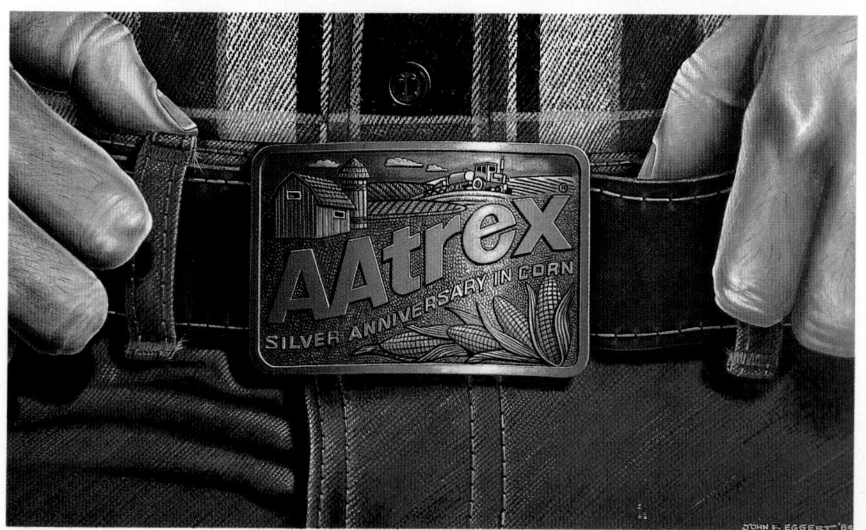

(212) 986-5680

Mendola LTD.

GRAYBAR BLDG. • 420 LEXINGTON AVE. • PENTHOUSE • NEW YORK, N.Y. 10170

BERNARD BERNHARDT

TED MICHENER

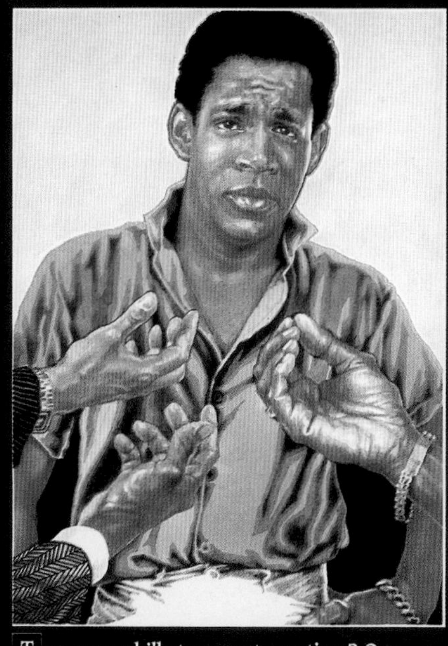

Too many bills to pay at one time? Our Scotia Plan* Consolidation Loan can help make all those payments easier to swallow by consolidating all your monthly payments and leaving you with one more manageable payment tailored to suit your budget. So ask us how a Scotia Plan Consolidation Loan can help you get it all together again.

Scotiabank
THE BANK OF NOVA SCOTIA

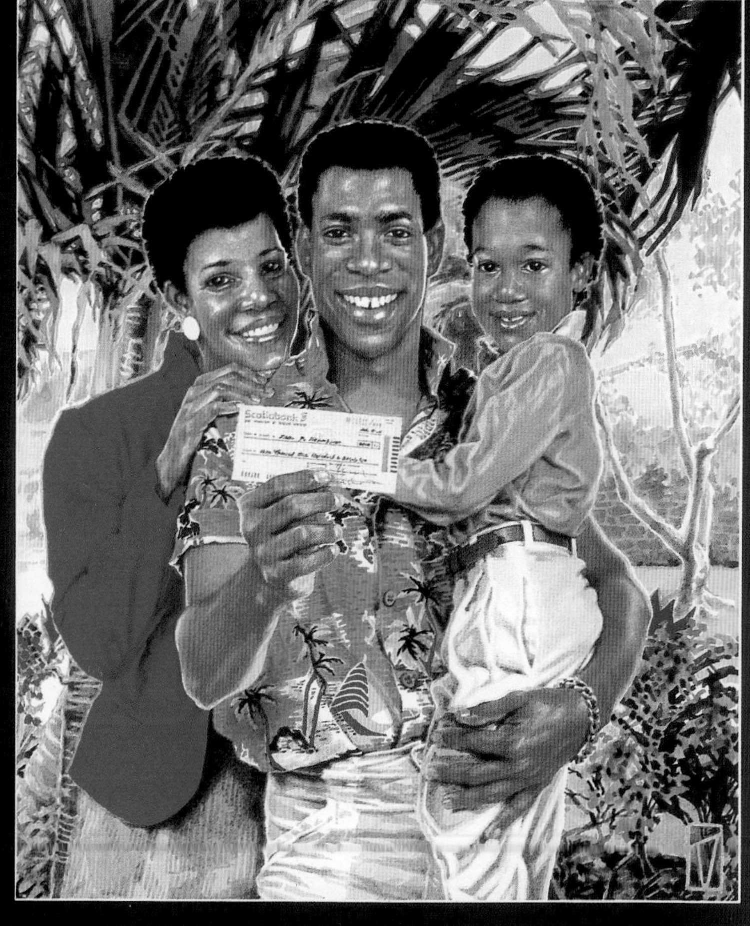

(212) 986-5680

Mendola LTD.

GRAYBAR BLDG. • 420 LEXINGTON AVE. • PENTHOUSE • NEW YORK, N.Y. 10170

MARK · WATTS INC.

ILLUSTRATION • TYPE • DESIGN

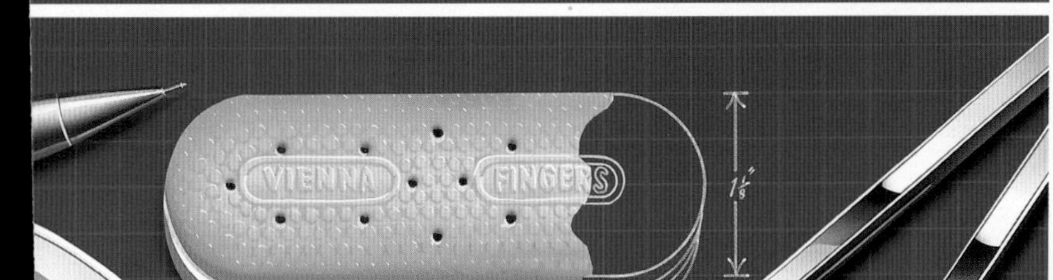

(212) 986-5680

GRAYBAR BLDG. • 420 LEXINGTON AVE. • PENTHOUSE • NEW YORK, N.Y. 10170

Mendola LTD.

ROGER METCALF

CLIFF SPOHN

8th National
Sports Collectors
convention
Dodgers
San Francisco

MATTHEW BENDER
FORECLOSURE
LAW BOOKS
LAW BOOKS
1040
Deed
Last WILL
BAYLIES PLEADING
A Celebration of Service
1887-1987

KIPP SOLDWEDEL

OPERATION-LIBERTY 1986

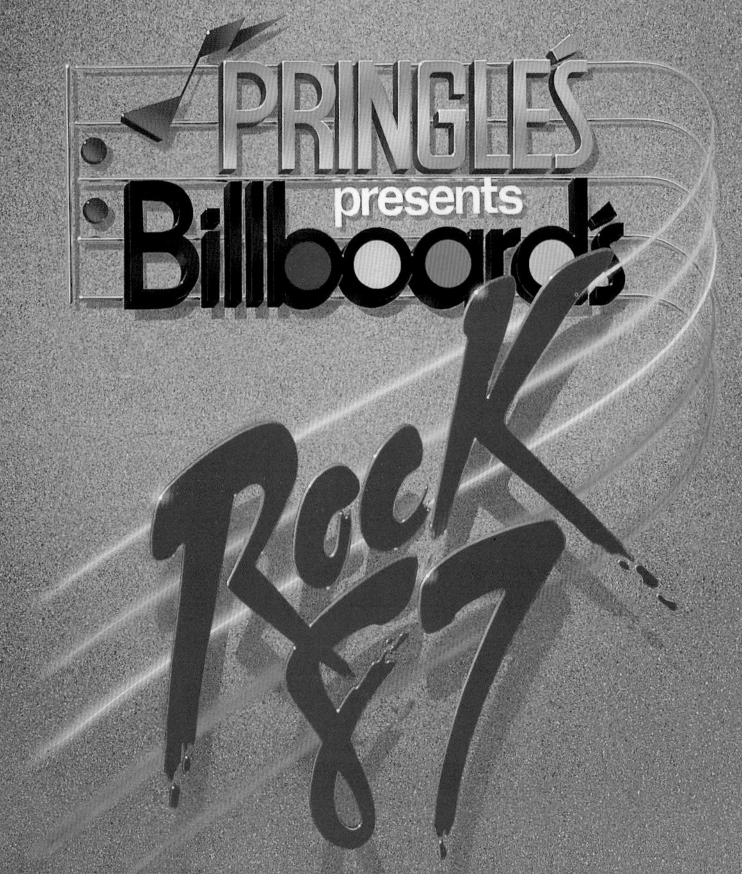

COUNTER

LYNCH

(212) 986-5680

Mendola LTD.

GRAYBAR BLDG. • 420 LEXINGTON AVE. • PENTHOUSE • NEW YORK, N.Y. 10170

TOM NEWSOM

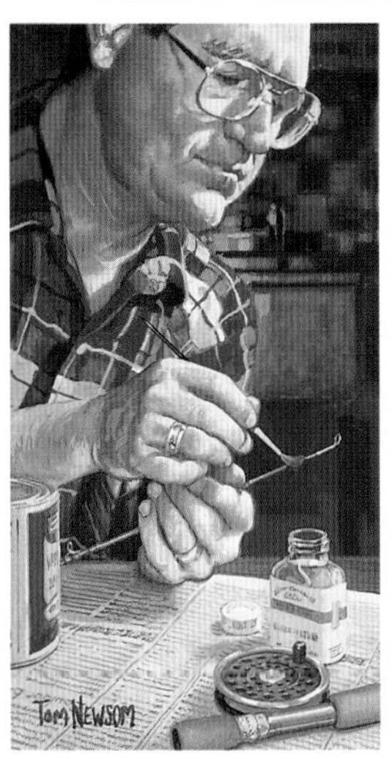

CAROL NEWSOM

JEFFREY TERRESON

MICHAEL SMOLLIN

(212) 986-5680

Mendola LTD.

GRAYBAR BLDG. • 420 LEXINGTON AVE. • PENTHOUSE • NEW YORK, N.Y. 10170

JOHN SOLIE

(212) 986-5680

Mendola LTD.

GRAYBAR BLDG • 420 LEXINGTON AVE • PENTHOUSE • NEW YORK, N.Y. 10170

JON ELLIS

BOB JONES

PETER FIORE

(212) 986-5680

Mendola LTD.

GRAYBAR BLDG. • 420 LEXINGTON AVE. • PENTHOUSE • NEW YORK, N.Y. 10170

DONNA DIAMOND

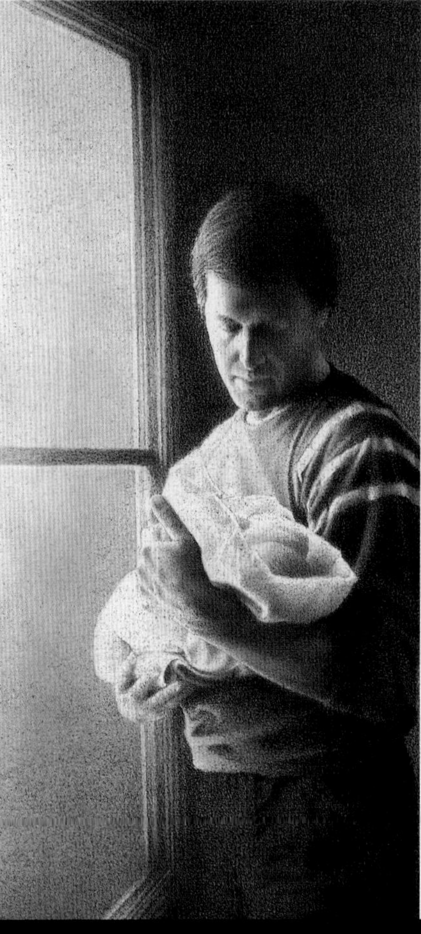

(212) 986-5680

Mendola LTD.

GRAYBAR BLDG. • 420 LEXINGTON AVE. • PENTHOUSE • NEW YORK, N.Y. 10170

JONATHAN MILNE

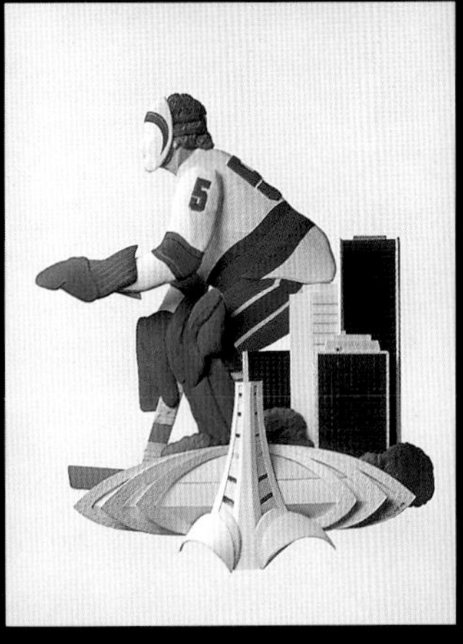

(212) 986-5680

Mendola LTD.

GRAYBAR BLDG. • 420 LEXINGTON AVE. • PENTHOUSE • NEW YORK, N.Y. 10170

MIKE MIKOS

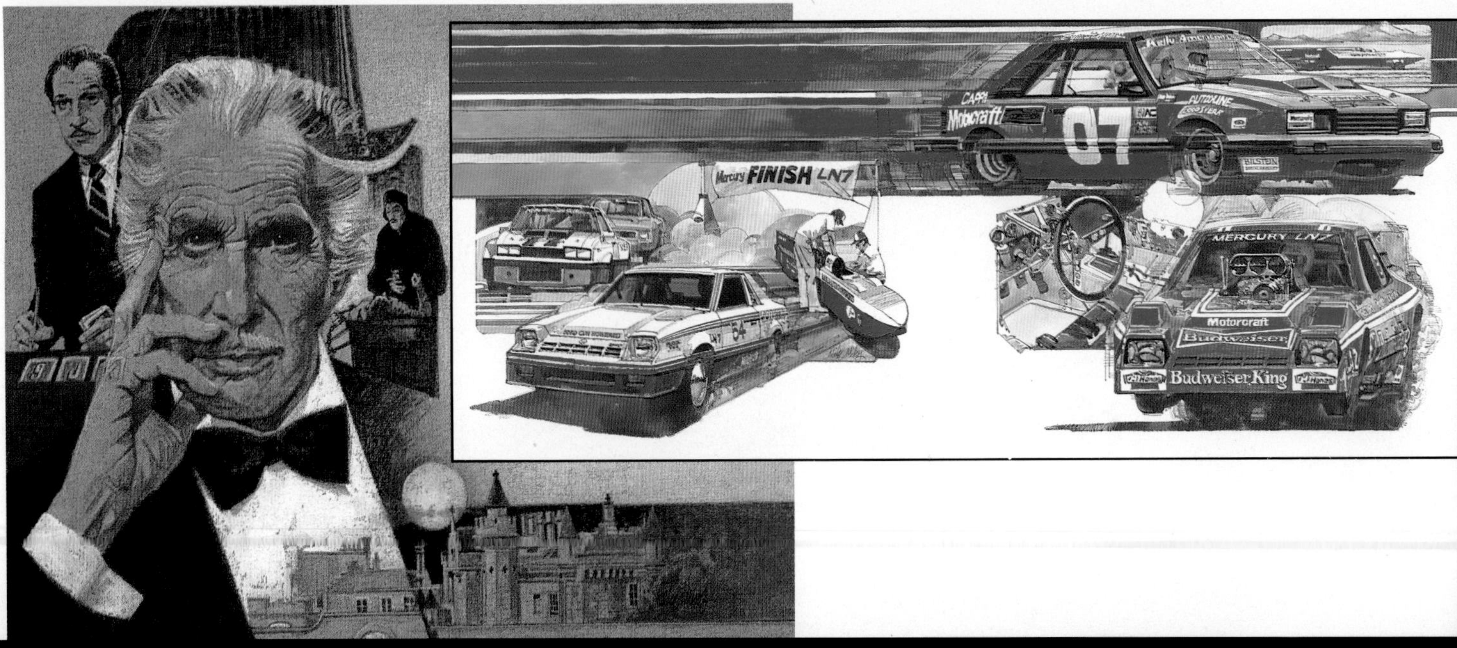

(212) 986-5680

Mendola LTD.

GRAYBAR BLDG. • 420 LEXINGTON AVE. • PENTHOUSE • NEW YORK, N.Y. 10170

JIM CAMPBELL

(212) 986-5680

Mendola LTD.

GRAYBAR BLDG. • 420 LEXINGTON AVE. • PENTHOUSE • NEW YORK, N.Y. 10170

PHIL FRANKE

DAVID SCHLEINKOFER

(212) 986-5680

Mendola LTD.

GRAYBAR BLDG. • 420 LEXINGTON AVE. • PENTHOUSE • NEW YORK, N.Y. 10170

GARRY COLBY

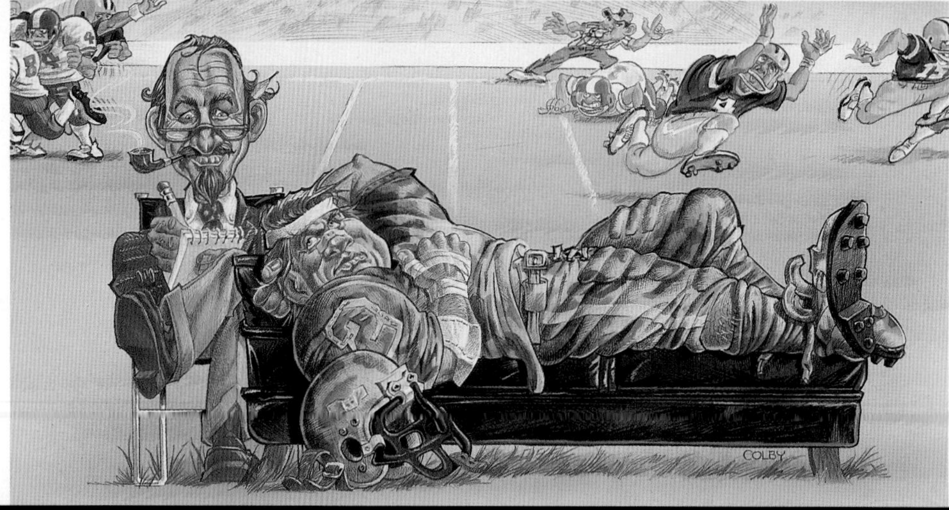

(212) 986-5680

Mendola LTD.

GRAYBAR BLDG. • 420 LEXINGTON AVE. • PENTHOUSE • NEW YORK, N.Y. 10170

JEFFREY MANGIAT

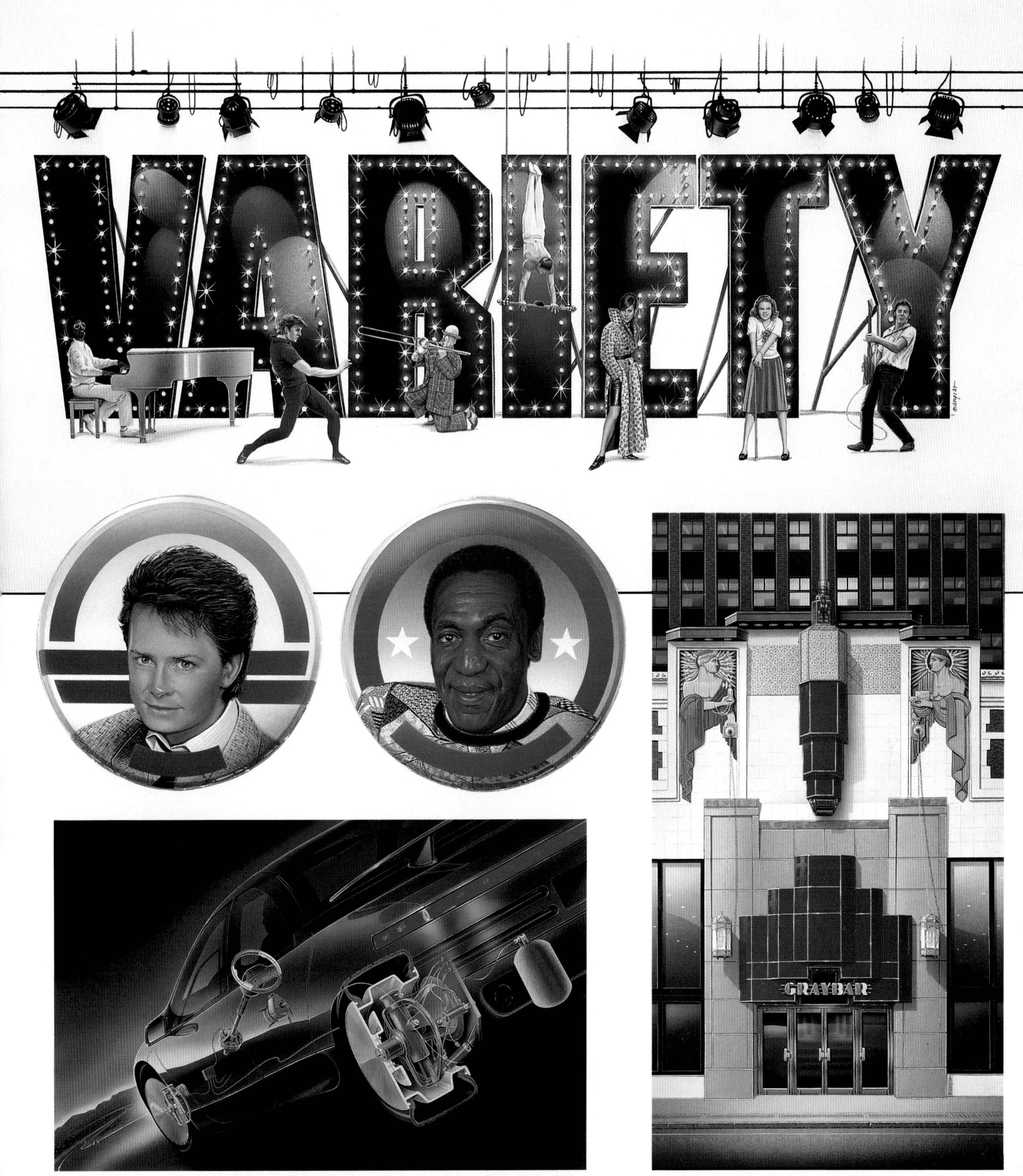

(212) 986-5680

Mendola LTD.

GRAYBAR BLDG. • 420 LEXINGTON AVE. • PENTHOUSE • NEW YORK, N.Y. 10170

CHARLES LILLY

(212) 986-5680

Mendola LTD.

GRAYBAR BLDG. • 420 LEXINGTON AVE. • PENTHOUSE • NEW YORK, N.Y. 10170

JIM DENEEN

PAUL ALEXANDER

(212) 986-5680

Mendola LTD.

GRAYBAR BLDG. • 420 LEXINGTON AVE. • PENTHOUSE • NEW YORK, NY 10170

GEOFF McCORMACK

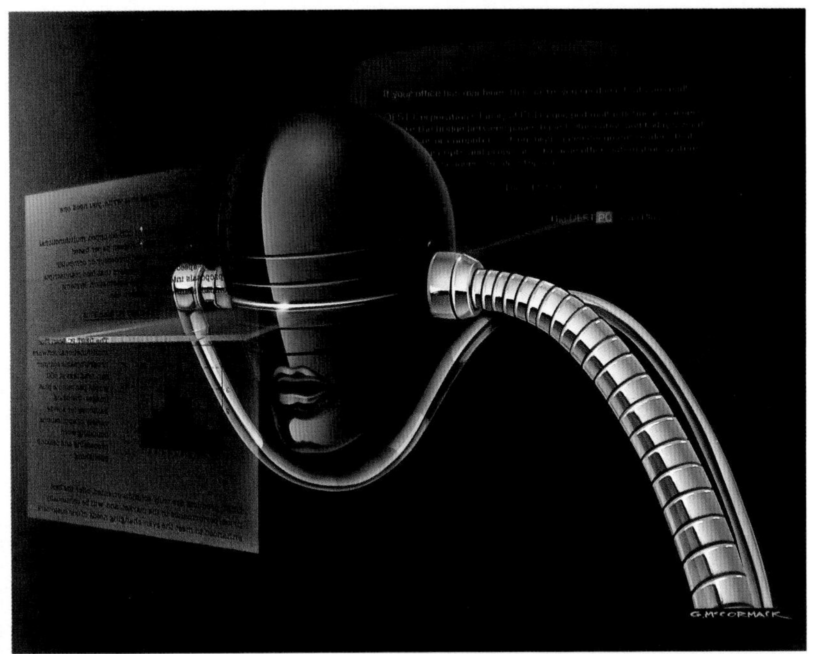

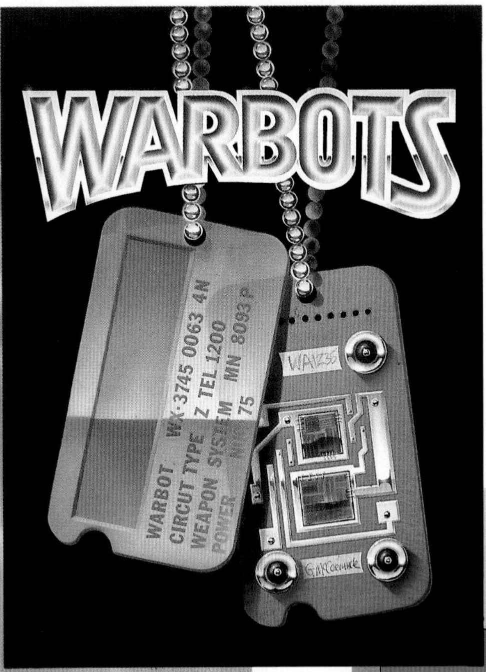

BOB BERRAN

The
Blue Cross
and
Blue Shield
HMO
The
Blue Cross
and
Blue Shield
HMO

AMSTEL light
AMSTEL light
IMPORTED
AMSTEL light

BILL
AT
DONNA
EDDIE
395
450
490
50

RICHARD LEECH

Porsche 959 6-cylinder, horizontally-opposed, four overhead camshafts, four valves per cylinder, water and air-cooled rear engine with twin turbochargers and intercoolers, variable all-wheel drive. 2850cc, 450hp. Estimated top speed: 190 + mph.
PORSCHE

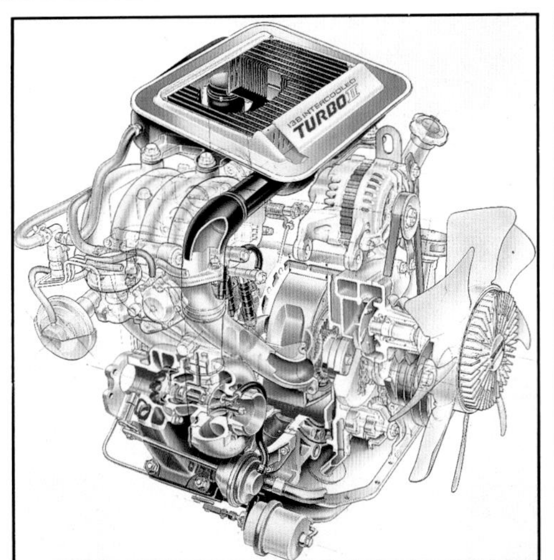

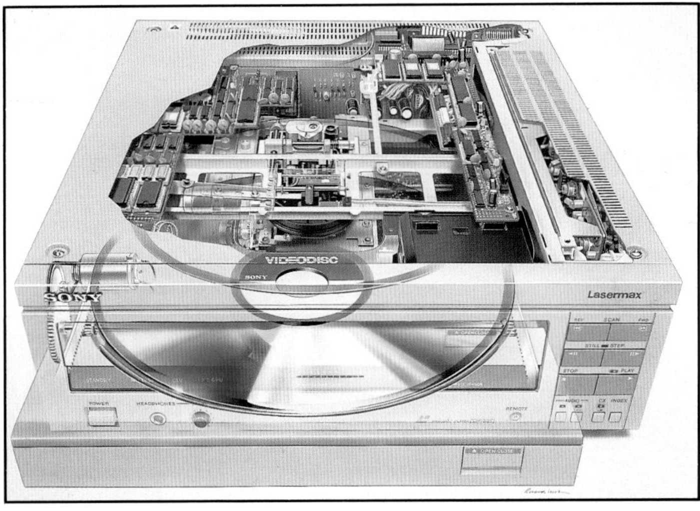

(212) 986-5680

Mendola LTD.

GRAYBAR BLDG. • 420 LEXINGTON AVE. • PENTHOUSE • NEW YORK, N.Y. 10170

DAVID HENDERSON

STEVE BRENNAN

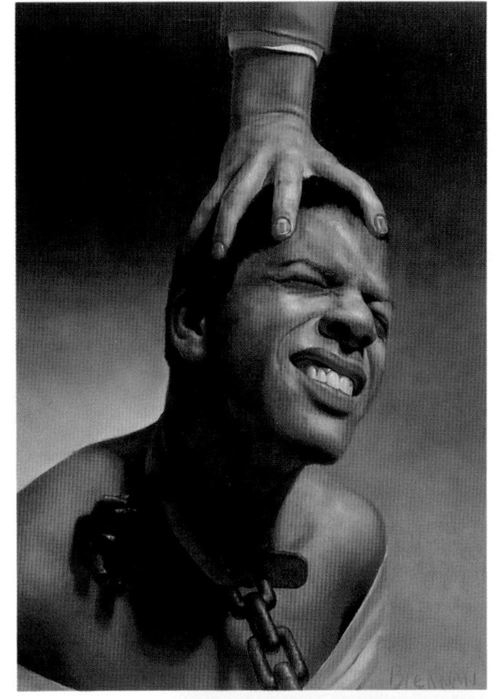

(212) 986-5680

Mendola LTD.

GRAYBAR BLDG. • 420 LEXINGTON AVE. • PENTHOUSE • NEW YORK, N.Y. 10170

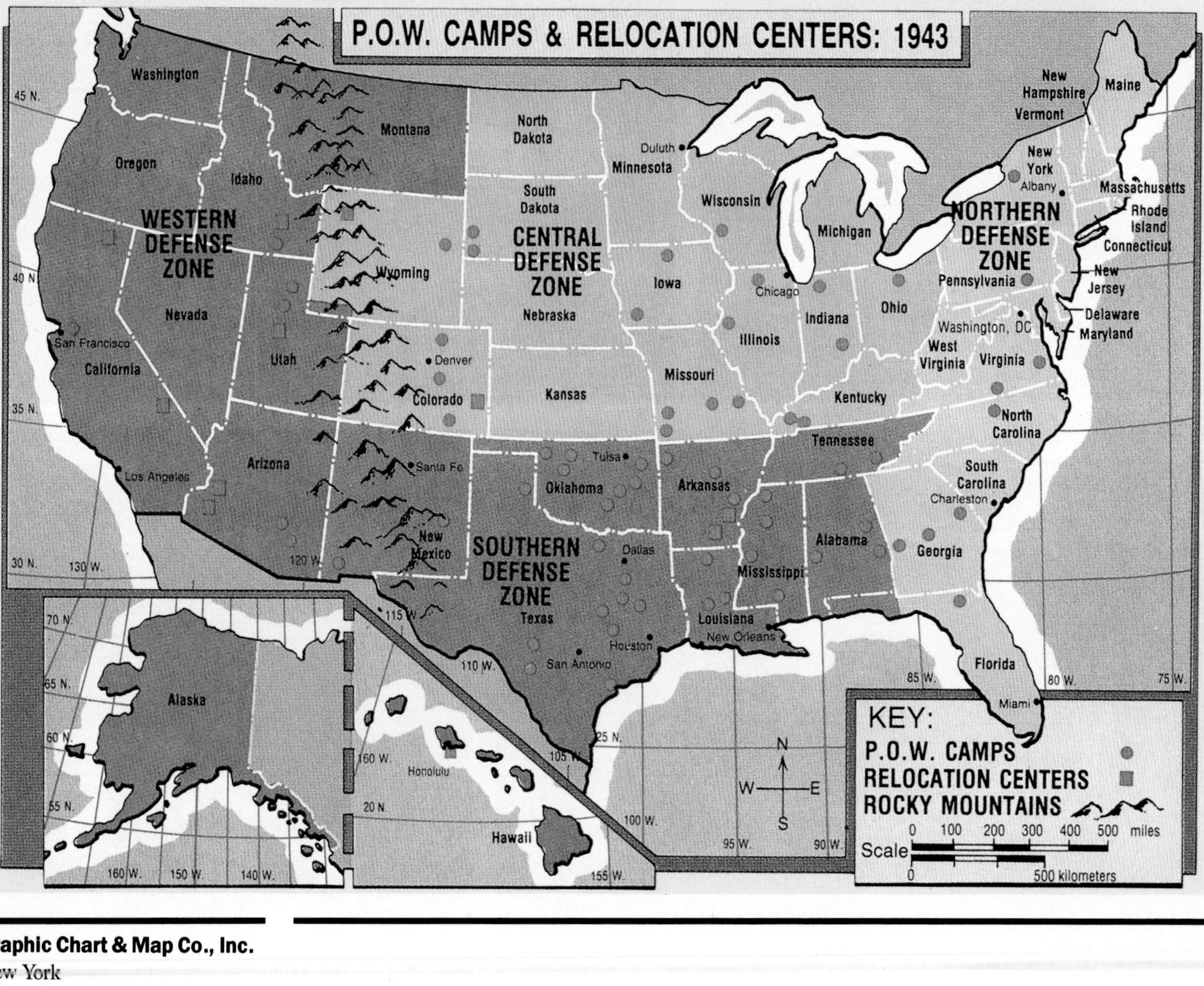

Graphic Chart & Map Co., Inc.

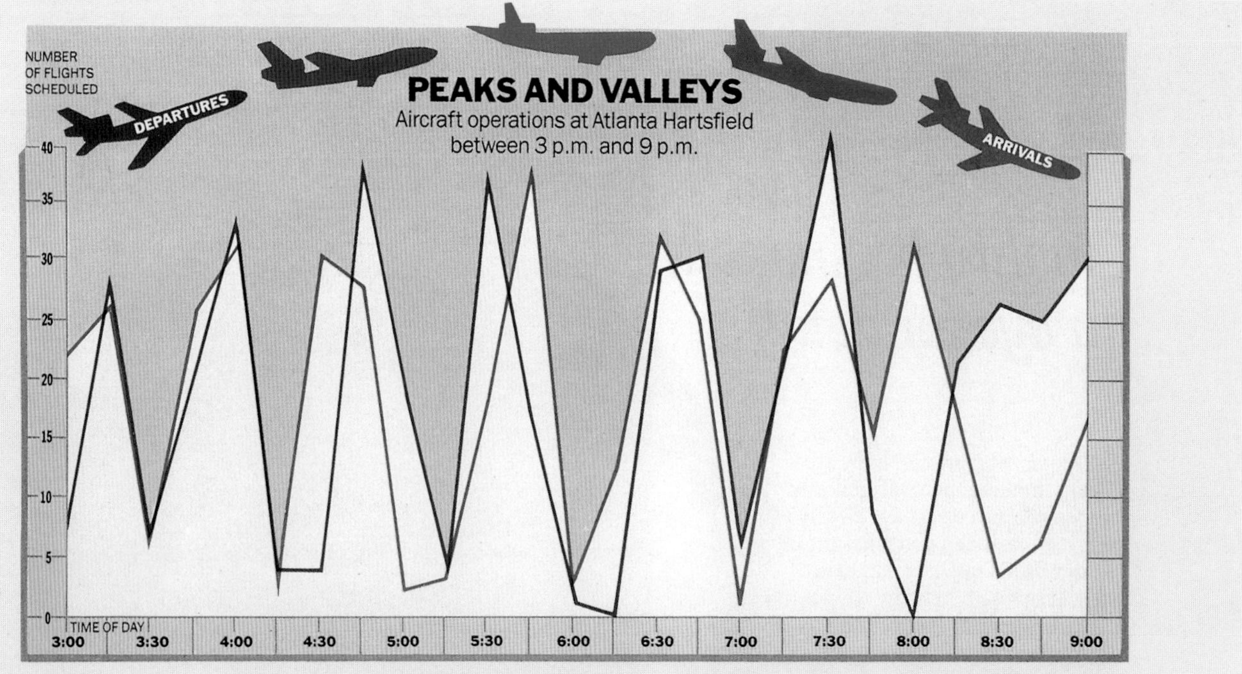

Graphic Chart & Map Co., Inc.
New York
(212) 463-0190
Los Angeles
(213) 475-7742
FAX in Studio

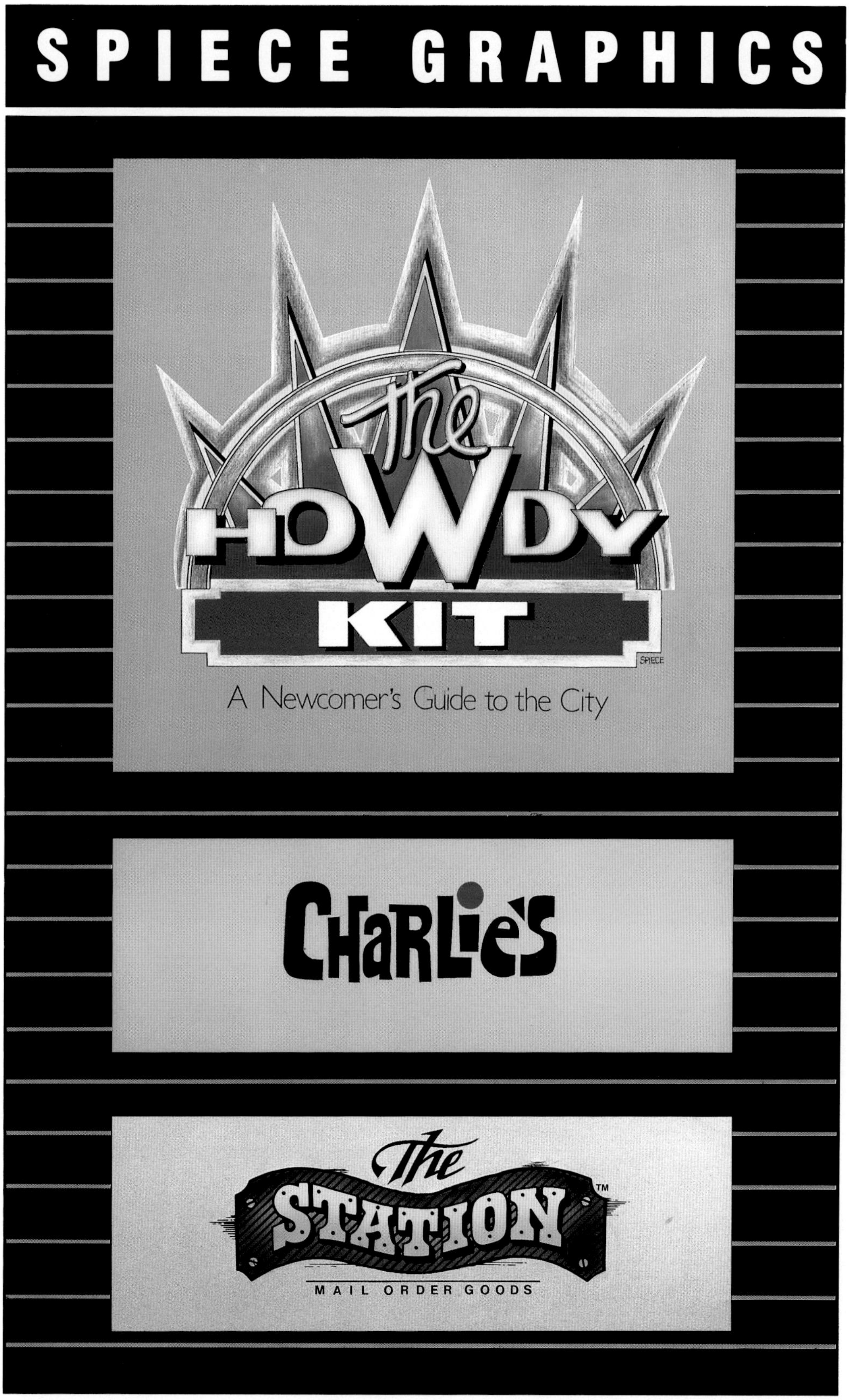

SPIECE GRAPHICS

The HOWDY KIT
A Newcomer's Guide to the City

CHaRLie's

The STATION™
MAIL ORDER GOODS

Spiece Graphics
1811 Woodhaven #7
P.O. Box 9115
Ft. Wayne, IN 46899
(219) 747-3916

Design and Lettering
Apple Macintosh® Computer and Telecopier in studio.

Member Graphic Artists Guild

Larry Taugher

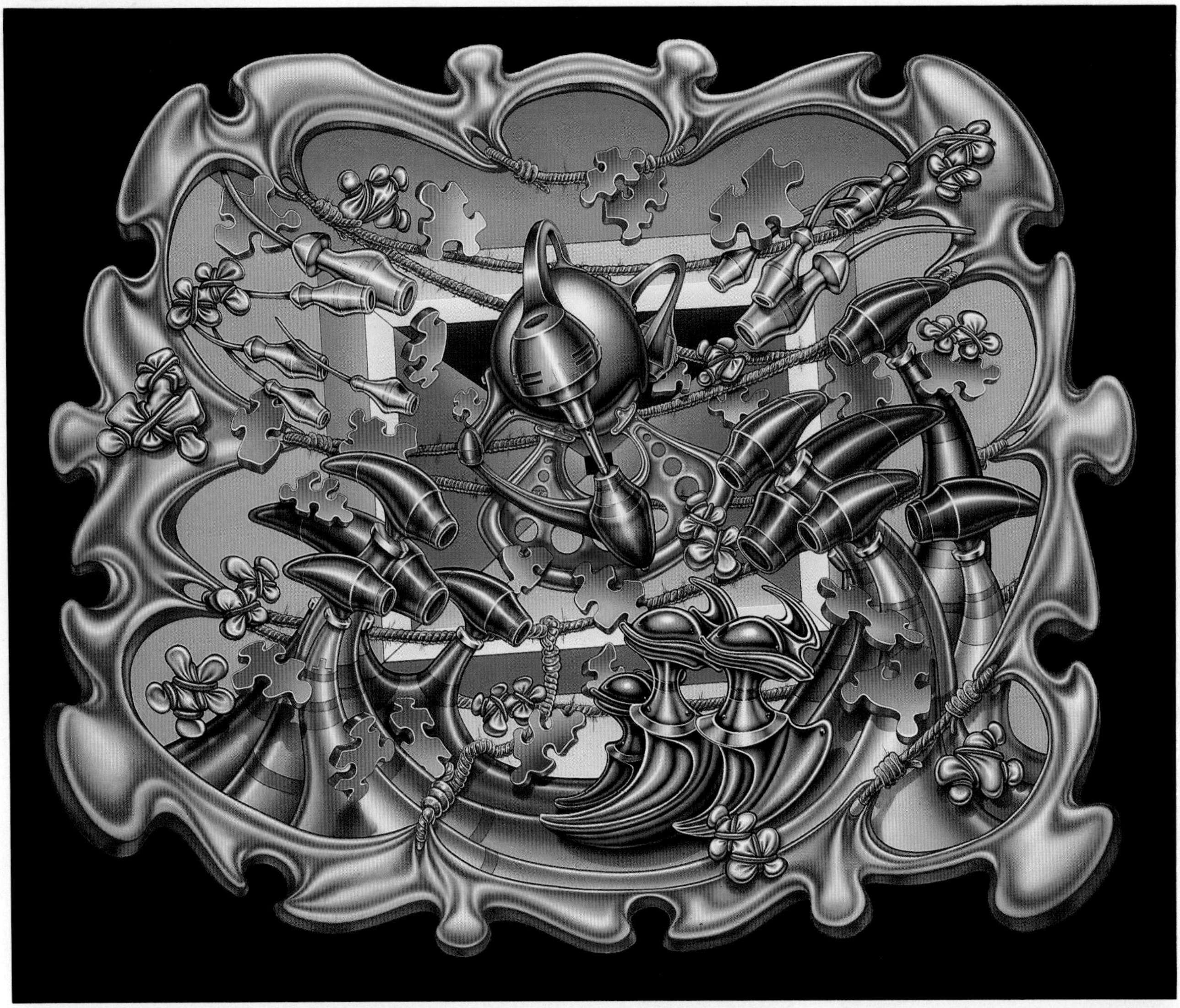

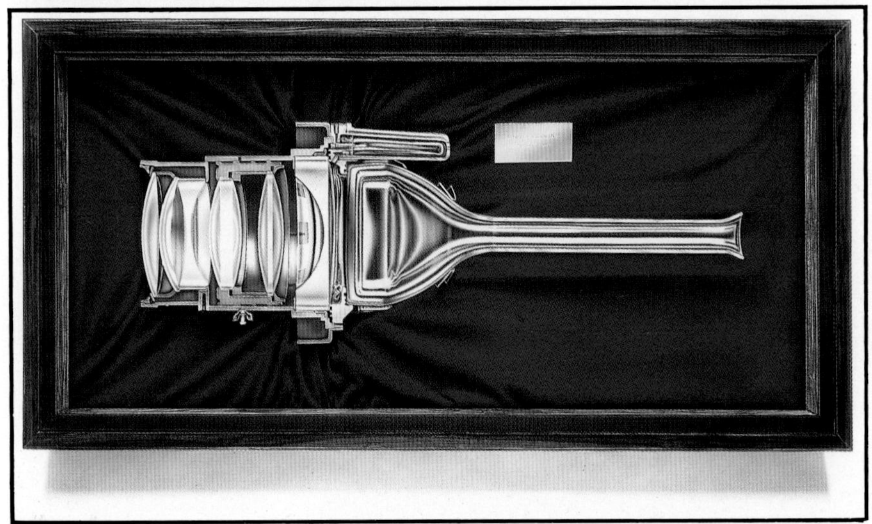

Larry Taugher
314 35th Street
Newport Beach, CA 92663
(714) 675-6932

Marc Rosenthal

Marc Rosenthal
#8 Route 66
Malden Bridge, NY 12115
(518) 766-4191

Clients include:
Altman & Manley Adver tising, AT&T, Coca-Cola, *Business Week, Fortune, New Woman, Savvy,* Simon & Schuster, *Psychology Today, Texas Monthly, The Boston Globe, The Washington Post.*

Awards:
CA Illustration Annual 1985
Print's Regional Design Annual 1985, 1986, 1987
Society of Publication Designers 1985
Print Casebooks #7
Humor '87
Creativity '87
American Illustration 6

Mary Badenhop

Mary Badenhop
807 Madison Avenue, Studio 4A
New York, NY 10021
(212) 861-4133

Children's illustration for books and fashion.

Clients have included:
Bloomingdale's, Macy's, Troll Publishing, Avon, Calendar of Kids Around the World, Barnum and Bailey, AC&R, North American Graphics, Burlington, Young & Rubicam, *McCall's,* Wrangler, Hush Puppies, Buster Brown, Ruth Scarf, Rowland Co., J.C. Penney, John Henry, The Gap, Lipman Advertising.

Publications:
New York Times, Washington Post, WWD, Earnshaws Review.

Owner of children's greeting card company, Pipsqueak Productions.

Member Graphic Artists Guild

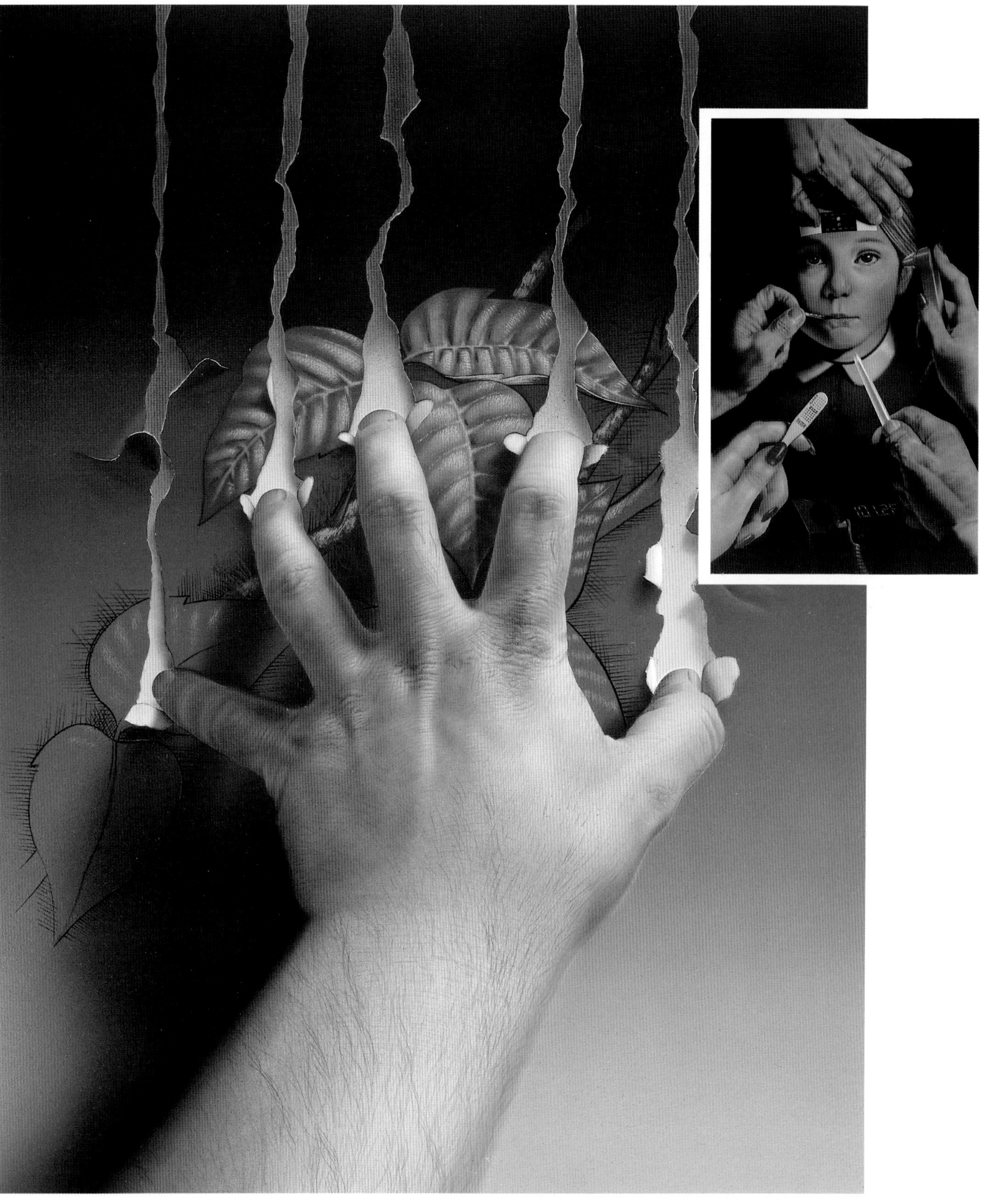

Steve Heimann
P.O. Box 406
Oradell, NJ 07649
(201) 345-9132

AWARDS:
Society of Illustrators
Art Directors Club of NJ

MEMBER:
Society of Illustrators

CLIENTELE:
Ciba-Geigy; McCann Healthcare; M.E.D. Communications; Grey Adv.; Gross, Townsend, Frank, Hoffmann; Rosenfeld, Sirowitz & Humphrey; Bozell, Jacobs, Kenyon & Eckhardt; Gianettino & Meredith; IBM; AT&T; Macy's; Squibb; Letraset; Pepsi; Champion International Corp.; Bendix; General Electric; Post Cereals; Lenox-Hill Brace; Diversitech General; Minnetonka; Lever Brothers; Levelor Lorenzes; Maruca; Mobil; Procter & Gamble; Reed & Carnrick; Warner-Lambert; *Medical Economics;* Hayden Publishing; Macmillan Healthcare; *Good Food Magazine;* Prentice-Hall Publishing; Scholastic; 1988 Olympics–Seoul; Antigua/Barbuda Postal Service; Dominica Postal Service; Grenada Postal Service; Sierra Leone Postal Service; Uganda Postal Service.

Jean Tuttle

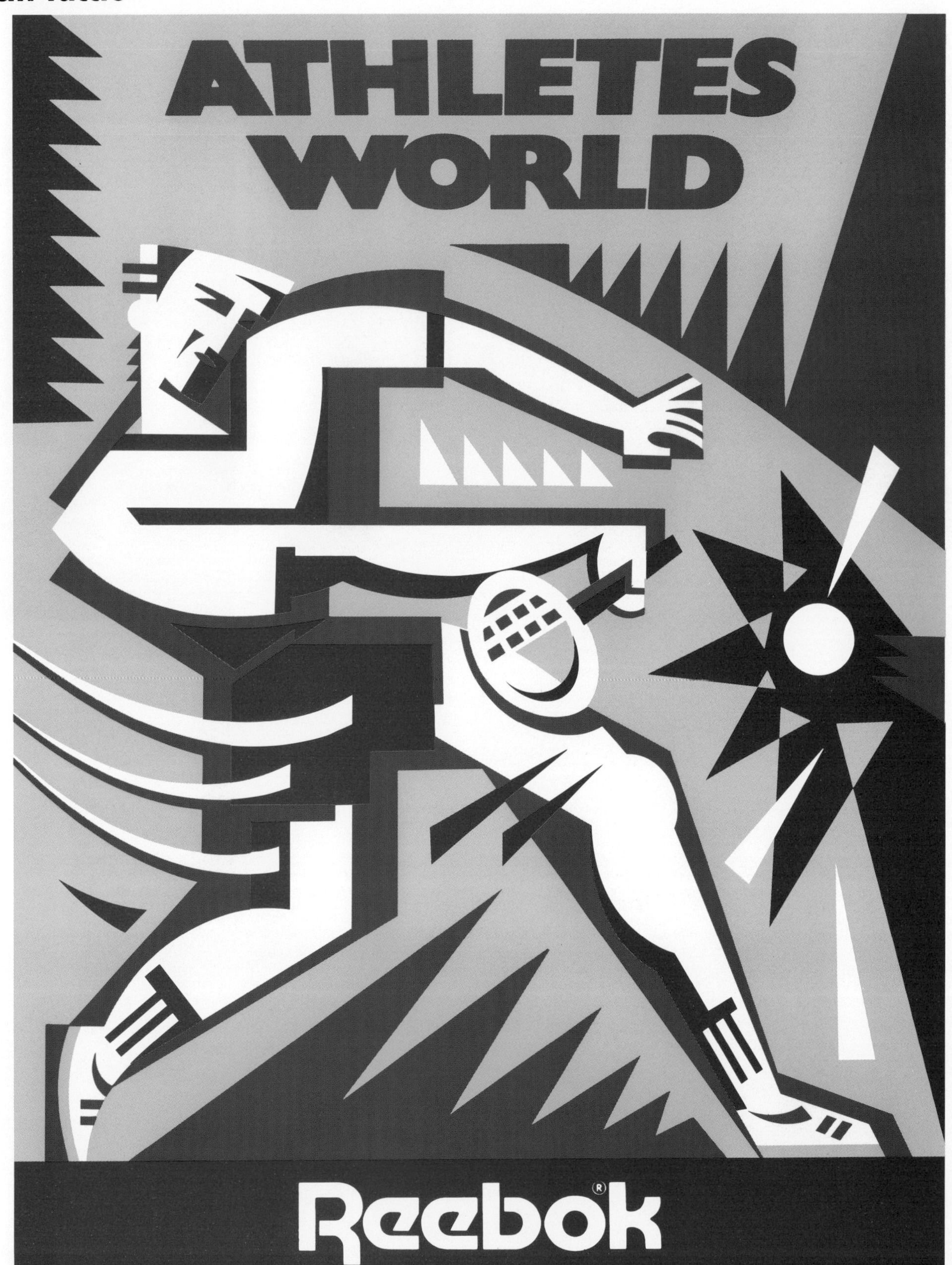

Jean Tuttle
227 West 29th Street, #9R
New York, NY 10001
(212) 967-6442

Clients include:
AT&T, *Boston Globe*, *Business Week*, Chase Manhattan, *Chicago Tribune*, Condé Nast, *Elle*, *LA Style*, *Marie Claire*, *McCall's*, *Money*, *Newsweek*, *New York Times*, *Psychology Today*, *Rolling Stone*, *Sports Illustrated*, *Wall Street Journal*.

Represented in Canada by Reactor Art & Design

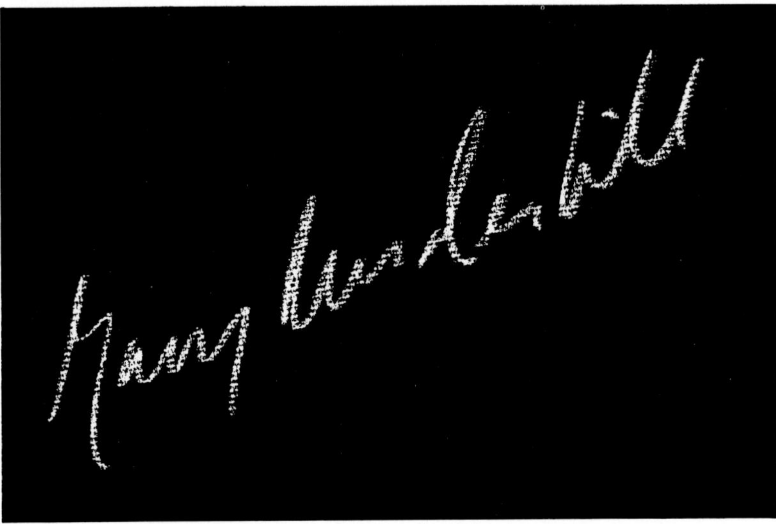

Gary R. Underhill
366 Belleville Avenue
Bloomfield, NJ 07003
(201) 680-9554

Marge Othrow

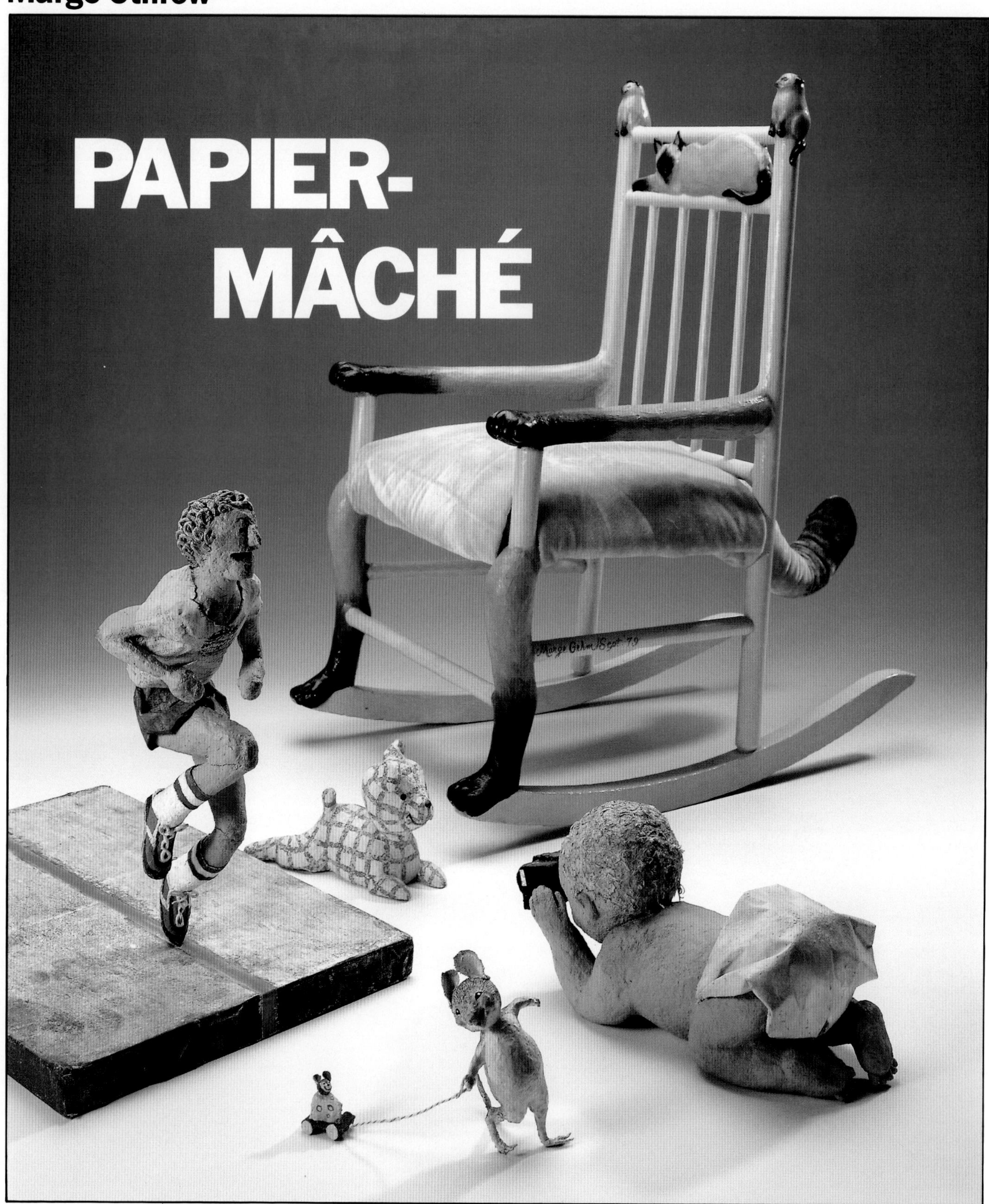

Marge Othrow
417 Washington Avenue
Brooklyn, NY 11238
(718) 789-1619

1973 Hallmark Gallery Craft Fair

1974 & 1976 Tiffany's windows

1979 Brooklyn Museum Community Gallery

1980 St. Anne's/Art Show

1984 "Saturday Morning Live" with Bill Boggs

1985 Tiffany's windows

1987 Society of Illustrators' first humor show

Steve Hofheimer

Visualize Design Studios, Inc.
102-25 67 Road, Suite 5E
Forest Hills, NY 11375
(718) 997-0399

Kay Life/Lifescapes

Kay Life/Lifescapes
419 Southwick Road, B7
Westfield, MA 01085
(413) 562-6418

Kathie Abrams
41 Union Square West
Room 1001
New York, NY 10003
(212) 741-1333

Humorous illustration for a variety of needs. Among my valued clients are corporate clients McNeil Labs, Chase Manhattan Bank, American Express, The Prudential, the American Cancer Society, US Trust, AT&T, and The Museum of Modern Art. Agency clients include Ogilvy & Mather, Backer Spielvogel Bates, Saatchi & Saatchi, and Cato DBG. Promotional work for Ogilvy & Mather Promotions, Rapp & Collins, Burson-Marsteller, and many others. Editorial and TV work for *The New York Times,* Broadcast Arts, and numerous magazines.

Member Graphic Artists Guild.

Daniela Wanda Maioresco

Daniela Wanda Maioresco
510 Main Street, #130
New York, NY 10044
(212) 838-2509

Graphic designer & illustrator

Born Bucharest, Romania. 1980 MFA, Romanian Academy of Fine Arts. Book designer and illustrator for major publishing houses in Bucharest.

Group shows in Denmark, France, Spain, Italy, Israel, USA, Canada. Works in private collections in USA; France; West Germany; Canada; and Romanian Museum of Engraving, Tulcea.

Living and working in USA since 1985. Clients include National Broadcasting Company and *The New York Times Book Review.*

Arthur Thompson

Arthur Thompson
39 Prospect Avenue
Pompton Plains, NJ 07444
(201) 835-3534

Graphic Artists Guild member

Clients:

Prentice Hall Press
Pro-Form Displays
Aetna Insurance
United States Tobacco
Jamaica National Investment Limited
CBS
Singer Sewing Machine
Martin Marietta
Houghton Mifflin
Crum and Foster Insurance
Sport Magazine
Lipman Advertising
Avon Books
Lipton Tea

JERALD J. SISTI

34 Wiedemann Ave.
Clifton, N.J. 07011
201-478-7488

A traditional approach with a contemporary twist.
A partial list of clients include:
ABC Broadcasting; AT&T; ABA Journal; A.M.Best; Blue Cross/Blue Shield; Bristol Meyers; Foote Cone & Belding/Leber Katz Partners; High Fidelity; Hoffmann La Roche; Lenox; Poppe Tyson; Prentice Hall; Swintec; Sony; and others.

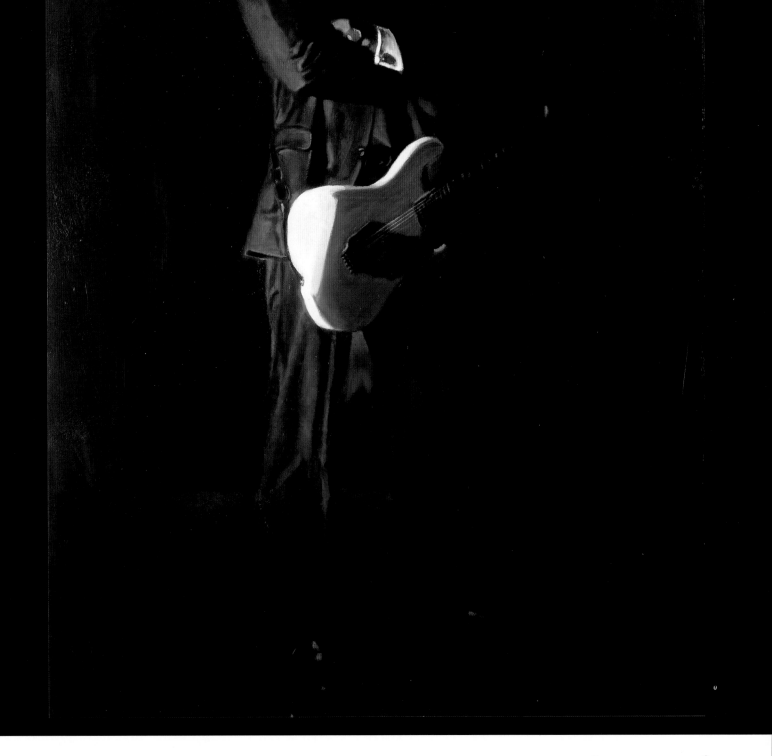

JERALD J. SISTI
34 Wiedemann Ave.
Clifton, N.J. 07011
201-478-7488

A traditional approach with a contemporary twist.
A partial list of clients include:
ABC Broadcasting; AT&T; ABA Journal; A.M.Best; Blue Cross/Blue Shield; Bristol Meyers; Foote Cone & Belding/Leber Katz Partners; High Fidelity; Hoffmann La Roche; Lenox; Poppe Tyson; Prentice Hall; Swintec; Sony; and others.

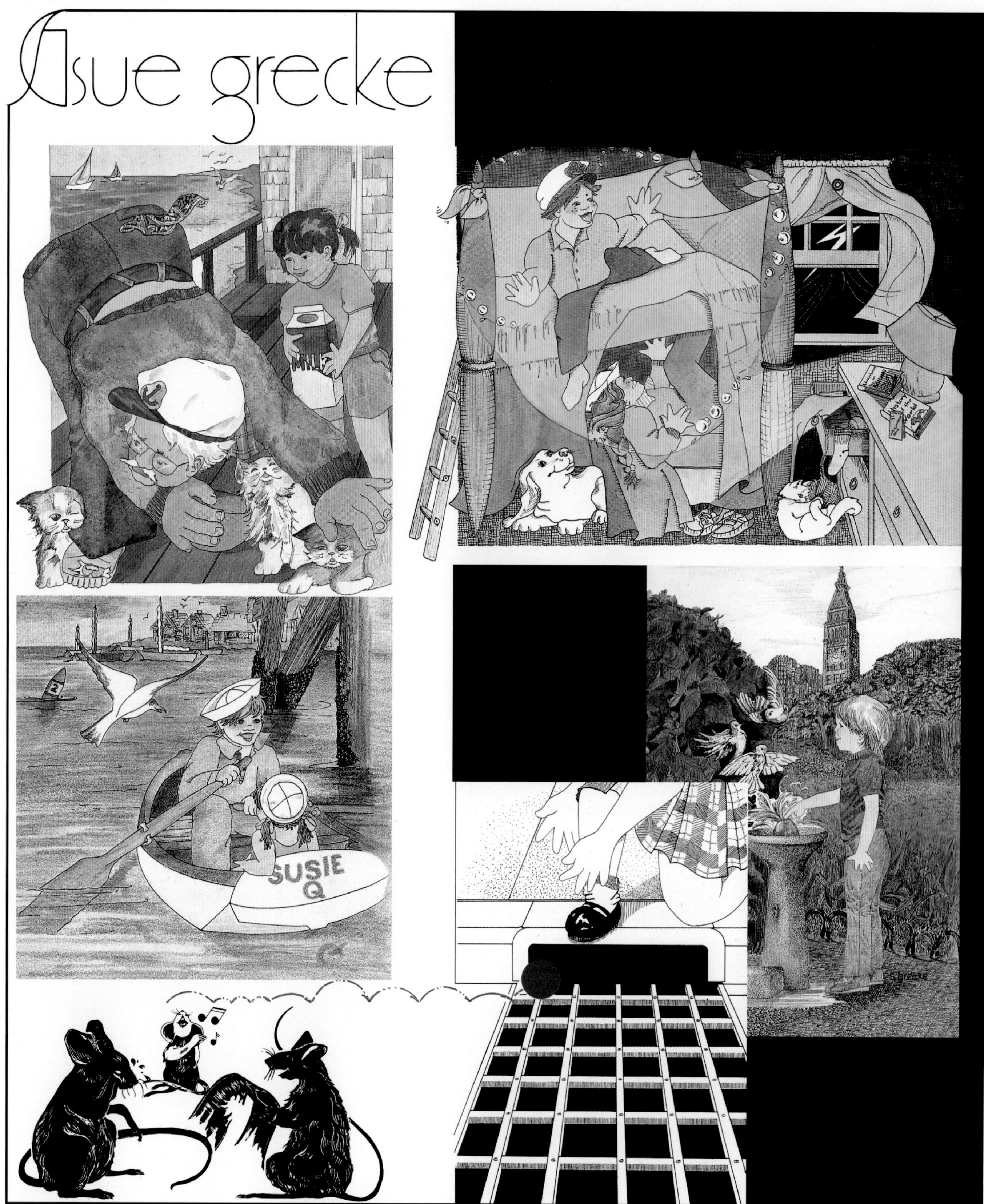

Sue Grecke
43-23 Byrd Street
Flushing, NY 11355
(718) 539-7394

Pen and ink, color wash, scratchboard for children's book and magazine illustration.

Please call for slide or portfolio presentation.

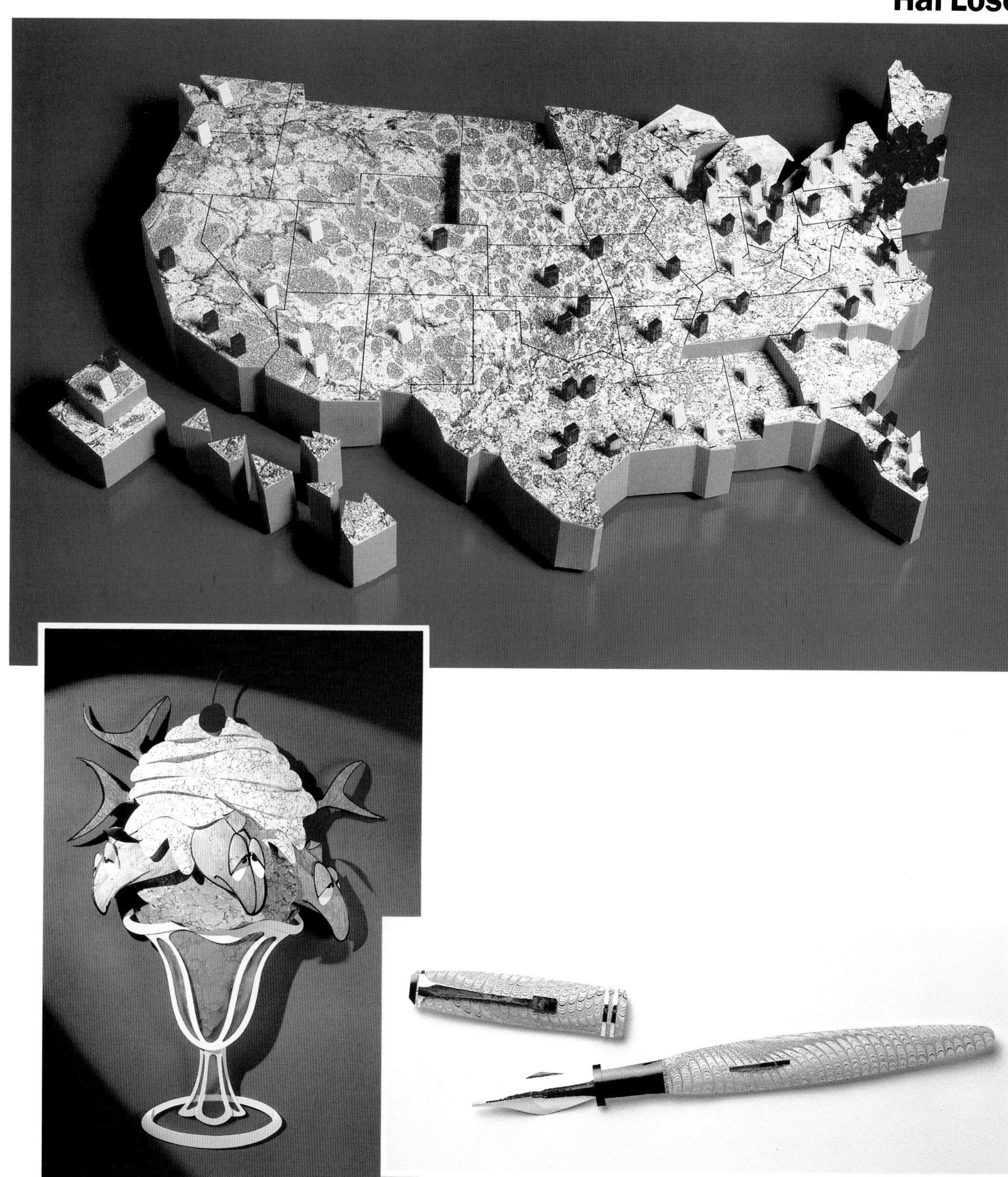

Hal Lōse
533 West Hortter Street
(Toad Hall)
Philadelphia, PA 19119
(215) 849-7635

designer and illustrator
☐ Paper sculpture
☐ Humorous illustration
☐ Graphic design

Joseph Cellini

Joseph Cellini
415 Hillside Avenue
Leonia, NJ 07605
(201) 944-6519

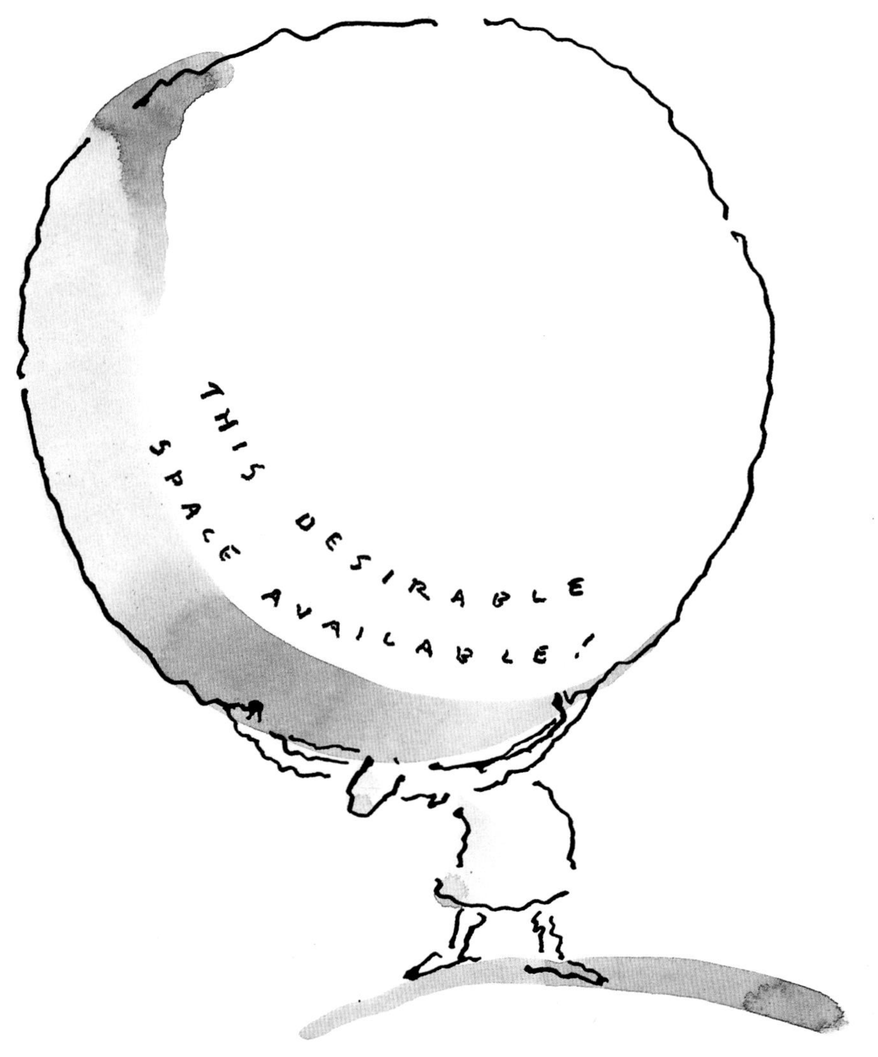

R.O. Blechman
2 West 47th Street
New York, NY 10036
(212) 869-1630

Paul Yalowitz

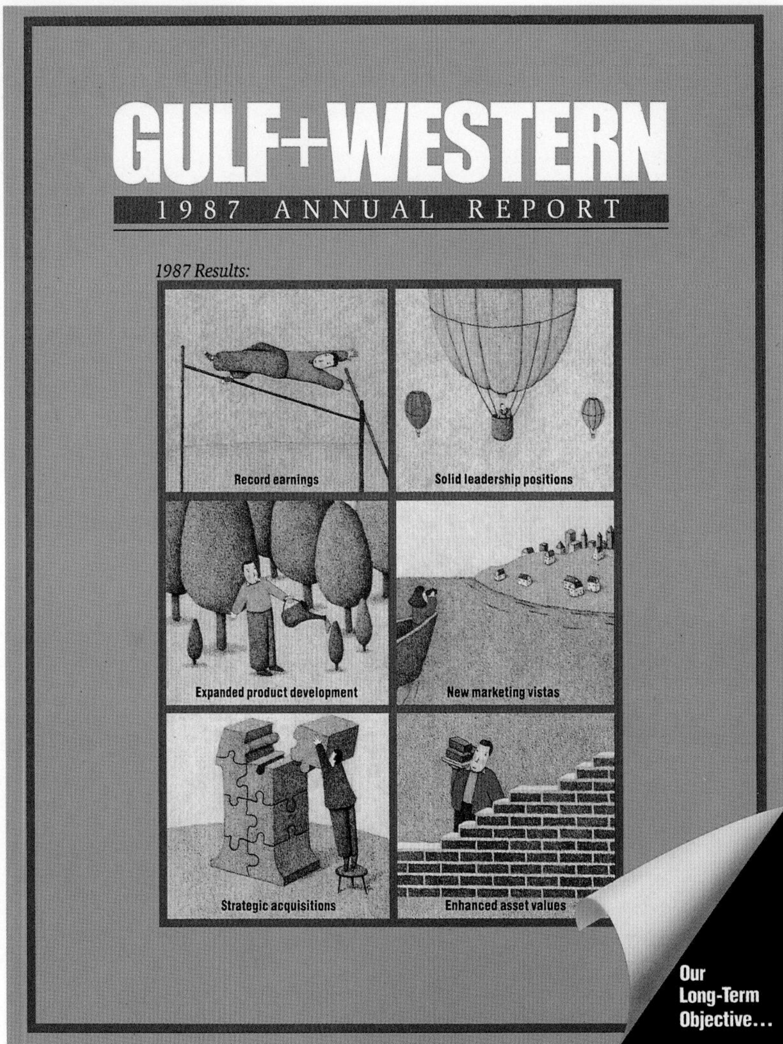

Paul Yalowitz
215 East 26th Street, Apt. #7
New York, NY 10010
(212) 532-0859

Margaret Ferraro
31-10 28 Road
Astoria, NY 11102
(718) 204-0097
Illustrator/Designer

"My professional interests center around using and further developing my ability to convey, through visual media, thoughts, ideas, and concepts."

Partial list of clients:

Scafa Tornabene Art Publishing Co., Levy International Publishing Co., Rainbow Program Enterprises (American Movie Classics and Bravo), Rainbow Gold Inc., Dynamic Graphics Inc.

Member Graphic Artists Guild.

Ken Krug

Ken Krug
60 Second Avenue, #22
New York, NY 10003
(212) 677-1572
(212) 691-5855

Clients include:

Time-Life; McGraw-Hill, King Features Syndicate; Archer Services; American Banker; NATPE Programmer; Home Satellite Marketing; and *Video Magazine*.

Work featured in *Child Magazine; The N.Y. Daily News Magazine;* and on several television shows including "Family Ties" and "Alf."

Work in Society of Illustrators show, "The New Illustration."

Member Graphic Artists Guild.

Alan Witschonke

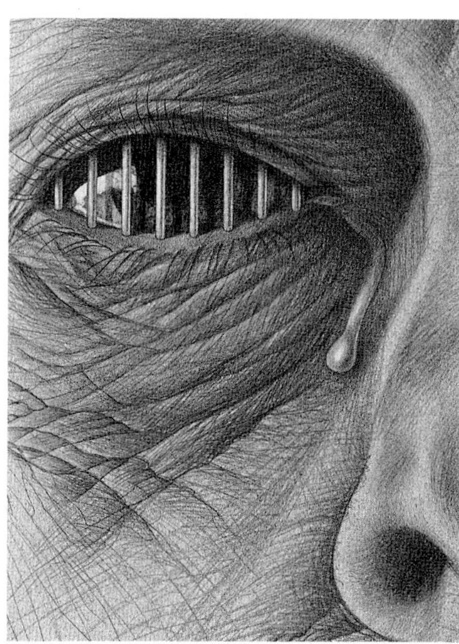

Alan Witschonke
The Artery
68 Agassiz Avenue
Belmont, MA 02178
(617) 484-8023

Art-buyers in New York City: To have my portfolio sent to your office, free of charge, call the N.Y. Portfolio Depot at (212) 989-8588.

Clockwise from top left:

1. Illustration for *PC Week* magazine article "Terminal Emulation" about chameleon-like ability of PC's.
2. One of a series of illustrations for Bildner's advertisements and direct-mail brochures.
3. Cover illustration for *Bostonia* magazine with the heading "American Perspectives."
4. Front-page illustration for *The Tab* newspapers about the elderly feeling imprisoned in their own homes.
5. Cover illustration for book *Hollywood Doesn't Live Here Anymore* by Robert Parrish, published by Little, Brown & Company.

Richard Brachman

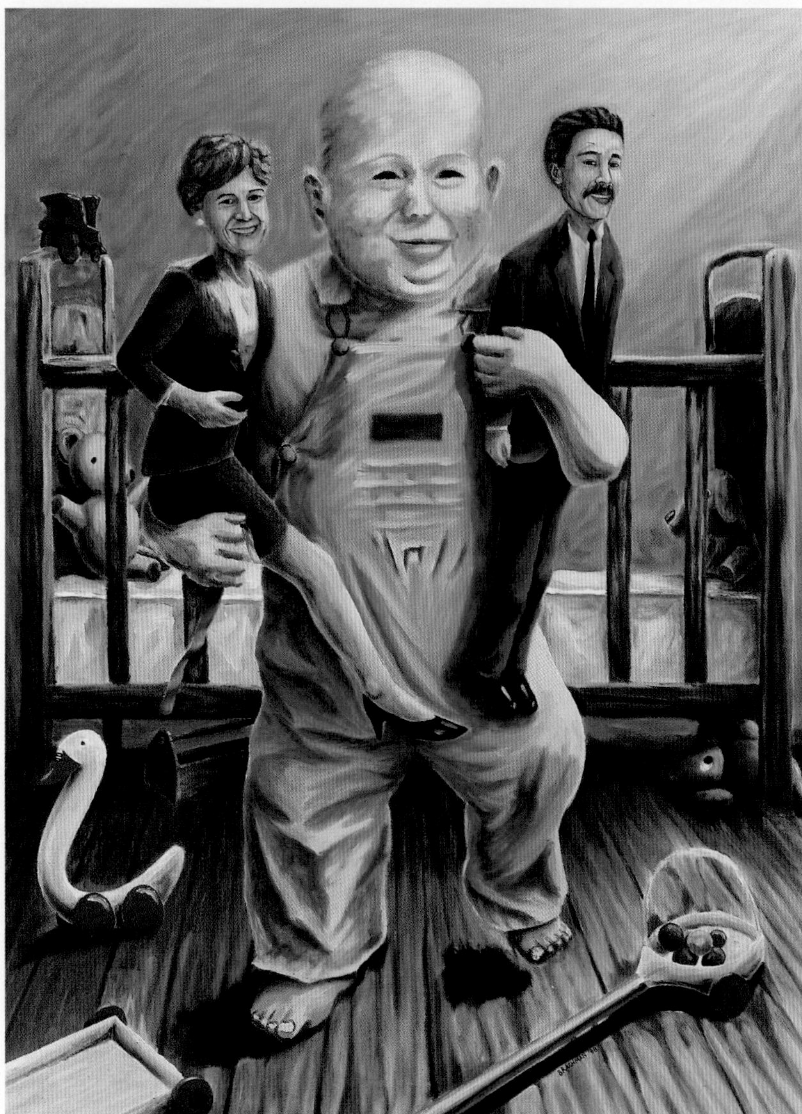

Richard Brachman
30-44 34th Street, #3F
Astoria, NY 11103
(718) 204-6879

Dorothy Leech
1024 Avenue of the Americas
New York, NY 10018
(212) 354-6641

Clients:
New York Times, New York News, MD Magazine, New Jersey Monthly, Publishers Weekly, Showcase Magazine, Kipling Press, Walker Books, Memorial Sloan-Kettering, AT&T.

Susan Detrich

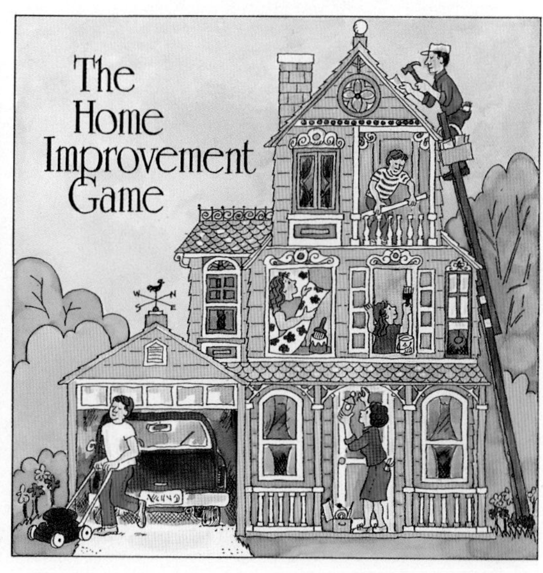

Susan Detrich
253 Baltic Street
Brooklyn, NY 11201
(718) 237-9174

Susan Detrich has been working in publishing and promotional graphics for over twenty years, concentrating on illustration since 1976. She loves the challenge of using odd-shaped spaces and working picture details around type.

Detrich's experience in design and in producing her own promotion pieces (including art and stripping corrections on 3- and 4-color flats) assures easy communication and a practical as well as imaginative solution.

Clients include:
Hanes, Ziff Davis Publications, Planter's Peanuts, Random House, Harcourt Brace Jovanovich, Harper & Row, Scribner's, Scholastic, design studios and retail businesses.

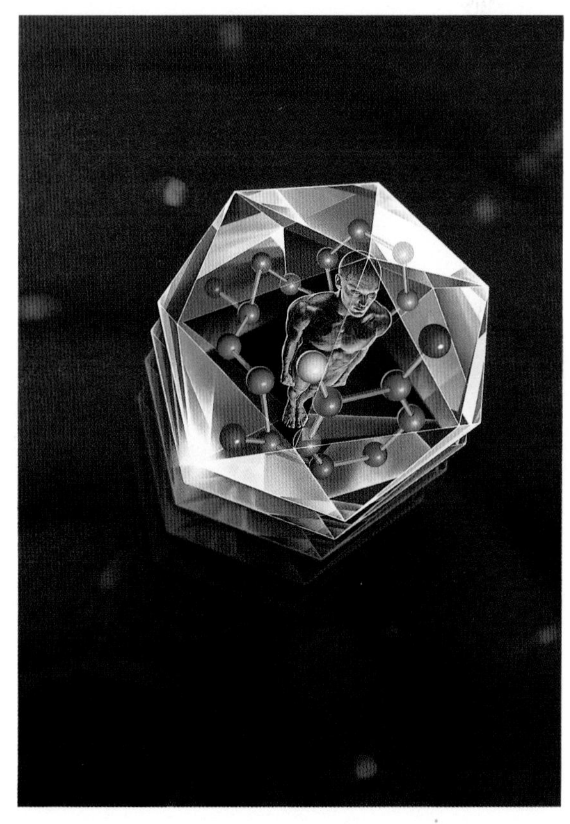

Kimmerle Milnazik
73-2 Drexelbrook Drive
Drexel Hill, PA 19026
(215) 259-1565

Shelley Matheis

Shelley Matheis
504 East Passaic Avenue
Bloomfield, NJ 07003
(201) 338-9506
People'd Illustration

Clients include:
Macmillan Publishing;
Cobblestone Publishing,
Inc.; *Cricket Magazine;*
Schmid; Soma Technologies.

Dan V. Romer

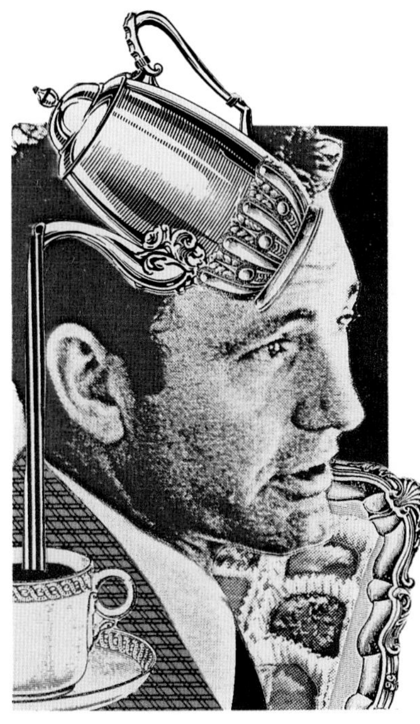

Dan V. Romer
125 Prospect Park West, #2A
Brooklyn, NY 11215
(718) 965-2524

COOK'S
MacUser
Metropolitan Home
Money
Ms.
The New York Times
Pentagram
Rio Casey
SAVVY
Schaeffer Boehm Ltd.
Travel & Leisure
Vanity Fair

Pressley-Jones Design

B Jones
ROBERT J. JONES

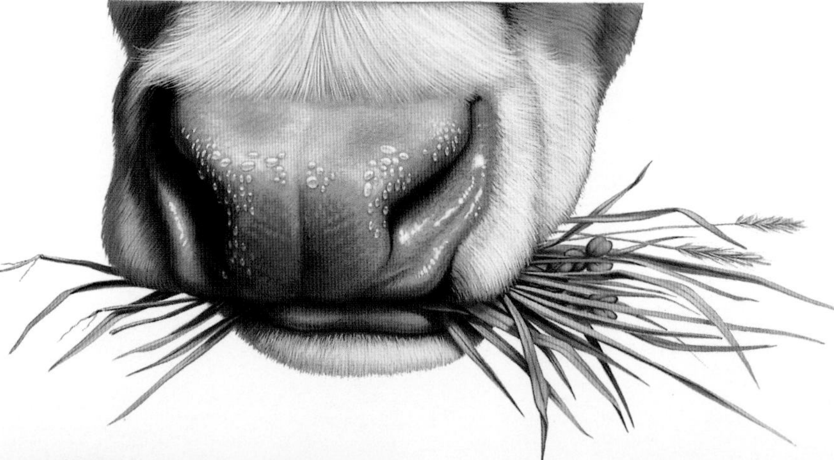

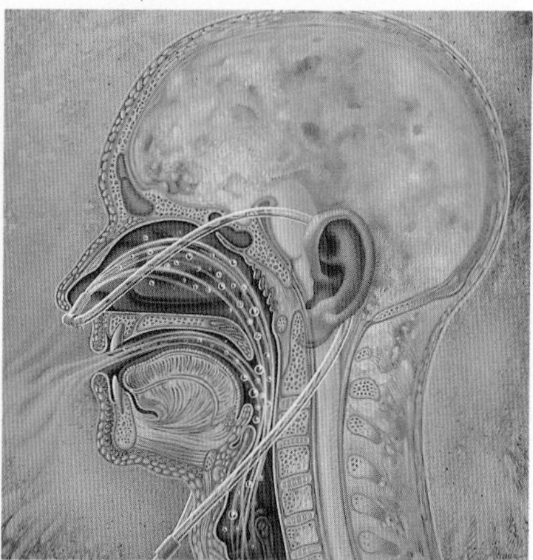

Pressley-Jones Design
47 West Stewart Avenue
Lansdowne, PA 19050
Contact: Robert Jones
(215) 626-1245

Clockwise, from upper right: ad, Pfizer Agricultural Division; *Philadelphia Daily News,* Supplement; cover, *Nursing Magazine;* poster, Campbell's Soup Company; mailer, American Cyanamid; ad for horse hoof medication.

Client list includes:

American Cyanamid, Bell of PA, Bethlehem Steel, Campbell's Soup, Certain-Teed, DuPont, Exide, Mack Truck, *Nursing Magazine,* Ortho, Pennsylvania Lottery, Pfizer, *Philadelphia Inquirer,* Rohm & Haas, Wyeth Labs

Works exhibited in:

Print's Regional Design Annual 1987, Art Directors Club of Philadelphia.

Represented in Philadelphia by Terry Putscher (215) 569-8890

Member Graphic Artists Guild

Steve Haimowitz
67-50 Thornton Placc
Forest Hills, NY 11375
(718) 520-1461
(914) 949-2955

Clients include:
IBM, Johnson & Johnson, Kleenex, Carnation, Russ Berrie and Co., Inc., *Tennis Magazine, Games Magazine, Spy.*

Member Graphic Artists Guild

Nancy Katsin

Nancy Katsin
17 East 31st Street
New York, NY 10016
(212) 213-0709

Client list available

Member Graphic Artists Guild

John Delaney
14 Castle Street
Saugus, MA 01906
(617) 233-1409

The illustrations of John Delaney are straight forward and strong in drawing and concept.

With a few select techniques, the artist will create contemporary or historical costume illustrations as well as wildlife animals and sport illustrations with which you can please your most discriminating editorial and advertising clients.

Write or call for a résumé or portfolio review.

Susan Gray

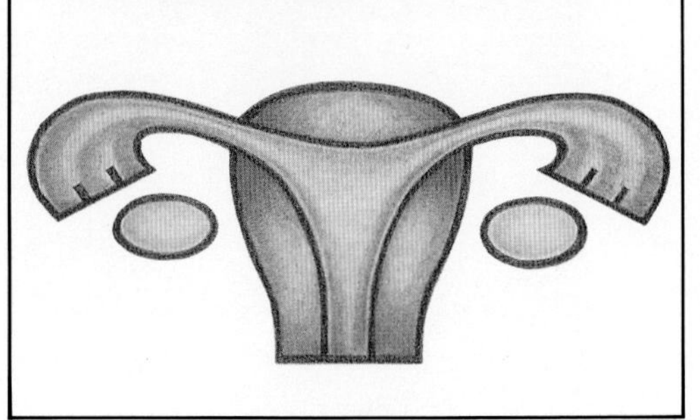

Susan Gray
42 West 12th Street
New York, NY 10011
(212) 675-2243
(212) 787-5400

Clients include:
Young & Rubicam
William Douglas
McAdams Inc.
McCann Erickson
J. Walter Thompson
Ogilvy & Mather
Milton Glaser, Inc.
Johnson & Johnson
Charles of the Ritz
Elizabeth Arden
McGraw-Hill
Doubleday
Harcourt Brace Jovanovich
Rodale Press, Inc.
Changing Times
Forbes
Fortune

Work exhibited:
Illustrators 27
Print

Member Graphic Artists Guild
Member Joint Ethics Committee

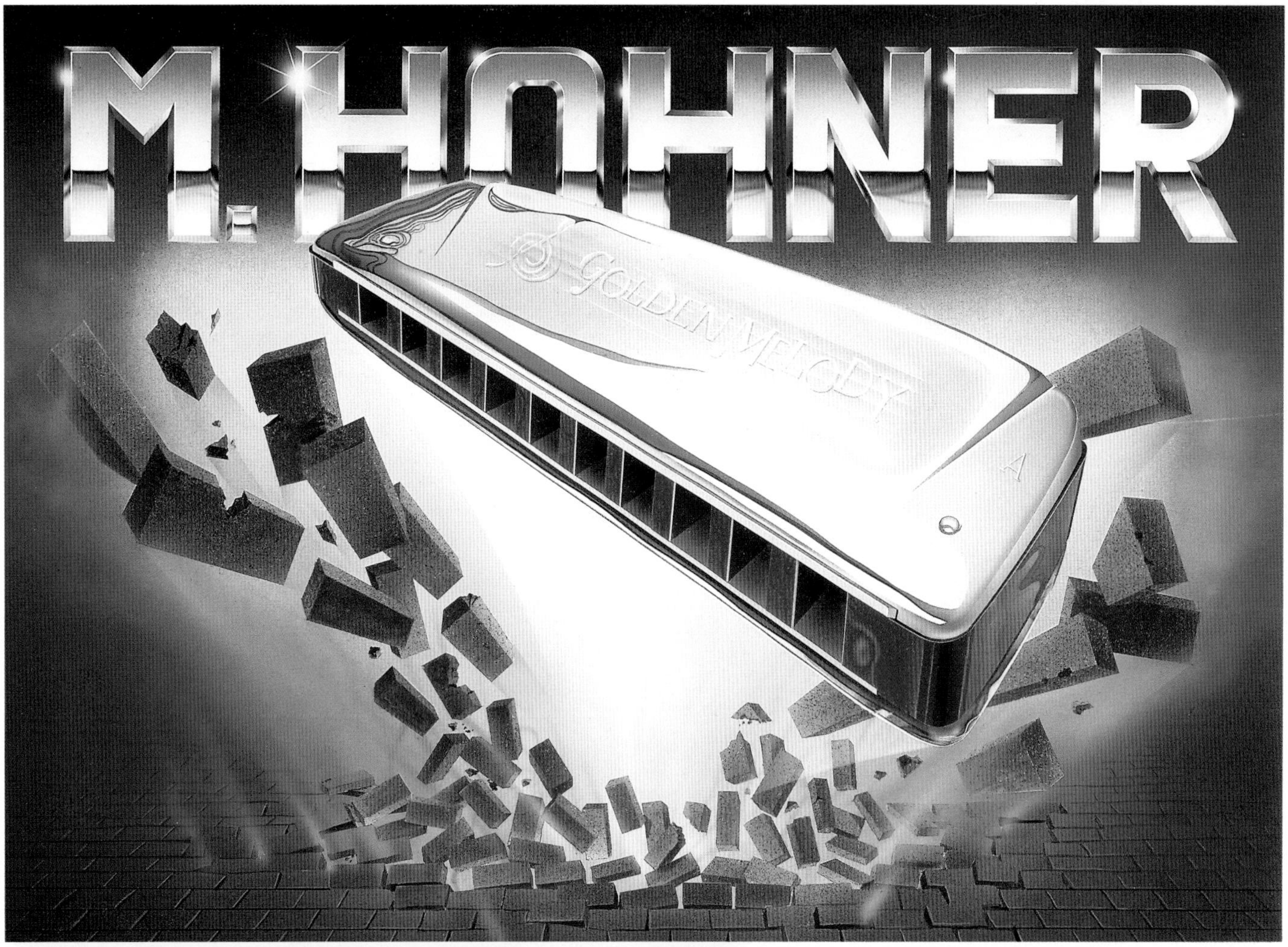

Sergio Roffo
42 Shepard Street
Boston, MA 02135
(617) 787-5861

Represented in New York by:
Hankins & Tegenborg
(212) 867-8092

Represented in Boston by:
Sheryl Beranbaum
(617) 437-9459

FAX machine available.

Airbrush illustration for advertising, promotion, lettering, and products.

A partial list of clients includes:
Cahners Publishing Company
Boston Edison Company
Cullinet Software
Polaroid Corporation
Hill Holliday C.C. Boston
The PennWell Publishing Company
Optikos Corporation
The Sheraton Corporation
MotionArt, Boston
Temple, Barker & Sloane
The Zayre Corporation
WGBH-TV, Boston

Concept to finished art. Quality work, accurate, fast, and on time.

Member Graphic Artists Guild

Wende Caporale

Wende Caporale
Studio Hill Farm, Route 116
North Salem, NY 10560
(914) 669-5653

American Council of Life Insurance
Chesebrough-Pond's
Doubleday
Guideposts
Harper & Row
Macmillan Publishing
New York
North American Philips
Publishers' Graphics, Inc.
Reader's Digest
St. Martin's Press
Scholastic, Inc.
Sports Illustrated
Tennis Magazine
Woman's Day
Xerox

Member:
Graphic Artists Guild
Pastel Society of America
Society of Illustrators

Represented in Connecticut by:
John Brewster Creative Services
(203) 226-4724/(203) 938-3935

Diane Vigée DeMeo
257 West 93rd Street,
Suite 5B
New York, NY 10025
(212) 663-9015

Wendy S. Braun

Wendy S. Braun
333 West 86th Street
New York, NY 10024
(212) 873-3311
(914) 961-3732

Work also appears in
CA Photography Annual
American Photography V

Can also been seen in
American Showcase 11

Peggy Dressel
11 Rockaway Avenue
Oakland, NJ 07436
(201) 337-2143
(201) 337-1838

Member Graphic Artists
Guild

Lisa Henderling

 Lisa Henderling

Represented by Artco

Gail Thurm and Jeff Palmer

Serving Clients in New York City:
232 Madison Ave. Suite 600
New York, NY 10016
(212) 889-8777
FAX in Office

Serving Clients outside New York City:
227 Godfrey Road
Weston, Connecticut 06883
(203) 222-8777
FAX # (203) 454-9940

Member Graphic Artist Guild

David Moses

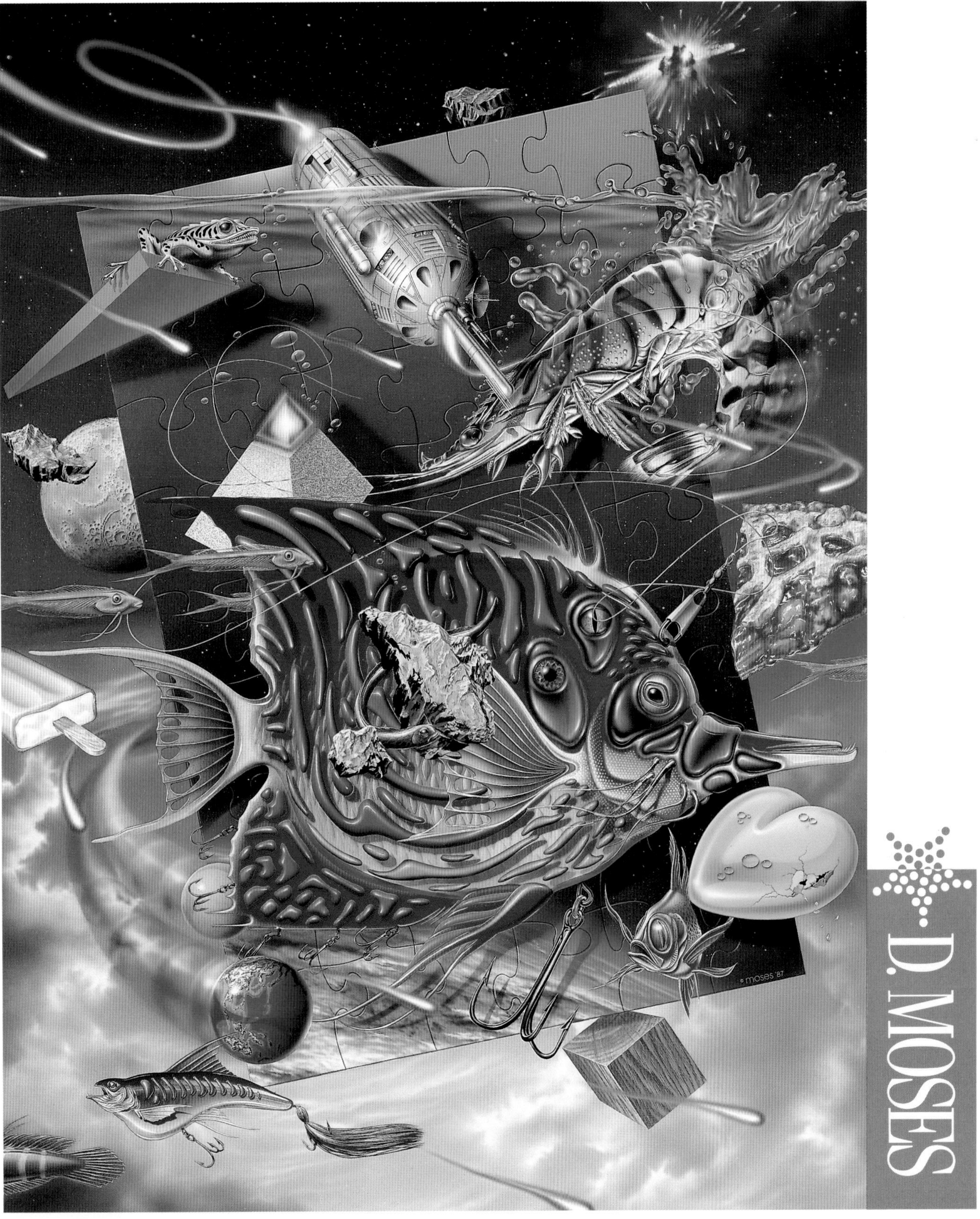

Will Sumpter & Associates
Artists and Photographers Representative
1728 N. Rock Springs Road, NE
Atlanta, GA 30324
(404) 874-2014
FAX available

David Moses's clients include: MSA, Pesi Cola, Seabrook, Chrysler Corp., Southwest Airlines, Holiday Inn, Dow Corning, CONAGRA, Kraft, Snapper, Hasbro.

The people in this portfolio would be proud to show up in yours.

Will Sumpter & Associates
Artists and Photographers Representative
1728 N. Rock Springs Road, NE
Atlanta, GA 30324
(404) 874-2014
FAX available

Drew Rose's clients include: Ryder Trucks, NAPA, Yamaha Sportswear, Snapper, Barons, Alliance, Blue Cross and Blue Shield, Reid-Rowell, St. Josephs, Asahi.

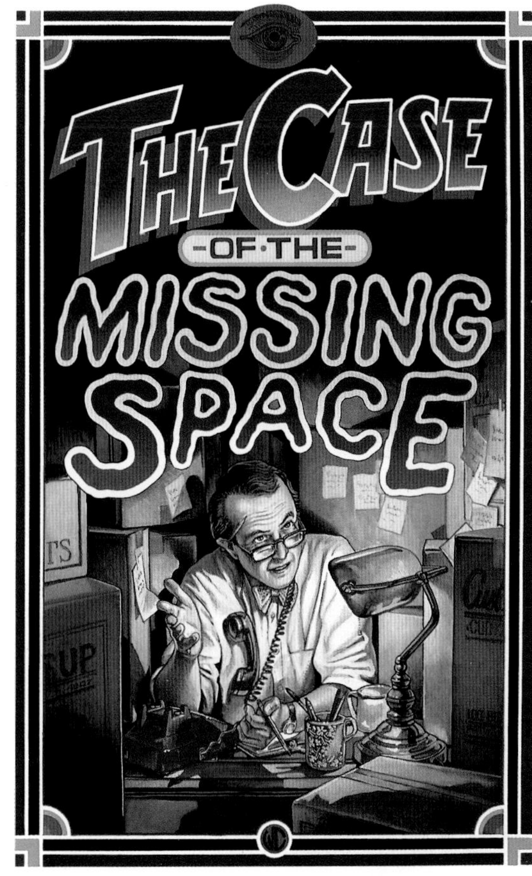

Will Sumpter & Associates
Artists and Photographers Representative
1728 N. Rock Springs Road, NE
Atlanta, GA 30324
(404) 874-2014
FAX available

Wayne Carey's clients include: Discover Card, Kellogg's, Delta, Kimberly Clark, GTE, AARP, UAW, Shakey's Pizza, Kraft, McDonald's, Cox, Siemans, CBN.

Will Sumpter & Associates
Artists and Photographers Representative
1728 N. Rock Springs Road, NE
Atlanta, GA 30324
(404) 874-2014
FAX available

Brenda Losey's clients include: *Smithsonian Magazine,* Eastern Airlines, Cox Communications, Hayes Microcomputer Products, Coca-Cola, John Harland Corporation, Marriott.

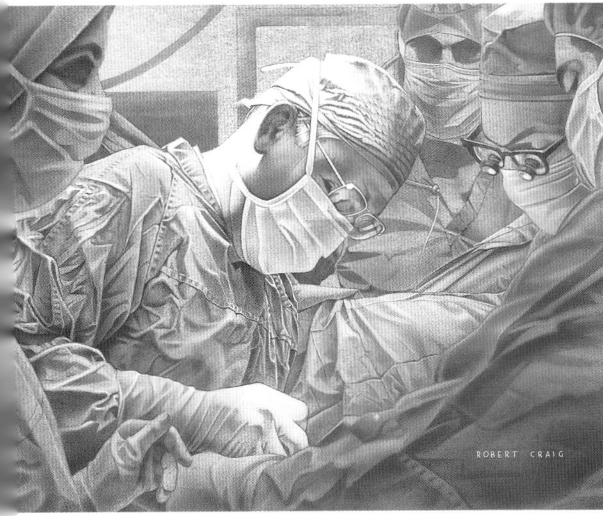

Will Sumpter & Associates
Artists and Photographers Representative
1728 N. Rock Springs Road, NE
Atlanta, GA 30324
(404) 874-2014
FAX available

Robert Craig's clients include: Mattel, Burroughs-Wellcome, Lorimar Productions, Warner Communications, RJR Nabisco, Gerber, Phillip Morris, Bassett Walker.

J. PITTMAN

Will Sumpter & Associates
Artists and Photographers Representative
1728 N. Rock Springs Road, NE
Atlanta, GA 30324
(404) 874-2014
FAX available

Jackie Pittman's clients include: American Express, Barnett Bank, Coca-Cola, *National Geographic,* Piedmont Aviation, Bojangle's, *Reader's Digest,* NCNB.

Hunting For A Home Loan?

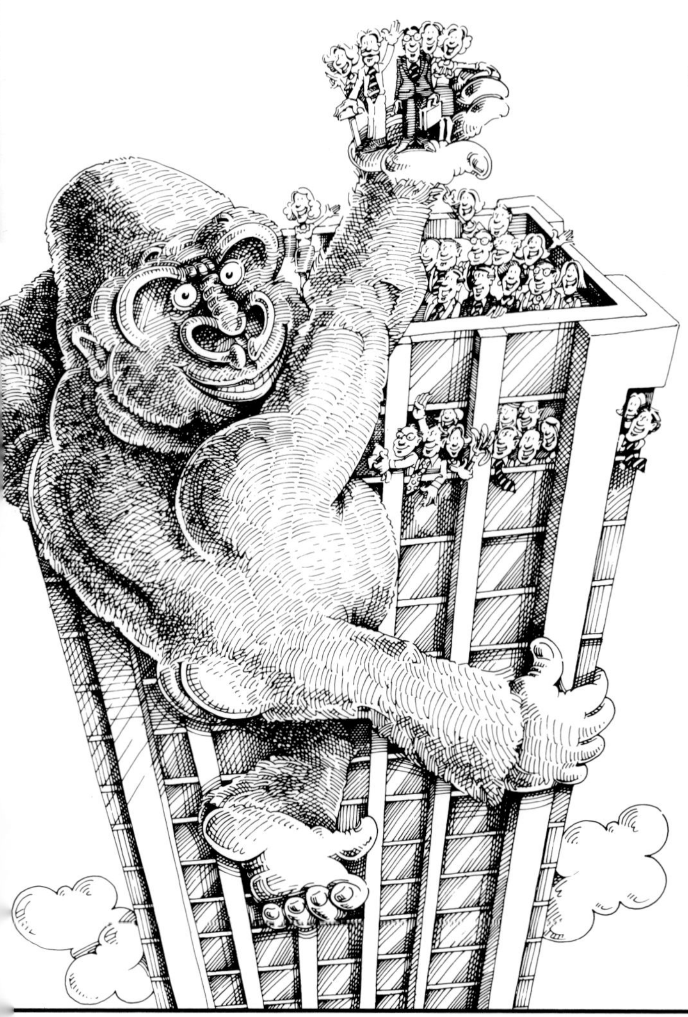

Will Sumpter & Associates
Artists and Photographers Representative
1728 N. Rock Springs Road, NE Atlanta, GA 30324 (404) 874-2014 FAX available

Philip Wende's clients include: Kellogg's, AT&T, New Jersey Bell, Southern Bell, Southwestern Bell, Coca-Cola, Hardee's, Turner Broadcasting Services.

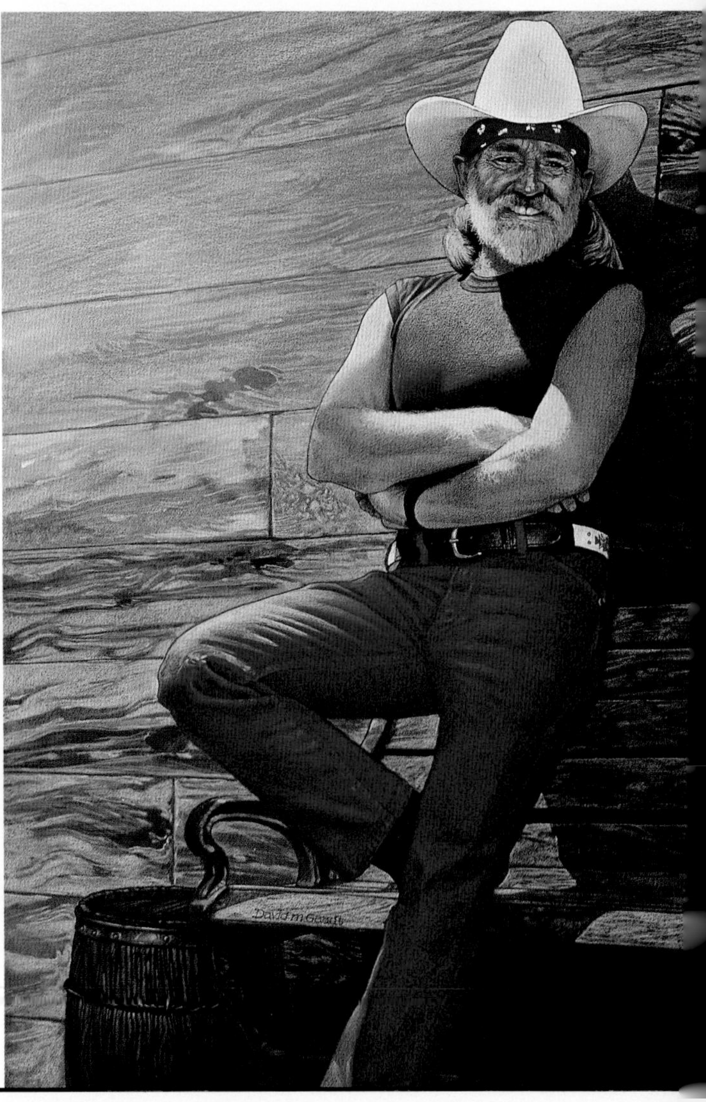

Will Sumpter & Associates
Artists and Photographers Representative
1728 N. Rock Springs Road, NE
Atlanta, GA 30324
(404) 874-2014
FAX available

David Gaadt's clients include: RJR Nabisco, Revell, Ryder Trucks, Bassett Walker, McDonald's, NFL, *Vanity Fair,* Wrangler, Coca-Cola, Paramount Pictures.

B.T. COLLINS

Will Sumpter & Associates
Artists and Photographers
Representative
1728 N. Rock Springs Road, NE
Atlanta, GA 30324
(404) 874-2014
FAX available

Britt Taylor Collins's clients include: RJR Nabisco, Coca-Cola, Lipton, U.S. Marine Corp., Inner Varsity Press, Cyanamid, Little Caesar's Pizza, Multmomah, WLS-Chicago.

Barbara Johansen Newman

Barbara Johansen Newman
Needham, MA
(617) 449-2767

Some favorite clients: *Miami Herald, Boston Magazine,* Whittle Communications, *Hartford Courant,* D.C. Heath and Co., *Ft. Lauderdale News, Sunshine Magazine, Bostonia, Upper Valley Magazine, Boston Globe, Detroit Free Press.*

Some favorite things: Pink and turquoise Formica, gangsters, Pez dispensers, miniature golf, cowboy junk, the Jersey shore, Elvis busts, Roy Rogers, and the theme song from "Car 54."

Some favorite quotes: "It's a good thing Barbara can draw, because she can't sing to save her life." Phil Newman. "It might choke Artie, but it ain't gonna choke Stymie." Stymie Beard in "The Pooch."

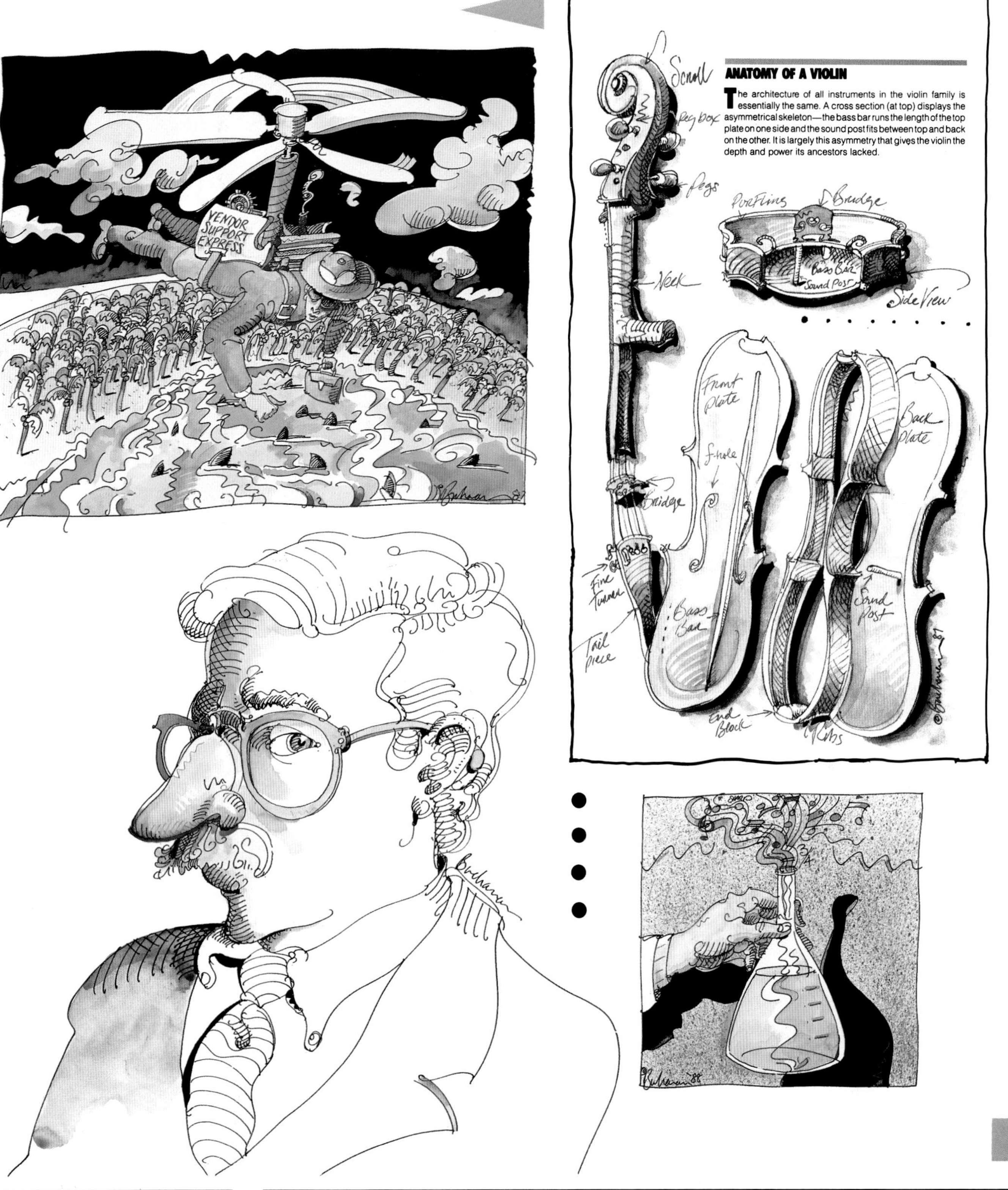
VENDOR
SUPPORT
EXPRESS
ANATOMY OF A VIOLIN
The architecture of all instruments in the violin family is essentially the same. A cross section (at top) displays the asymmetrical skeleton—the bass bar runs the length of the top plate on one side and the sound post fits between top and back on the other. It is largely this asymmetry that gives the violin the depth and power its ancestors lacked.
Scroll
Peg box
Pegs
Neck
Bridge
Side View
Front plate
f-hole
Bridge
Fine Tuner
Bass Bar
Tail piece
Back plate
Sound Post
End Block
Ribs

Yvonne Buchanan
411 14th Street
Brooklyn, NY 11215
(718) 965-3021

Clients:

AT&T; Ford Foundation; J.P. Martin Associates; Cato-Johnson; N W Ayer; Hearst Publications; Condé Nast; Fairchild Publications; Ziff-Davis; Montcom Publications; Grey Communications; *T.V. Guide;* McGraw-Hill; *New York Times; Village Voice;* McCaffery and Ratner; Dancer, Fitzgerald; Gannett Publications; Jonson Pedersen Hinrichs & Shakery; Peat Marwick; Chase Manhattan.

Polly M. Law

Please don't lick this comp, the markers will run.

Polly M. Law
309 West 93rd Street
New York, NY 10025
(212) 866-3754

Graphic Artists Guild
Society of Illustrators

Comps, Animatics, and Storyboards

Malcolm Farley

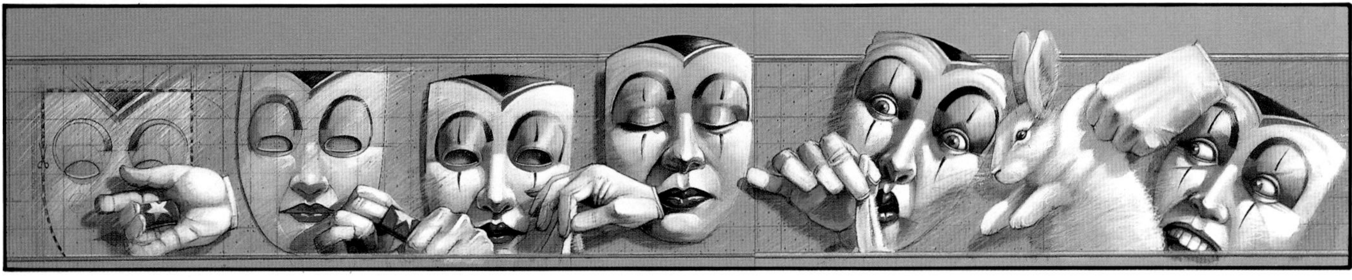

Malcolm Farley
3870 Newland Street
Wheat Ridge, CO 80033
(303) 420-9135
(303) 832-2666

Clients:
Pepsi USA, Siemen's, AT&T, U.S. West, American Healthcare Association, Coors Brewery, Viking Press, Credit Suisse, Citicorp, Rocky Mountain National Park, Diner's Club, Great West Life, Blinder-Robinson International, Major Indoor Soccer League, Platinum Rainbow Records.

Bachrun LoMele

Bachrun LoMele
100 Washington Street
Hoboken, NJ 07030
(201) 963-4572

Saksa Art & Design, Inc.

Saksa Art & Design, Inc.
41 Union Square West
Suite 1001
New York, NY 10003
(212) 255-5539

Specializing in collage, photomontage, handcoloring & type design.

Clients include:

Adler & Adler, *Aim Plus Magazine*, Avon, Bantam Books, Basic Books, Berkley Publishing Group, Carroll & Graf, *Connecticut Magazine*, Consumer Reports, Doubleday & Company, Estée Lauder, Fromm International, Insurance Review, Farrar Straus & Giroux, Gargoyle Graphics, Harcourt Brace Jovanovich, HBO, Henry Holt Books, McGraw Hill, New American Library, *New Jersey Monthly*, W.W. Norton, Oxford University Press, Pucci International, Warner Books, Van de Steeg Associates.

Member Graphic Artists Guild, Type Design.
Portfolio also available.

Peter Kuper

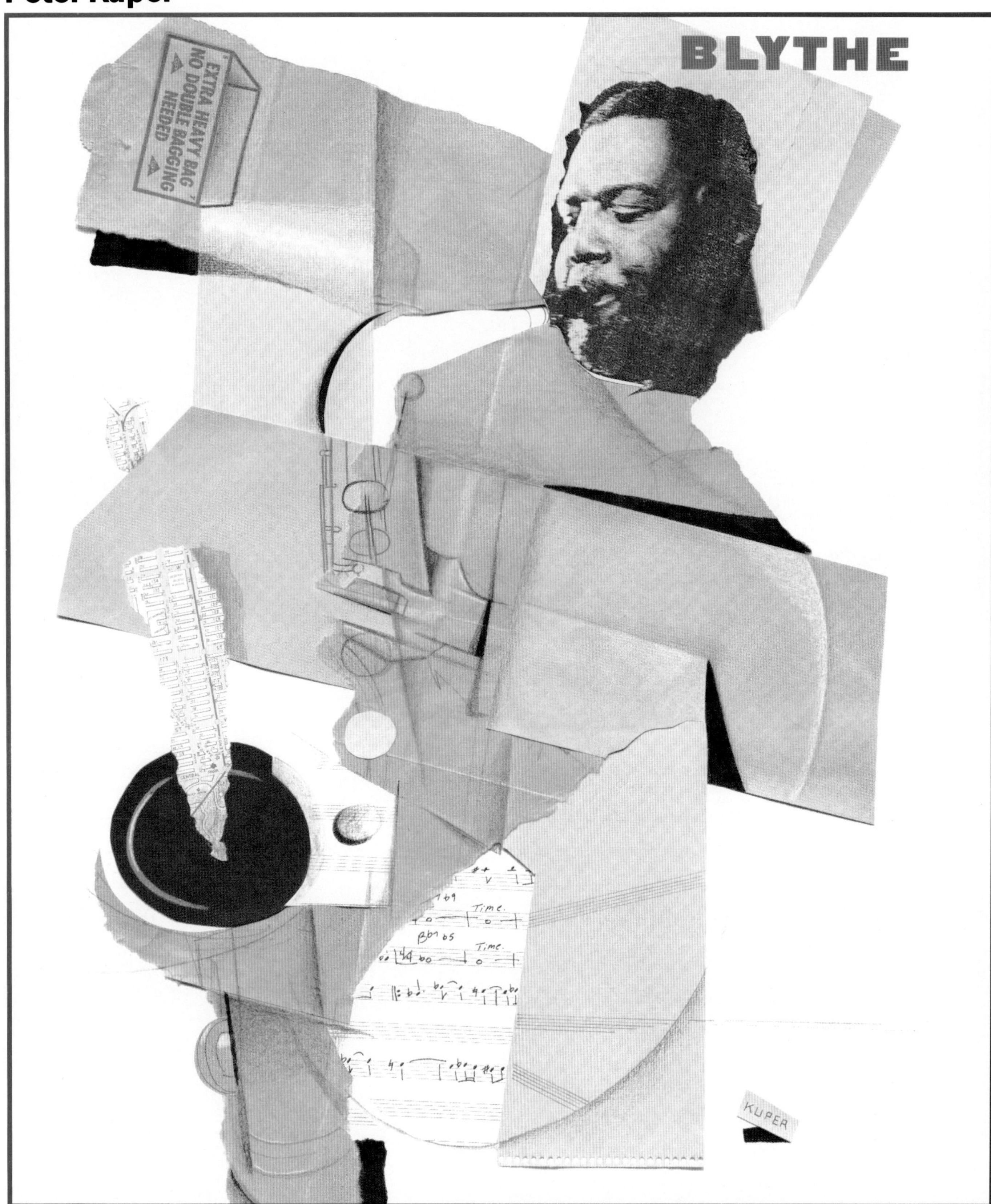

Peter Kuper
250 West 99th Street, #9C
New York, NY 10025
(212) 864-5729

Clients include:
CBS Records (above)
Revlon
Frito-Lay
Time
Fortune
Business Week
Travel & Leisure
Simon & Schuster

Awards include:
Creativity '86
Humor '87
Society of Publication Designers
Society of Newspaper Designers

A feature article appears in the March/April, 1987, issue of *Print*.

Member Graphic Artists Guild

CUSHWA
How to infiltrate leading companies throughout America.

Tom Cushwa
303 Park Avenue South
Apt. 511
New York, NY 10010
(212) 228-2615

Clockwise from upper left:

One of a series of ads for *Advertising Age*.
Illustration about Saturday morning television for *Business Week*.
Cover art for software catalog.
Logo for Cushwa's Studio bowling shirt (available free with every purchase).
Cover art for *Daily News* Sunday supplement.

Other clients include:

Cato-Johnson, Y & R, Grey Direct, William Esty Co., Manufacturers Hanover Trust, RCH&L, *New York Times*, *Connecticut Magazine*, *Games Magazine*, Children's Television Workshop, Pop Shots Inc., Van Brunt Advertising.

For additional samples see *American Showcase 9, 10, 11*.
Member Graphic Artists Guild

Mirko Ilić

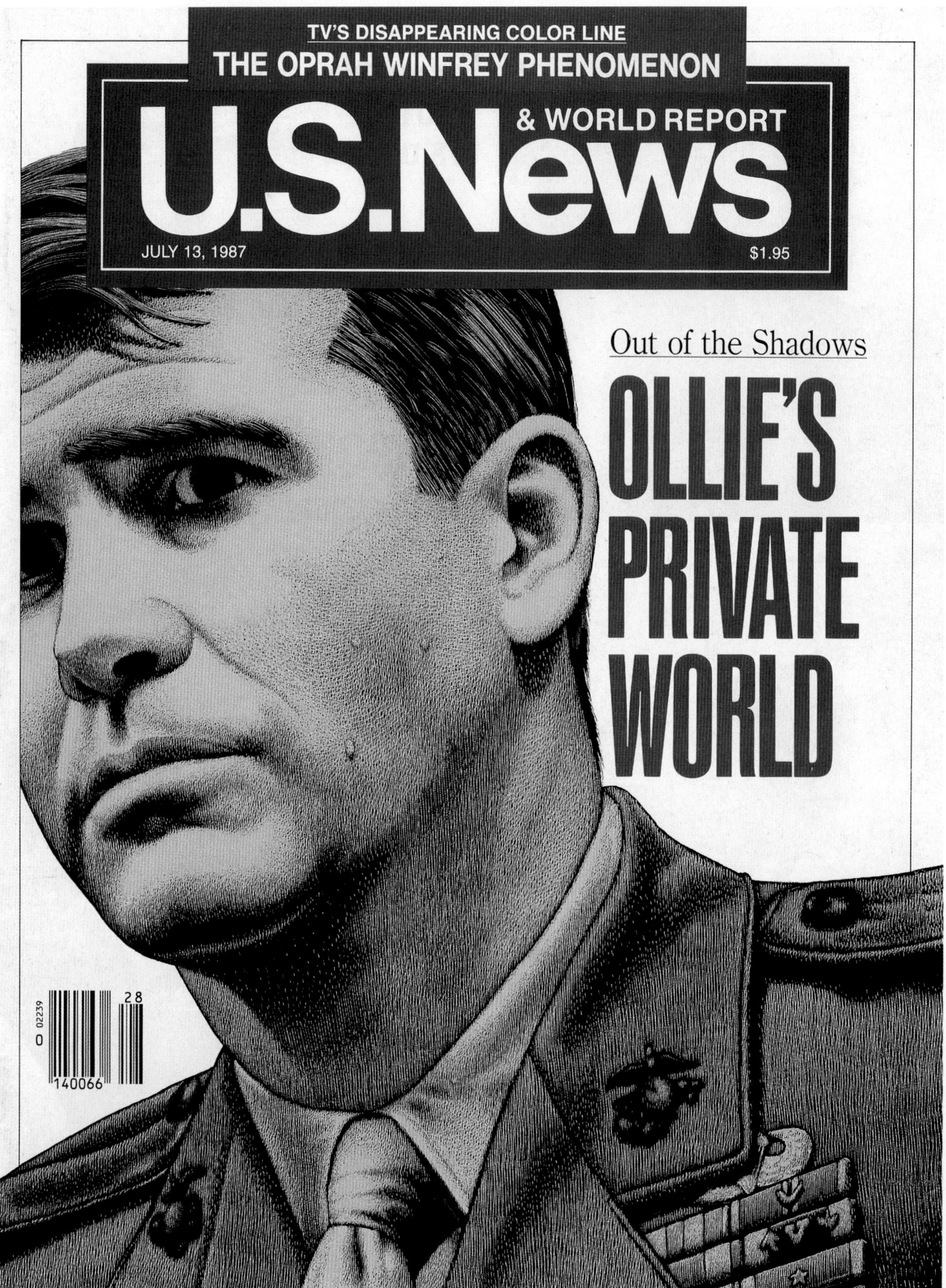

Mirko Ilić
548 Hudson Street, #3
New York, NY 10014
(212) 645-8180

Clients:
American Management Association
Boston Globe
Business Month
Connoisseur
Inc.
L.A. Times
Manhattan inc.
Money
Ms.
New York Times
Psychology Today
Random House
Time
U.S. News & World Report
Wall Street Journal
Washington Post
WBMG Inc.

Tom Bloom
235 East 84th Street
New York, NY 10028
(212) 628-6861

I ink therefore I am.

Philip A. Scheuer

Philip A. Scheuer
126 Fifth Avenue
New York, NY 10011
(212) 620-0728

Clients include:
American Lung Association
Business Week
CBS
Chicago Tribune
Discover
Forbes
Games
Holt, Rinehart and Winston
Howard Marlboro Group
Money
National Lampoon
Newsweek
Random House
Robinson & St. John
Scholastic Inc.
State Street Bank
USA Today
Whittle Communications
Wilson, Haight & Welch
Workman Publishing

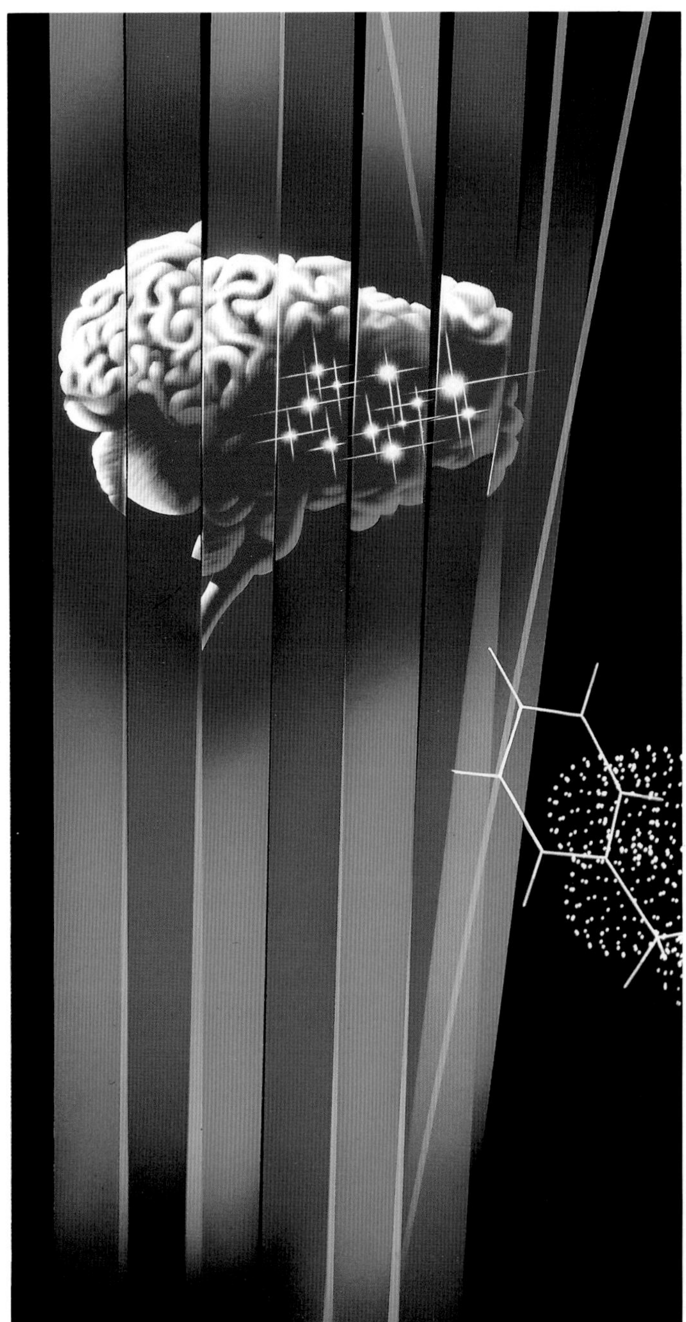

1

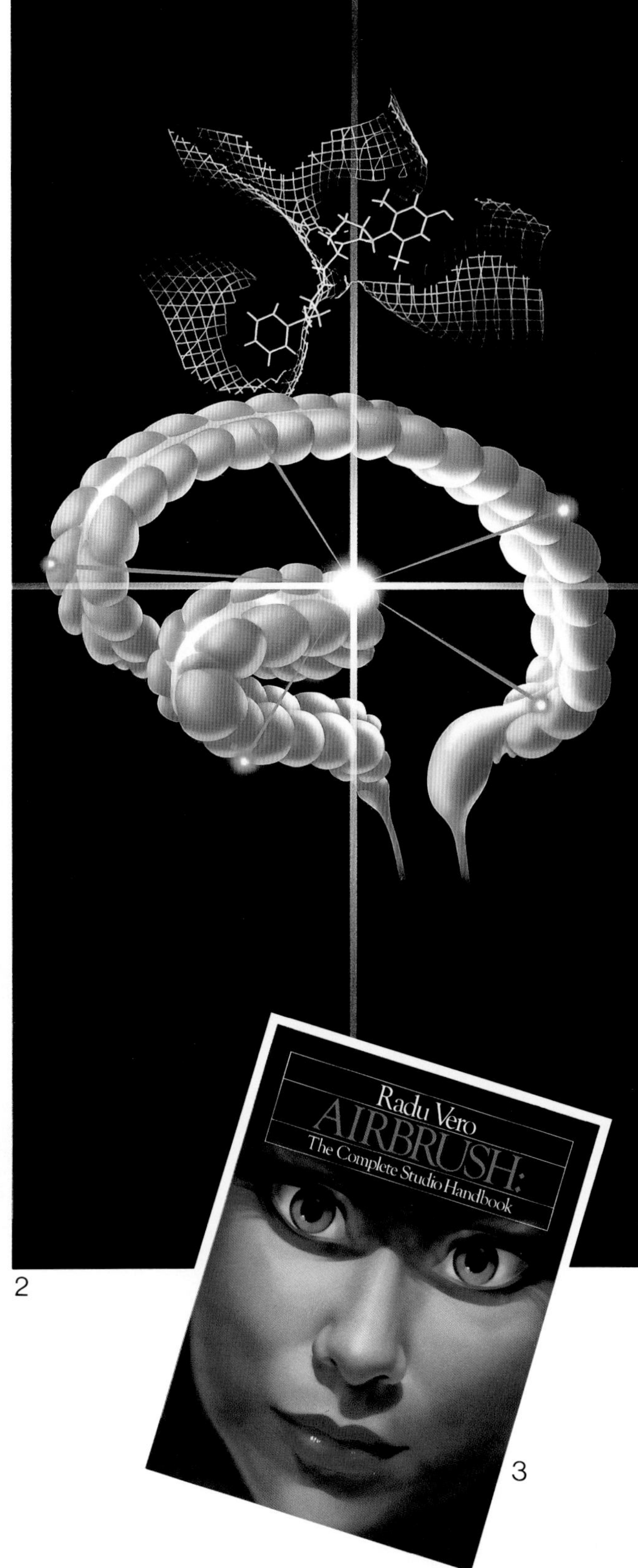

2

3

1. and 2. Brain illustrations from "New Ideas for the future from Searle"
© 1986 by G.D. Searle & Co.
3. Cover of the airbrush book by Radu Vero © 1983 by Watson Guptill Publications

Radu Vero
345 East 80th Street
New York, NY 10021
(212) 628-2152

Conceptual art and design for medical, scientific, and architectural illustration and video.

Bill Russell

Bill Russell
227 West 29th Street, 9R
New York, NY 10001
(212) 967-6443

I draw apples, too, and do illustrations for books, magazines and newspapers, advertising, corporate brochures, and logos. Call for portfolio.

Partial list of clients: AT&T; *Adweek; American Banker;* Apple Computer; Bata; Coca-Cola; CW Communications; *Eastern Review;* The Franklin Library; *Marie Claire; Manhattan inc; New England Monthly; Newsweek; The New York Times; PC Magazine;* Prentice Hall Press; *Spy;* The South Street Seaport; *Stereo Review;* Stewart, Tabori and Chang Publishers; The Stratford Festival; *Toronto Magazine; The Village Voice; The Wall Street Journal;* Whittle Communications.

Represented in Canada by Reactor Art and Design.

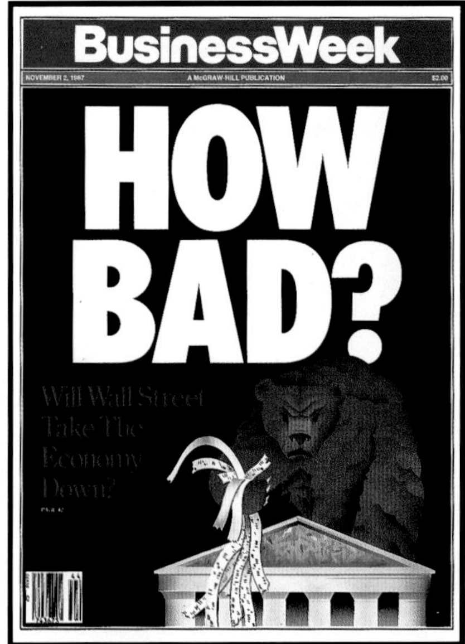

Bob Scott
106 Lexington Avenue, #3
New York, NY 10016
(212) 684-2409

Represented in Chicago by
Connie Koralik
(312) 944-5680

Clients include:

Anthony Russell Design; Bernhardt/Fudyma; *Boston Globe, Business Week;* Clarke/Thompson; CW Communications; DeSantis Design; DynaSoft; *Newsweek;* Peat Marwick Corporation; R.C. Cola; *Sports Illustrated;* St. Martins Press; *Travel & Leisure;* Whittle Communications.

Susan Hunt Yule

Susan Hunt Yule
176 Elizabeth Street
New York, NY 10012
(212) 226-0439

Clients include:

Albert Frank-Geunther Law, Coty, DCA Advertising, Dancer Fitzgerald Sample Inc., Della Femina Travisano & Partners, *Diversion Magazine*, Doremus & Co., Doyle Dane Bernbach, FCB/Leber Katz Partners, Hill & Knowlton, Ketchum Communications, Kolker Talley Hermann Inc., Krupp/Taylor USA, L'Oreal, Lotus Minard Patton McIver, Lowe Marschalk, Malone Advertising, Marlboro Marketing, Muir Cornelius Moore, *The New York Times*, Newmark Posner & Mitchell, Ogilvy & Mather, Rapp & Collins: SSC&B, Scali McCabe Sloves, Steve Phillips Design Inc., Sudler & Hennessey, Trout & Ries.

You can see more of my work in *Graphis Annual 1986, American Showcase 10* and *11*, and *The Black Book 1980, 1982-86* and *1988*.

Reynold Ruffins

Reynold Ruffins
15 West 20th Street
New York, NY 10011
(212) 627-5220

Above illustrations done for:

Gourmet, U.S. Postal Service (Cato/Johnson Y & R), Beneficial Finance (Gips & Balkind & Associates).

Partial list of clients:

Time-Life; Pfizer; *Fortune;* Y & R; BBDO; McCann-Erickson; Wells, Rich, Greene; Coca-Cola; McDonald's, V W of America; IBM; CBS; Amtrak; *The New York Times;* CONOCO; NABISCO; Pan Am.

Lyn Martin

Lyn Martin
P.O. Box 51972
Knoxville, TN 37950-1972
(615) 694-8246

Clients have included:
The Great American Chocolate Chip Cookie Company; Little Debbie Snack Cakes; John Harland Company; American Trends Corporation; Ogilvy & Mather Direct; World Carpets; A.L. Williams Company; Beecham Laboratories; Special Instruments Laboratories, Inc.; City of Oak Ridge, Tennessee; City of Knoxville, Tennessee; Tennessee Valley Authority; Oak Ridge National Laboratories.

Member Graphic Artists Guild

Elizabeth Sayles
16 East 23rd Street
New York, NY 10010
(212) 777-7012

Clients:
Middlesex News, *New Video Magazine*, New York Hospital-Nutrition Information Center, UNICEF, Diane Von Furstenberg Studio, *Woman's Day*.

Member: Graphic Artists Guild

Ernest S. Albanese

Ernest S. Albanese
136 Park Avenue, Apt. 2
Hoboken, NJ 07030
(201) 659-9335
Member Graphic Artists Guild

Clients:
Allivest Video
Armour
Avalon Books
Bordeaux Wines
Citibank
Florida Gold Orange Juice
Fruit of the Loom
Hosiery Sales
Macmillan Publishing
Nabisco
Peter Pan Records
Planters Peanuts
Silver Burdett & Ginn
Sony Corporation

Jim Ceribello
11 West Cedarview Avenue
Staten Island, NY 10306
(718) 317-5972

Member Graphic Artists Guild

Phyllis Tarlow

Phyllis Tarlow
42 Stratford Road
New Rochelle, NY 10804
(914) 235-9473

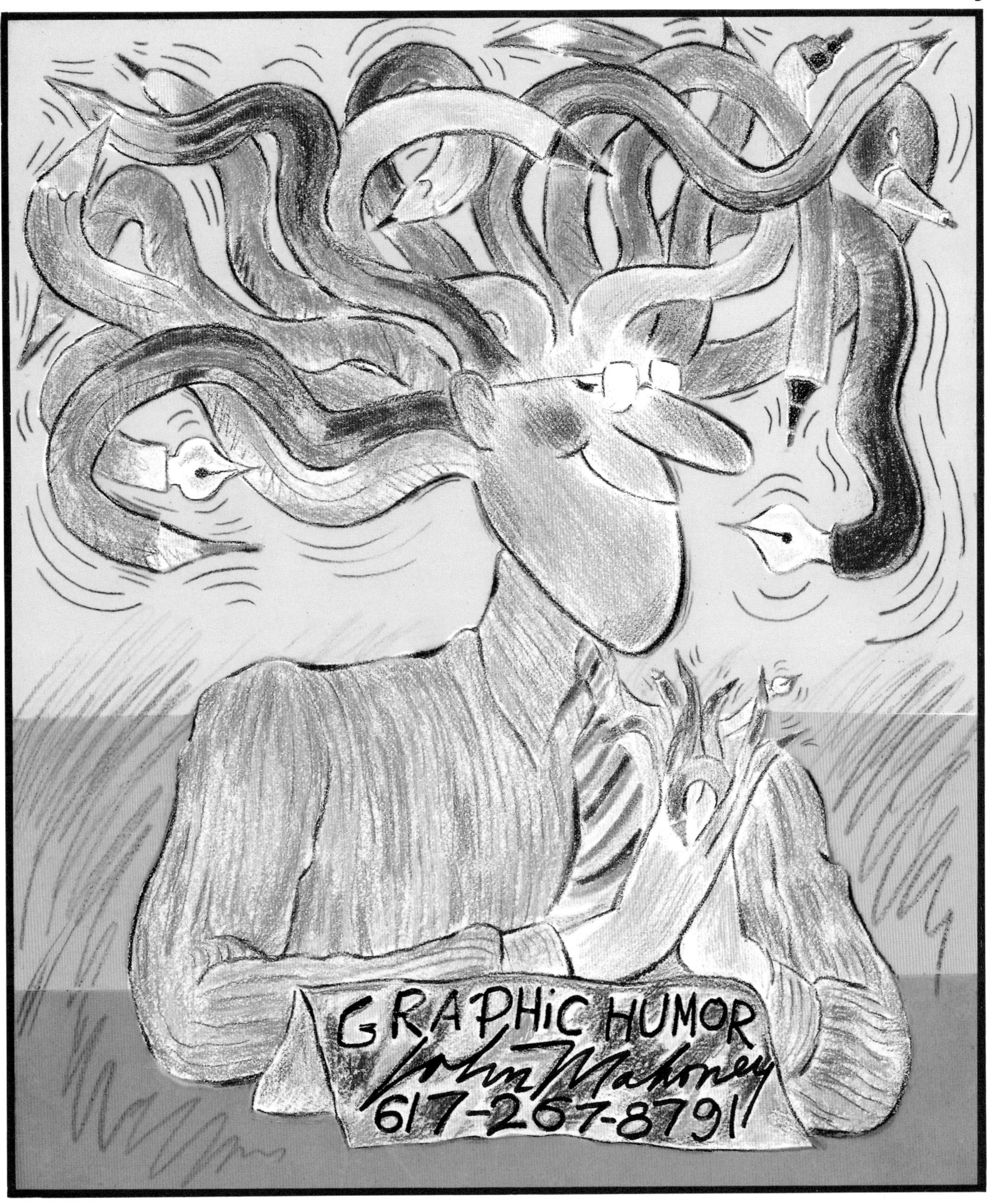

John Mahoney
77 W. Brookline Street
Boston, MA 02118

Arnold Adv., Cabot, HBM/Creamer, HHCC, Maher/Hartford, Ogilvy & Mather, Cahners Publishing Co., *PC Week, Digital Review, New England Business Magazine, Reader's Digest, Boston Magazine, Sportscape,* Computer World, Houghton Mifflin, Boston Edison, Genrad.

Member Graphic Artists Guild

The Dynamic Duo Studio, Inc.

The Dynamic Duo Studio, Inc.
Arlen Schumer &
Sherri Wolfgang
313 East Sixth Street
New York, NY 10003
(212) 254-8242

Comic books are an indigenous American art form with a unique verbi-visual vocabulary, and are read and loved by anyone and everyone, demographically. That's why comic book art sells.

As The Dynamic Duo, we combine our backgrounds in graphic design, drawing, and painting with an extensive knowledge of the comic book medium to bring its aesthetic to advertising art in new ways–codifying images and themes from popular culture for fun solutions to trade, consumer, and editorial illustrations.

The frames above are from an animated spot we co-wrote, art directed, and designed. Other areas of expertise include: commercial and film storyboarding; logo design and hand lettering; audio-visual, animation, and book design.

To view more work, see *American Showcase Illustration 11*.

John Bowdren

John Bowdren
437 West 53rd Street, Apt. 2B
New York, NY 10019
(212) 265-9260

Clients include:

Ogilvy & Mather, McCann Erickson, *Reader's Digest,* Metropolitan Opera, *U.S. Life,* Associated Press, *Alfred Hitchcock's Mystery Magazine, Twilight Zone Magazine,* The K.S.F. Group, *Boston Magazine,* Friendship Press, *High Fidelity Magazine, The New Leader.*

Terry Allen

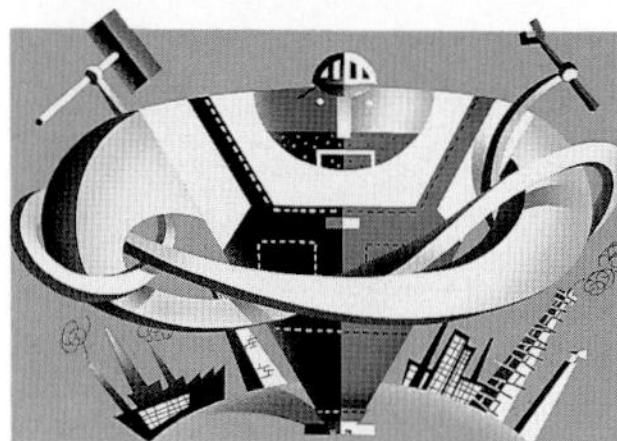

Terry Allen
164 Daniel Low Terrace
Staten Island, NY 10301
(718) 727-0723

Clockwise from right:
1. Koppel & Scher
2. *The Boston Globe Magazine*
3. *The Atlantic*
4. Koppel & Scher
5. *Rolling Stone & Esquire*, Germany
6. Promotion

Member Graphic Artists Guild
FAX in studio

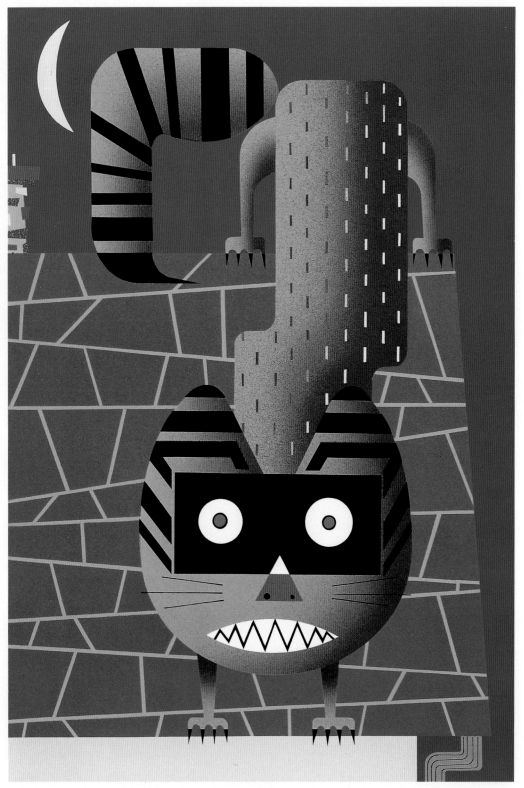

Guy Billout
225 Lafayette Street
Suite 1008
New York, NY 10012
(212) 431-6350

Beth Jennings

Beth Jennings
469 Palisade Avenue
Jersey City, NJ 07307
(201) 795-9483

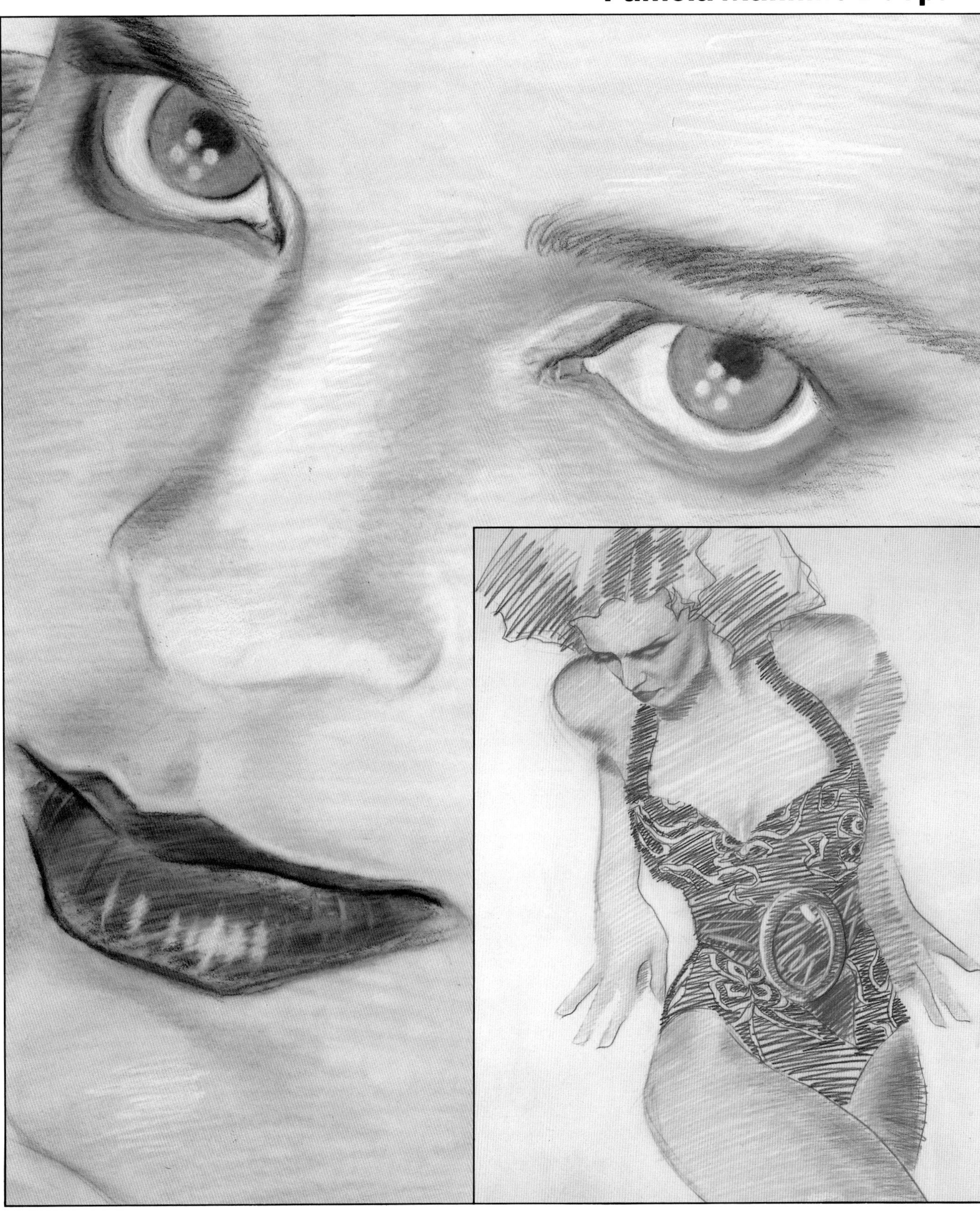

Pamela Mannino DeSpain
344 East 63rd Street
New York, NY 10021
(212) 486-2315
Prismacolor drawings

Fashion
Cosmetics
Animatics
Editorial

Member Graphic
Artists Guild
Graduate of
Pratt Institute

Award of Merit
The School Art
League, Inc. 1983

Craig Berman Illustration
16 Taylor Street
Dover, NJ 07801
(201) 366-4407

Illustration projects include:

Melniker-Uslan Productions, Major Films, Inc., Lightyear Entertainment [RCA], Columbia Pictures, DIC Animation, Silverstone Associates & BMW, CBS/Jim Jensen's All Stars.

Awards:

Art Directors Club of NJ

Memberships include:

Art Directors Club of NJ; Graphic Artists Guild; The S•W•A•N Organization/ Self-Employed Writers and Artists Network, Inc.; Society of Illustrators.

Craig Berman Illustration
16 Taylor Street
Dover, NJ 07801
(201) 366-4407

Illustration projects include:

Melniker-Uslan Productions, Major Films, Inc., Lightyear Entertainment [RCA], Columbia Pictures, DIC Animation, Silverstone Associates & BMW, CBS/Jim Jensen's All Stars.

Awards:

Art Directors Club of NJ

Memberships include:

Art Directors Club of NJ; Graphic Artists Guild; The S•W•A•N Organization/ Self-Employed Writers and Artists Network, Inc.; Society of Illustrators.

Marika Hahn

Marika Hahn
11 Riverside Drive
New York, NY 10023
(212) 580-7896

Clients include:
D'Arcy Masius Benton & Bowles
Ogilvy & Mather Direct
Dancer Fitzgerald Sample
Young & Rubicam
Revlon
Avon
Estée Lauder
Simon & Schuster
Ballantine Books
Fawcett
Bloomingdale's
Family Circle
Good Housekeeping
Glamour

Member of the Graphic Artists Guild

Marty Coulter Studio
10129 Conway Road
St. Louis, MO 63124-1239
(314) 432-2721

Telecopier in studio.

Specializing in Architectural Illustration.

Clients include:
Innsbrook Properties Inc.
MCA Recreation/Planning & Development LA
Hellmuth Obata & Kassabaum
Peckham Guyton Albers & Viets
Pearce Corporation
Brown Shoe Company
Wohl Shoe Company
Missouri Botanical Garden
Monsanto Company
Anheuser-Busch Companies Inc.
Trammel Crow Company
Washington University School of Medicine

Member Graphic Artists Guild, New York Society of Renderers

Kimble Pendleton Mead

Kimble Pendleton Mead
125 Prospect Park West
Brooklyn, NY 11215
(718) 768-3632

Tom Sciacca

Joan Sigman
336 East 54th Street
New York, NY 10022
(212) 421-0050
(212) 832-7980

Represents:
Tom Sciacca
(718) 326-9124

Clients include:
New York magazine, *Vogue*, Bantam Books, *New York Woman*, Whittle Communications, TDM Theatre Ensemble, *New York Times Book Review*, New American Library, NRG Productions.

Robert Goldstrom

Joan Sigman
336 East 54th Street
New York, NY 10022
(212) 421-0050
(212) 832-7980

Represents:
Robert Goldstrom
(718) 768-7367

Clockwise from top:
1. Scholastic/Safari Poster
2. Doubleday/Azazel
3. Geer DuBois/BASF
4. Grove Press

Joan Sigman
336 East 54th Street
New York, NY 10022
(212)421-0050
(212) 832-7980
Represents:
John H. Howard
(212) 832-7980

Clockwise from left:

1. Weidenfeld & Nicolson NY
2. *Essence*
3. *PC Magazine*
4. *Manhattan inc.*
5. *Stereo Review*

Deborah Blackwell

Deborah Blackwell

Deborah Blackwell
3 River Street
Sandwich, MA 02563
(508) 888-4019

every
part
counts
Any part, regardless of individual function or size, is critical to the overall smooth operation of goal-oriented public service.
With the continued commitment and unified dedication of each part, we take pride in our achievements ... in a job well done.
Jim Gillum, Sheriff
PASCO COUNTY SHERIFF'S OFFICE
JIM GILLUM, SHERIFF

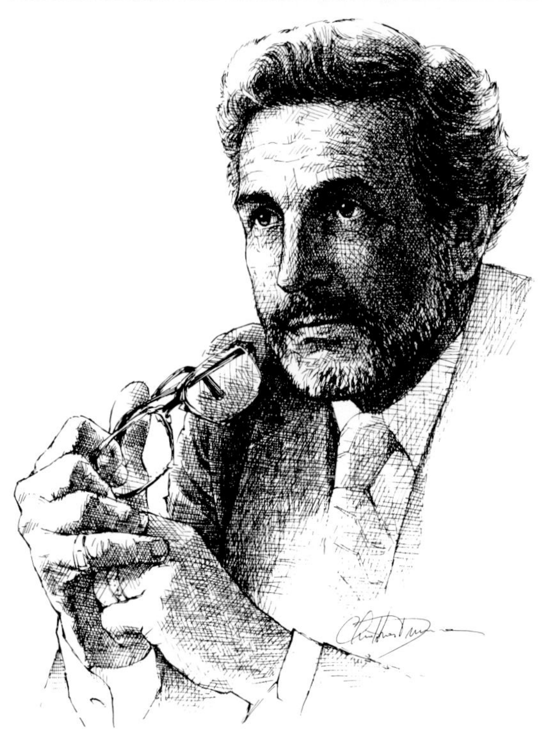

Christopher Dunne
5105 Doe Court
Golden Acres
New Port Richey, FL 34654
(813) 856-2049

Via illustration, a designer can create new worlds, explore different methods of perception, and stir emotional response through visual stimulation. No technical restrictions confine original art developed to fit a client's unique and individual needs. A diverse background in graphic communication has broadened my capabilities as an illustrator and simplifies collaboration with other design professionals. My professional disciplines encompass creative portraiture, various color and line techniques, general illustration, line conversion rendering, logotype development, and graphic design incorporating illustration. Client lists, line art samples, color portfolio, and further information available on request. I am a member of the Graphic Artists Guild and active in my local chapter.

Robert Burger

Robert Burger
County Rt. 519
RD2, Box 38
Stockton, NJ 08559
(609) 397-3737

Represented in New York by American Artists (212) 682-2462

Represented in Philadelphia by Deborah Wolfe Ltd. (215) 232-6666

Clients include:

Time & Life Inc., E.F. Hutton, Allied Corporation, Universal Studios, *Psychology Today,* Viking/Penguin, Bantam Books, *Discover,* Elizabeth Arden, Philip Morris, Avon Books, United Artists, American Express, *Money Magazine, Flying,* and *Sport.*

Awards for book jacket design, advertising campaign, magazine cover design, and lettering design.

Member of the Graphic Artists Guild

CLIENT: ATLANTIC RECORDS

Rosanne Percivalle
430 West 14th Street
Studio 413
New York, NY 10014
(212) 663-2480

Member Graphic Artists Guild and Society of Illustrators

Created for Art Director Bob Defrin at Atlantic Records, this album entitled "Chicago Jazz Summit" was in concept to be the largest baby grand piano, with instruments emerging, making it the tallest structure within the city of Chicago.

Research and creative input in hand, I submitted the first round of sketches. Bob liked the way I had the piano straddling the river, but pressed for further perfection.

Playing with the perspective and my xerox machine I created two more finished comps. The xerox idea got great response and with that Bob's "I love it, let's go with it."

I combined xerox, collage, and my own painting techniques to create a fun illustration and a successful cover.

Roger T. De Muth

Roger T. De Muth
De Muth Illustration/
Design Studio
4103 Chenango Street
Cazenovia, NY 13035
(315) 655-8599 Studio
FAX/Telecopier in studio

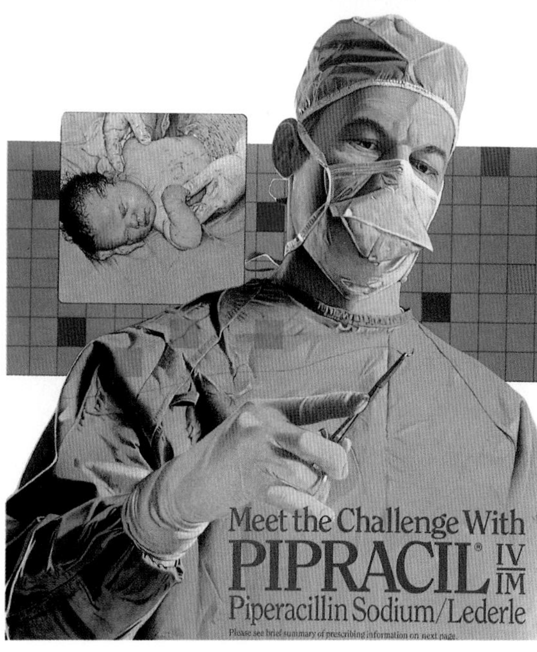

Meet the Challenge With
PIPRACIL® IV IM
Piperacillin Sodium/Lederle

Sal Catalano
114 Boyce Place
Ridgewood, NJ 07450
(201) 447-5318

Clients include:

National Audubon Society; Ciba Geigy; American Motors; CBS; NBC; Coca-Cola; General Foods; N.Y. Zoological Society; Canada Dry; ABC; Time-Life; Pepsi Cola; Citibank; Travenol; U.S. Government; Upjohn; Lederle; Pfizer; Winthrop; Burger King; IBM; Dupont; United Artists; Panasonic; Sony; Borden; McGraw-Hill; RCA; TWA; McNeil; Squibb; Wyeth; Sterling; American Distillers; N.J. Bell; Paramount Studios; Merck; The Rockefeller Group; Paine Webber; Doyle Dane Bernbach; J. Walter Thompson; Grey; Ogilvy & Mather; Marsteller; Benton & Bowles; Foote Cone & Belding; Kallir, Philips, Ross; McCann Erickson; *TV Guide; Reader's Digest; Redbook;* Avon Books; National Wildlife Federation; *N.Y. Times; Field & Stream;* Stainmaster® Dupont; Pipracil® Lederle.

Heather Taylor

Heather Taylor
(516) 477-2997

Clients include:
Avon Cosmetics, Ballantine Books, *The Daily News, Family Circle, International Food & Wine Magazine*, Harmony Books, *House Beautiful, Modern Bride Magazine*, NBC, *New Jersey Monthly, Scholastic, Seventeen Magazine, Time.*

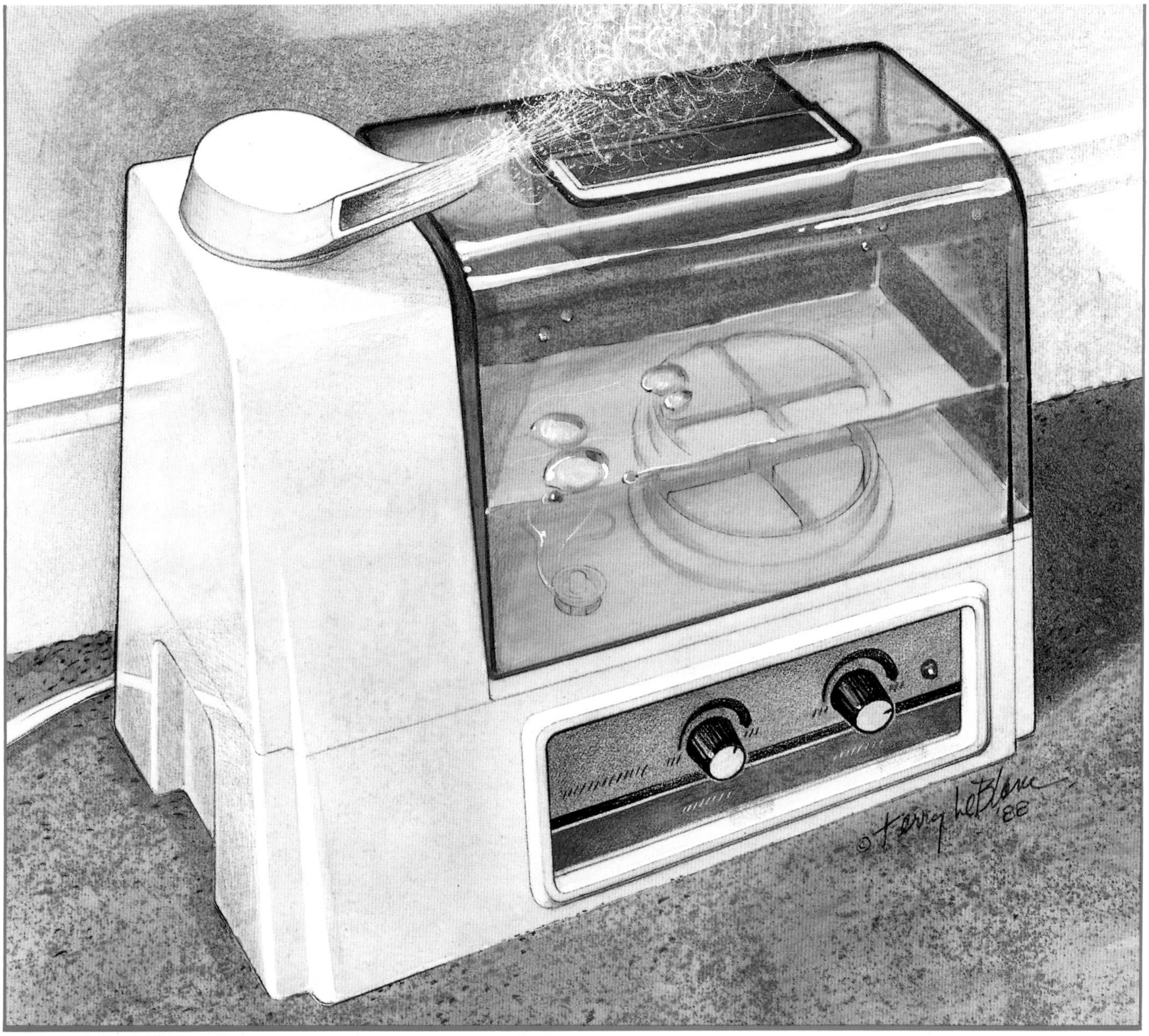

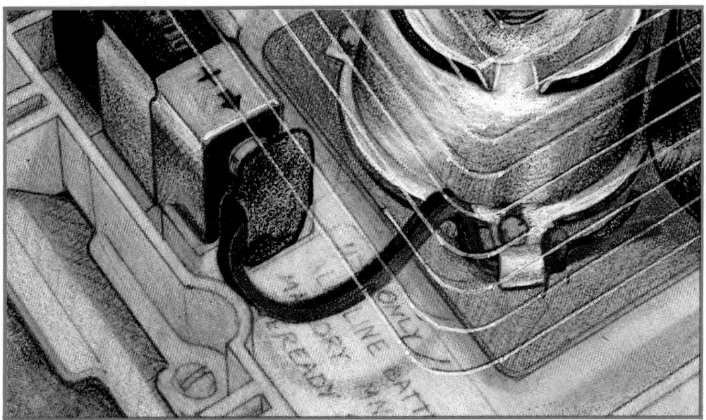

Terry LeBlanc
65 Eustis Street
Cambridge, MA 02140
(617) 864-0932

Member/past president
Graphic Artists Guild, Boston

3-D Product Illustration
• Color: colored pencil and markers
• Precision B/W: ink or pencil
• Cut-away, exploded, x-ray views
• A high level of technical understanding
• Solutions that show how things function

Clients:

Aerospace Museum (CA), Alfa Laval, Apollo Computer, Boston Whaler, Cahners Publishing, Ciba Corning, Costar, Dennison Mfg., Doremus/Boston, DRK Adv., Draper Lab (Apollo, Polaris), Dynatech, EPG/Gulf & Western, Hasbro Industries, HBM/Creamer, Ilex, Instron, ITP/Boston, Jason Grant Adv., Laser Science, Lexicon, NEC Electronics, Peckham, Polaroid, Raben Publishing, Raytheon, Roberts & Dana Adv., Wetzel Assoc., Whitman & Howard.

Daniel Abraham

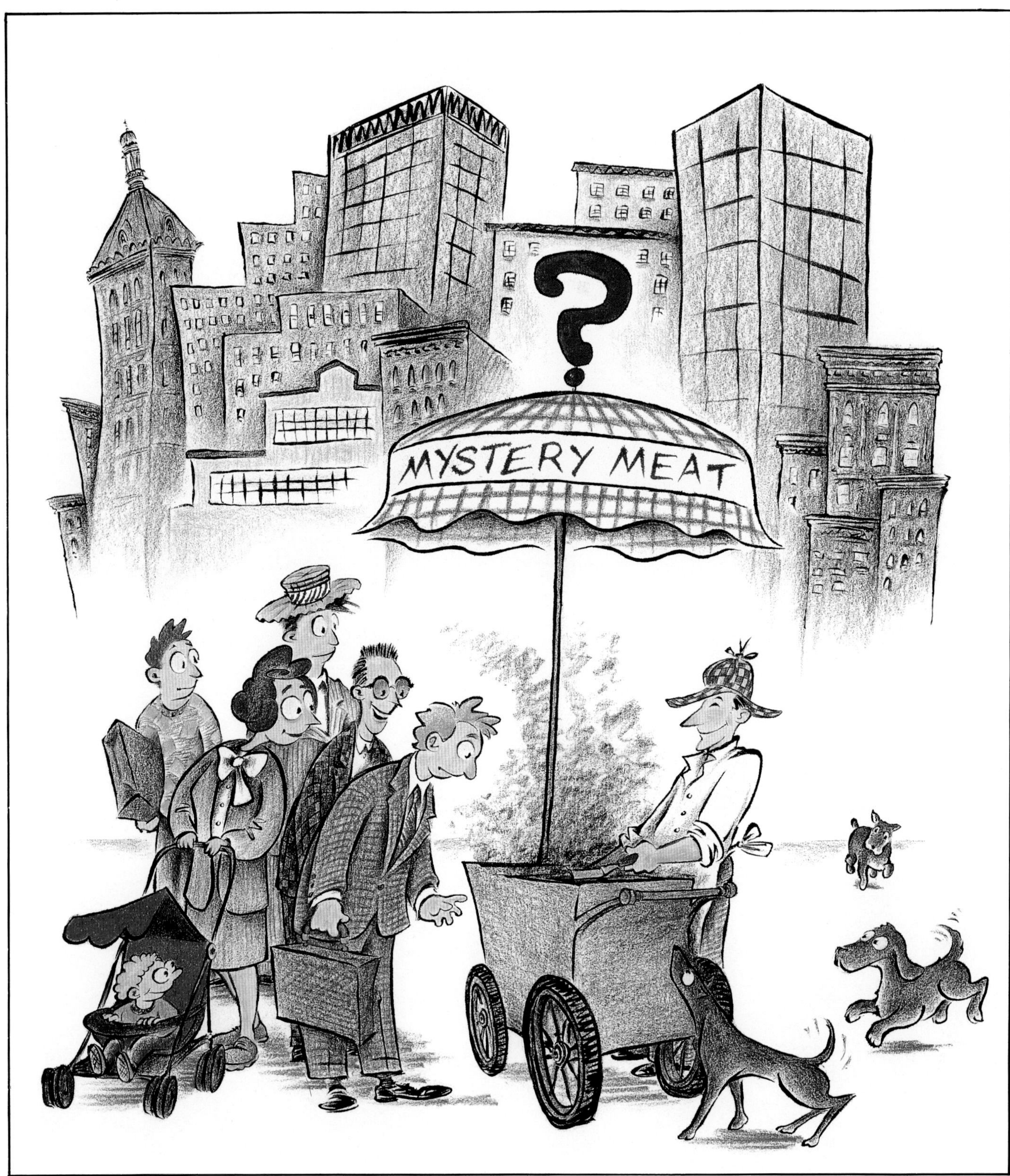

Daniel Abraham
Box 2528
Rockefeller Center Station
New York, NY 10185
(718) 499-4006

You want to harpoon 'em?
Get me to cartoon 'em,
You'll get a whale of
a response.

It's truth, not a rumor;
You sell best with humor,
So let me attend to your
wants.

Just serve up your
problems,
For I love to gobble 'em;
They're brain food that
get me to think.

You'll get a solution
And wit in profusion,
With coquille board,
brushes and ink.

Member Graphic Artists
Guild

Jennifer Collins
(212) 260-1920

George Schmidt

George Schmidt
183 Steuben Street
Brooklyn, NY 11205
(718) 857-1837

Illustration
Portrait
Landscape

David G. Klein
273 Prospect Park West
Brooklyn, NY 11215
(718) 788-1818

Illustration – Engraving – Scratchboard

New York Times, Forbes, Bulletin of the Atomic Scientists, Franklin Library, Inx., Society of Illustrators.

FAX services available.

Ron Lieberman

Ron Lieberman
109 West 28th Street
New York, NY 10001
(212) 947-0653

Illustration Design
Illustration Concept

SHOWN HERE: (Left row-top to bottom) Ad for the U.S. Economic Census; Illustration of disco night-life. (Right row) "The Big Five"/Editorial illustration for *Venture Magazine*, Auto market trade ad for *The Washington Post*, illustration for a tropical cruise.

CLIENTS INCLUDE: FCB/Leber Katz Partners, Diener/Hauser/Bates, BBDO, Ogilvy & Mather, R.J. Gibson Adv., Citibank, Merrill Lynch, *N.Y. Times, GEO, Esquire, Dunn's Business Month,* Random House, Condé Nast, Dell Publishing, CBS Records, Warner Bros. Records, and NBC/ Saturday Night Live.

ADDITIONAL SAMPLES ARE SHOWN IN: Graphic Artists Guild Directory 4; American Showcase 6, 7, 8, 10 & 11; Black Book 1984 & 1986; RSVP 12 & 13.

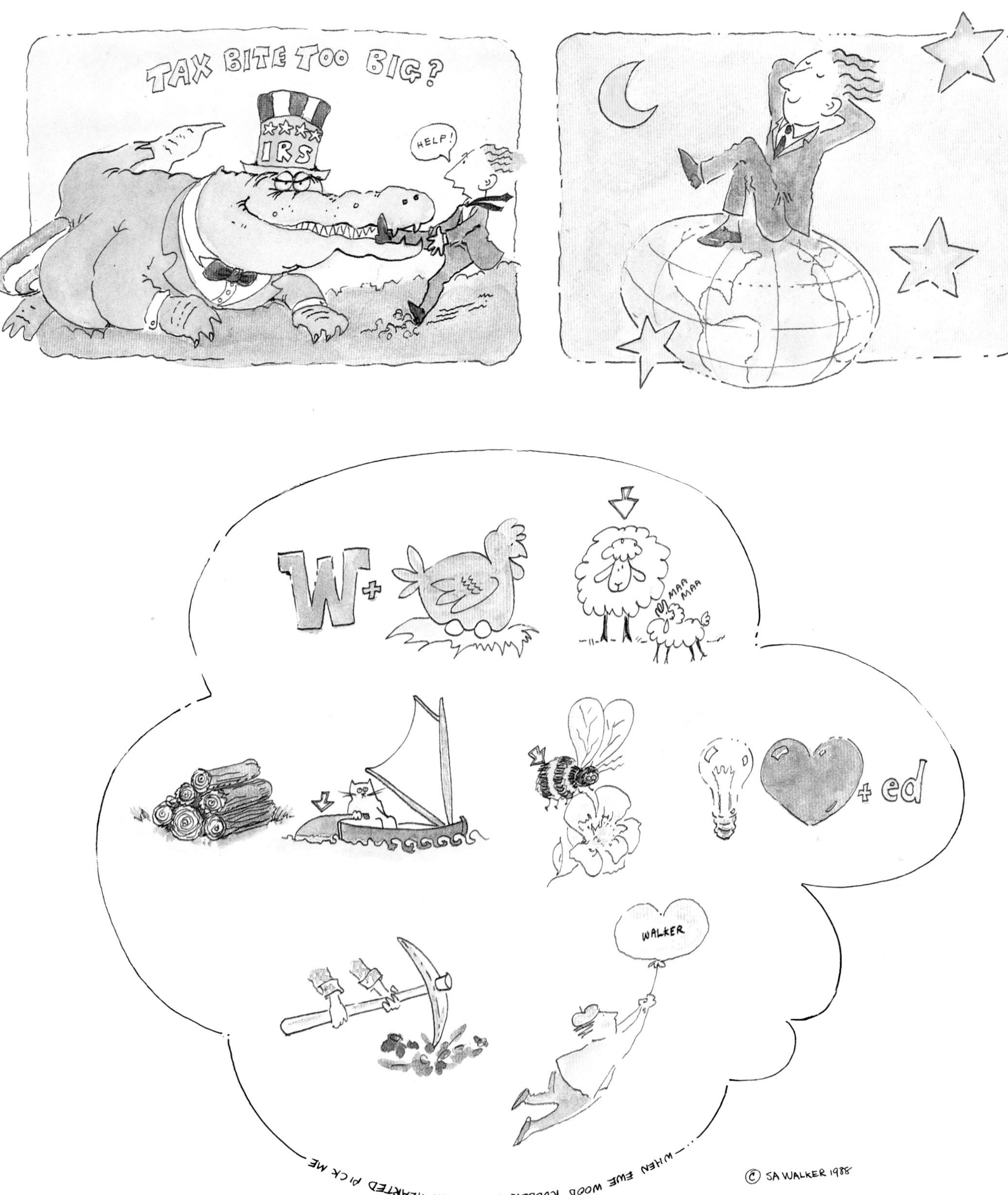

S.A. Walker
8 Gifford Court
Salem, MA 01970
(508) 745-6175

Capabilities:

Illustration
Light-hearted illustration
Cartoons
Political cartoons
Storyboards
Animation design
Identity design & support
Application design for interactive computer/video projects
Consultation

Clients:

Advest
Baybanks
Cramer
Directronix
Kroeger
Indiana Bell
New England Telephone
New York Telephone
North Star
Stop & Shop

Marsha E. Levine

Marsha E. Levine
140-55 34th Avenue, #4-P
Flushing, NY 11354
(718) 445-9410

Realistic pen and ink drawings or with color, for advertising, editorial, publishing, and corporate use. Specializing in portraits, naturalistic themes, and food-related drawings.

Graphic Artists Guild

Dana Schreiber

Dana Schreiber
89 Saint James Place
Brooklyn, NY 11238-1802
(718) 638-3505
(203) 693-6688
FAX 718-636-1458

See *American Showcase 11*
Graphic Artists Guild
Society of Illustrators

"Exciting solutions! Reliable." Sharon Kaminer, Institute for Counseling & Human Development.

"Genuine concern for our needs–makes us all look good." William Chickering, Chick-Green Associates.

"Professional, consistantly meets deadlines." Susan Kotarba, Kotarba Design.

"Thorough, competent, good service you can count on." Charles Viera, Long Island University.

Clients Include:

Brooklyn Botanic Garden
Brooklyn Museum
Citibank, N.A.
Crazy Eddie, Inc.
Doug Cramer Productions
NBC
Pratt Institute
RKO General
Time Equities, Inc.
3M Media Network

Nancy Lee Walter

Tarantula

Where is your skeleton? The tarantula's is outside its body and covered with hair. The skeleton holds the spider up and protects its insides.

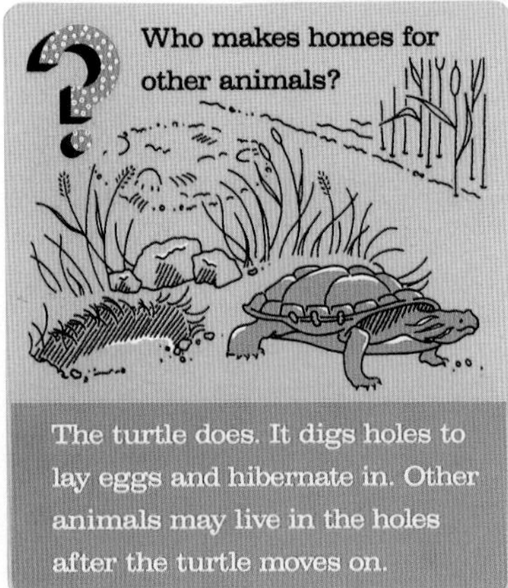

Who makes homes for other animals?
The turtle does. It digs holes to lay eggs and hibernate in. Other animals may live in the holes after the turtle moves on.

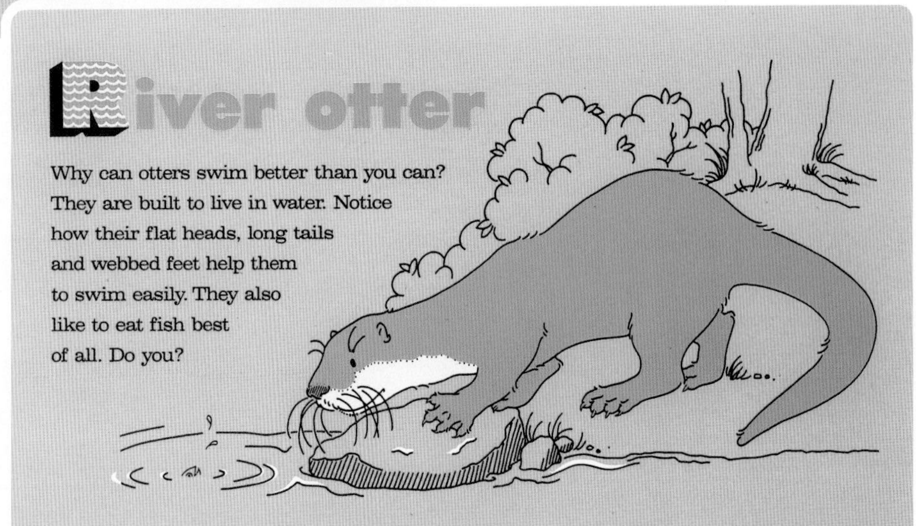

River otter
Why can otters swim better than you can? They are built to live in water. Notice how their flat heads, long tails and webbed feet help them to swim easily. They also like to eat fish best of all. Do you?

Marjorie Boccio, designer
Nancy Lee Walter, illustrator

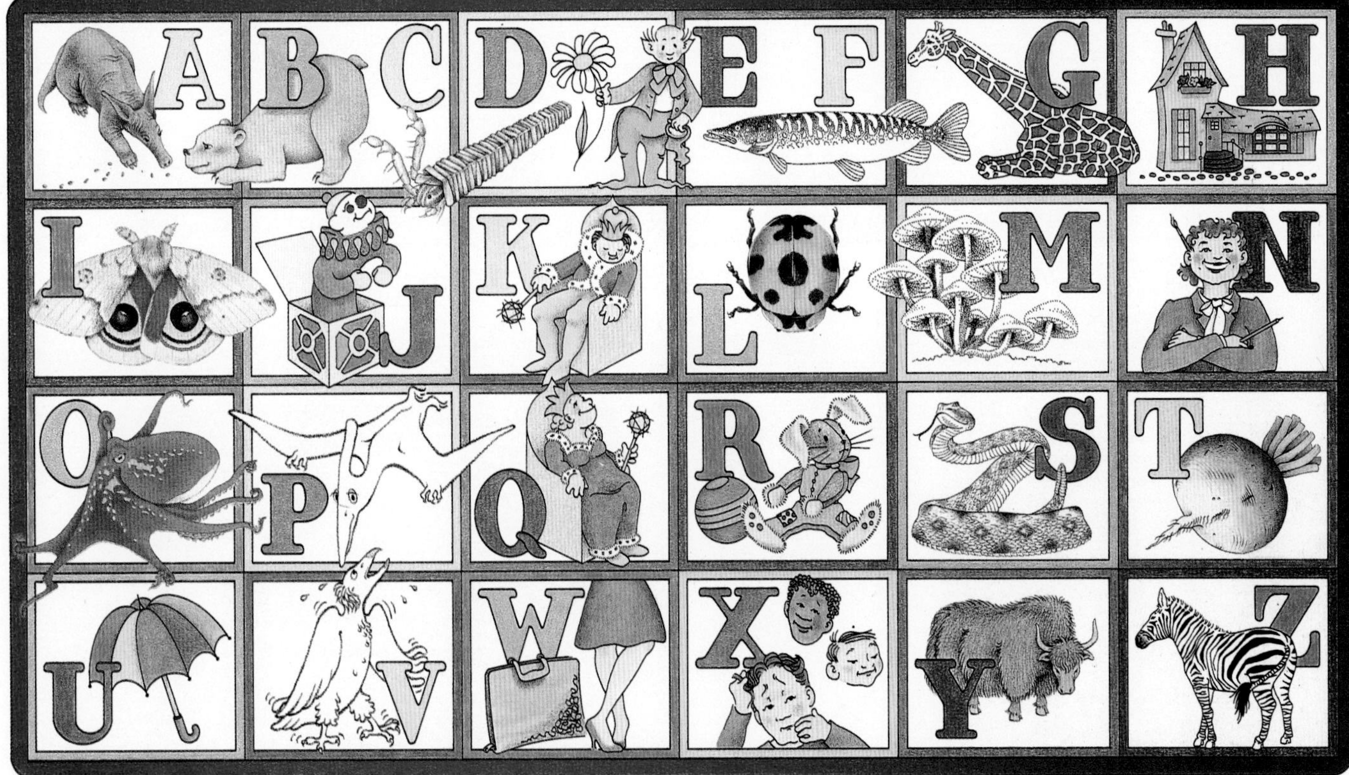

Nancy Lee Walter
P.O. Box 611/391 Popular
Elmhurst, IL 60126
(312) 833-3898

Services: cartoon-style children's and editorial subjects, science, animals. Watercolor, gouache, ink, graphite, colored pencil. Samples are available on request.

Accounts: General Exhibits & Displays • Lincoln Park Zoo • *World Book* • *Childcraft* • *Encyclopedia Britannica/Comptons* • Nystrom/Eyegate • David C. Cook Publishing Company

Rob Saunders

Rob Saunders
368 Congress Street, 5th floor
Boston, MA 02210
(617) 542-6114

Image-smith at your disposal.

Member Graphic Artists Guild

Ideas created for:

Boston Globe; Reader's Digest; Psychology Today; Money; Inc.; Changing Times; Smithsonian; Hartford Courant; Lotus; BYTE; Common Cause; New Age; Sportscape; Sylvia Porter's Personal Finance; Polaroid; Reebok; Sheraton; Honeywell; AT&T; Fidelity Investments; Digital; Ocean Spray; Bank of Boston; Harvard Business School; John Hancock Mutual Life; Children's Television Workshop; Little, Brown & Co.; D.C. Heath; Ziff-Davis; and others.

Best of Show, New England Press Association Awards 1987; New York Art Directors Club 1987; Creative Club of Boston Design Show '84, '86, '87

See also: *American Showcase 11, Adweek Portfolio 1987, Designsource/ Worksource '85 - '88*

Lilla Rogers

Lilla Rogers
483 Henry Street
Brooklyn, NY 11231
(718) 624-6862

To view more work:
American Showcase 7 and *11*
Adweek Portfolio 1988
RSVP 9-12
American Illustration 4 and *7*

Albert Frank-Guenther Law, *American Health, Applause, Archaeology,* BBDO, *Beauty Digest,* Benton & Bowles, Bergdorf Goodman, *Bride's, Child, Children, Connoisseur, Elle, Essence, Family Circle, Health, HG, High Fidelity,* IBM, *Ladies' Home Journal,* Macy's, Merrill Lynch, *Metropolitan Home, Minnesota Monthly, Moviegoer, Ms.,* Neiman-Marcus, Neville Lewis Associates, *New Woman, New York, New York Daily News, New York Times, New York Woman, Parents,* Pantheon Books, *PC World,* Portal Publications, *Psychology Today, San Francisco Focus, San Jose Mercury, Sassy, Savvy, Self, Seventeen, Signature,* Time Inc., *Travel & Leisure, TWA Ambassador, US Air, Vanity Fair, Vogue Knitting, Walking, Weight Watchers,* Whittle Communications, *Women's Sports & Fitness, Working Mother, Working Woman,* YM.

Katherine A. Ginzel
17 Allerton Street
Plymouth, MA 02360
(617) 746-1099

Clients include:

Gillette, Carter's Baby Clothing Co., and Rainbow Arts, publisher of Ginzel Bears™, a line of greeting cards conceived, designed, and executed by Ms. Ginzel.

Member of the Graphic Artists Guild, The Creative Club of Boston, and the Illustrators Group of Boston.

Portfolio available upon request.

STUDIO • 23
ARTISTS

612 Argyle Road, No. 6H, Brooklyn, NY 11230
718 • 434 • 0503

STUDIO
December, 1986

Gary Halsey

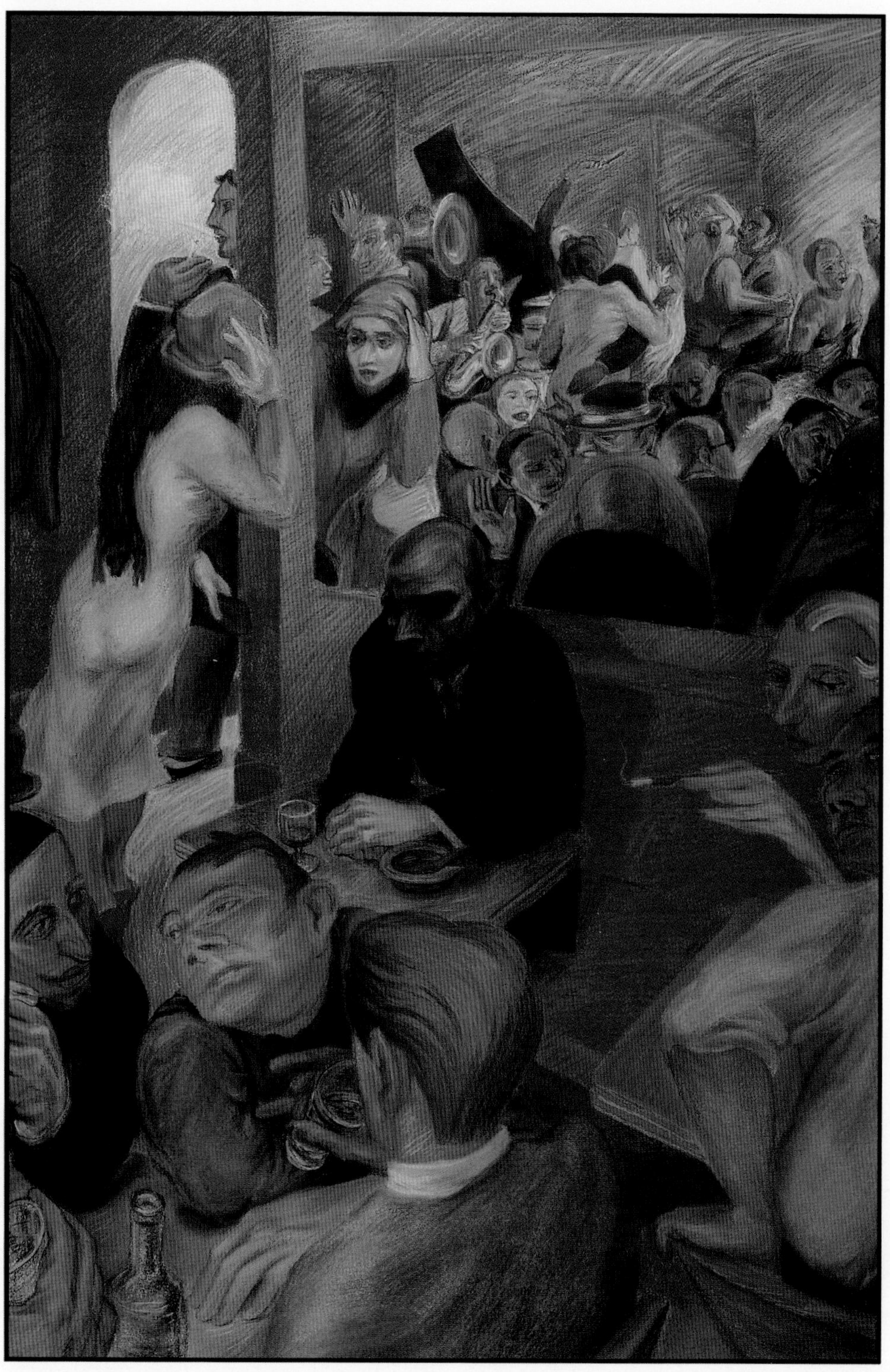

Gary Halsey
176 St. Johns Place #8
Brooklyn, NY 11217
(718) 857-1798

Above: Cover illustration of *Steppenwolf,* Herman Hesse, Penguin Books, London, © 1987.

Member Graphic Artists Guild

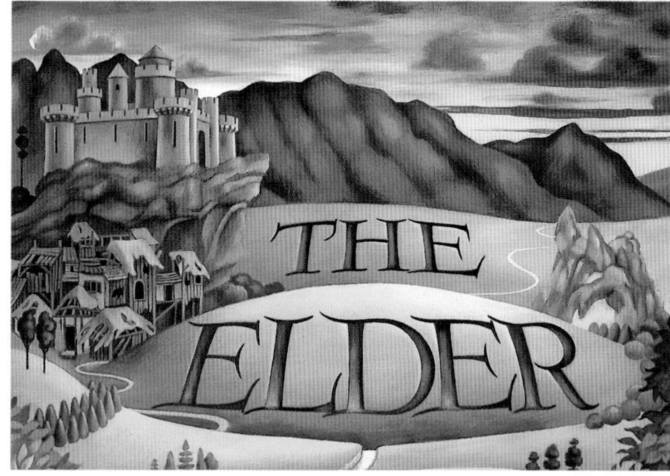

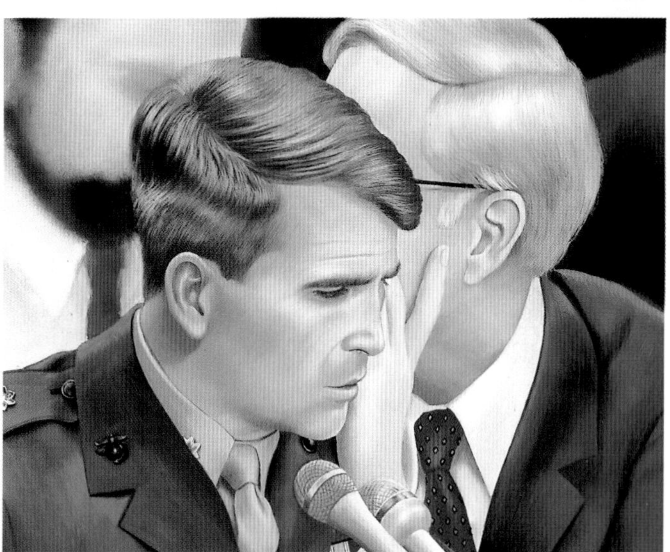

Mona Conner
One Montgomery Place, #8
Brooklyn, NY 11215
(718) 636-1527

Pat Grant Porter

Pat Grant Porter
28 West 69th Street
New York, NY 10023
(212) 799-8493

Advertising & editorial art

Clients include:

Avon, *Barron's, Children's Digest,* Crown, Aldine DeGruyter Publishing, Franklin Watts, The Gallagher Group, The Girl Scouts of America, Harcourt Brace Jovanovich, Houghton Mifflin, J.C. Penney, Alfred A. Knopf, Laidlaw Brothers, Little, Brown & Company, Macmillan, Marc O'Polo/IF, National Council on Drug Education, Pantheon, Mrs. Pauls Kitchens, Reynolds Wrap, Rob Roy/Clothes for Boys, Scholastic Book Services, Scott Towelettes, United Nations Publications, Vanguard Records, The Viking Press, Western Publishing Co.

Member Graphic Artists Guild

Meryl Meisler
553 Eighth Street
Brooklyn, NY 11215
(718) 768-3991

Illustration on Photography

Joel Cadman

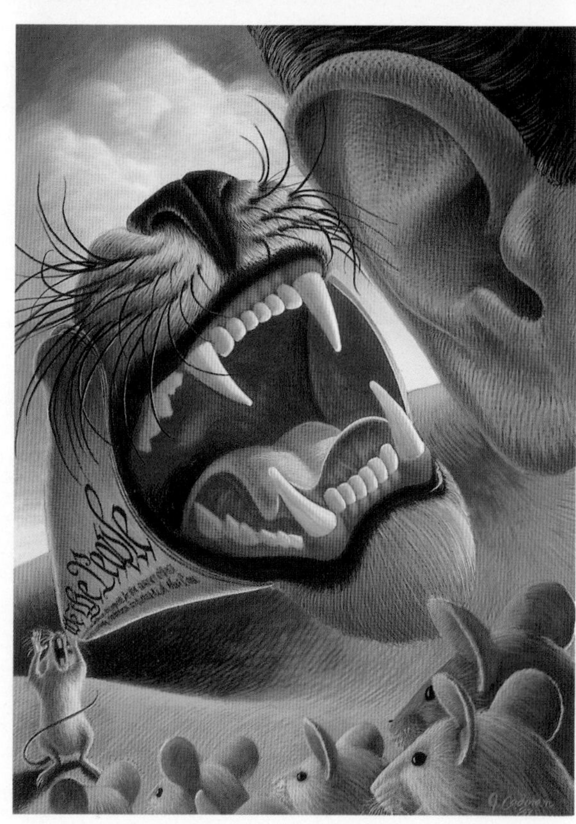

Joel Cadman
515 West 48th Street, 1RE
New York, NY 10036
(212) 586-9829

- Editorial
- Book Cover
- Poster
- Album Cover

Clients include:

- Suzuki of America Automotive Corporation
- Designory Inc.
- Transamerica Life Co.

Steve Henry
7 Park Avenue
New York, NY 10016
(212) 532-2487

Penny Carter

(212) 772-3715

Brian Ajhar

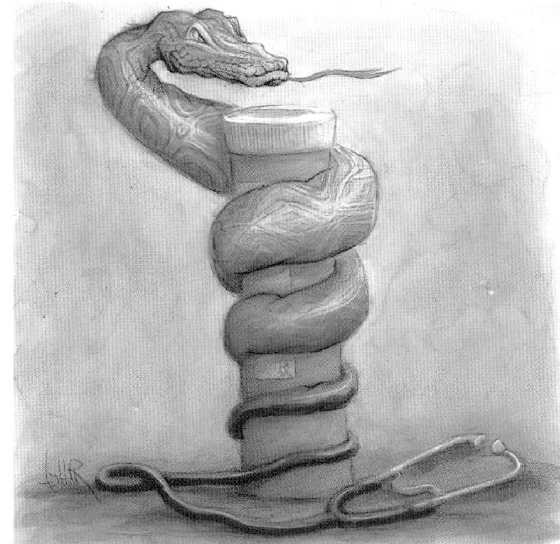

Brian Ajhar
321 East 12th Street, #30
New York, NY 10003
Represented by:
Pamela Korn
(212) 529-6389

Partial Client List Includes:
Advertising:
DDB Needham
J. Walter Thompson
FCB/Leber Katz Partners
Scali, McCabe, Sloves
General Foods
General Electric Corporation
McDonald's
Chase Manhattan

Editorial and Publishing:
Time
Forbes
Sports Illustrated
Newsweek
Changing Times
Oxford Press
William Morrow Publishing
Harvard University
New School for Social Research

Work also appears in:
CA Illustration Annual
Graphis Annual
Humor '87
American Illustration
Society of Illustrators Annual
Print's Design Annual

Can also be seen in:
The Creative Blackbook 1988
American Showcase 9, 10 & 11

Nazz Model Construction

Photo: NORA SCARLETT

Nazz Model Construction
159 Second Avenue
New York, NY 10003
"Specializing in Miniatures"
Represented by:
Pamela Korn
(212) 529-6389
Can also be seen in:
American Showcase 8
Corporate Showcase 6

Partial Client List Includes:

McCann-Erickson
Black & Decker
Sony
Playmobile
Vestron Video
Long, Haymes & Carr
Pilot Life
Marine Midland Bank
Financial Technologies
International
City of New York
Barbara Brown Design
TPF&C
Time Magazine
Business Week
Atlantic Monthly
Psychology Today
Sylvia Porter's
Personal Finance
Video Review
Outlook
Personal Computing
Satellite Marketing
Dun's Business Month
Drug Topics
Medical Economics
Computer Merchandising
McGraw-Hill
Bantam Books
William Morrow & Company
Crown Publishers

Jeff Moores

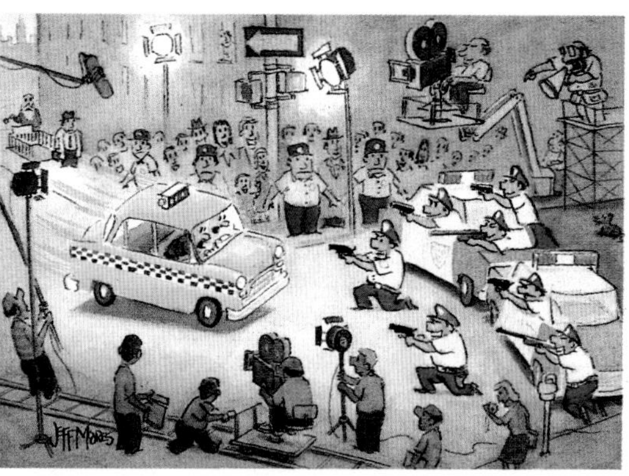

Jeff Moores
72 South Maple Avenue
Springfield, NJ 07081

Represented by:
Pamela Korn
(212) 529-6389

Partial Client List Includes:
AT&T
American Express
Bell Communications
International Olympic Committee
Manufacturers Hanover Trust
Chemical Bank
New York Times
McGraw Hill
Business Week
Money Magazine
Reader's Digest
New York Magazine
Washingtonian
Field & Stream
Food & Wine
Golf Magazine
Emergency Medicine
Medical Economics

Work also appears in:
CA Illustration Annual '87
Print's Design Annual '87
Society of Illusrators *Humor '87*
Creativity '87

Can also be seen in:
American Showcase 11

Jeffrey Bellantuono

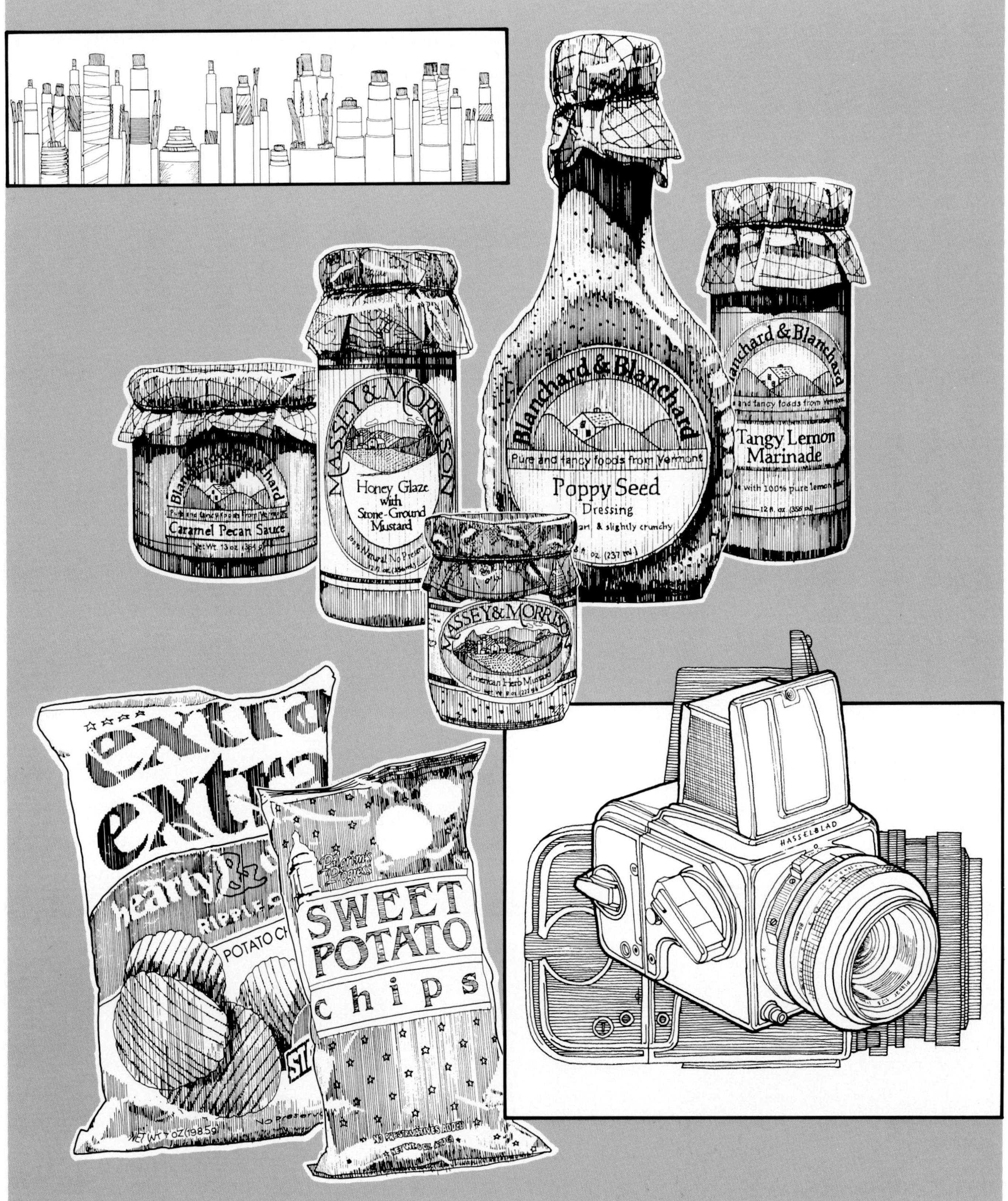

Jeffrey Bellantuono
27 Varmor Drive
New Britain, CT 06053
(203) 562-8433

These are some of the clients/affiliate accounts I have had the pleasure of working with:

Taunton Press/*Fine Homebuilding Magazine*
Cablec Corporation
First Federal Savings of Waterbury
First National Supermarkets
Saab-Scania of America
General Electric/Black & Decker Housewares
Stauffer Chemicals
Union Carbide
Fusco Corporation
Westville/New Haven Chamber of Commerce
...and other creative agencies

Call or write for a full portfolio review and up-to-date samples.

Member Graphic Artists Guild
Telecopier transmission available

Marlies Merk Najaka

Marlies Merk Najaka
241 Central Park West
New York, NY 10024
(212) 580-0058

Clients include:

Bologna International; *Business Week; Archaeology;* Avon; *Family Circle;* Harcourt Brace Jovanovich; Lally, McFarland & Pantello; Houghton Mifflin Co.; Fones & Mann; *Food & Wine; Good Food;* McGraw-Hill; NBC Inc.; *Redbook;* Scholastic; *Homes International; Signature;* The Putnam Publishing Group; *Young Miss;* The Scribner Book Companies.

Exhibitions:

Cooper-Hewitt Museum, Society of Illustrators

Professional associations:

Graphic Artists Guild, Society of Illustrators

To view more work:

Adweek Portfolio Showcase #9

H. B. Lewis

H. B. Lewis
P.O. Box 1177
New York, NY 10011
(212) 243-3954
(203) 535-3632
FAX 203-535-2160

• Traveling portfolio available
• Member Graphic Artists Guild

Clients include:

ABC; American Express; Amtrak; Avon Books; Biederman Advertising Inc.; *Business Week;* Cabot Advertising; CBS; Dancer, Fitzgerald & Sample; D'Arcy, McManus & Masius; Dayton-Hudson Corporation; *Diversions; Dun's Business Month; Eastern Review; Esquire; Family Circle; Forbes;* High Tech Marketing; ITT; J. Walter Thompson; Ketchum; Metropolitan Life Ins. Co.; *Money; Newsweek; New York; The New York Times;* Ogilvy & Mather; Poppe Tyson; *Redbook;* Ross Roy Advertising; Rubin Postaer & Assoc.; Scholastic; *Successful Meetings;* 13-30 Corporation; *Time;* W.B. Doner & Co.; *Working Mother; US Air;* Ziff Davis.

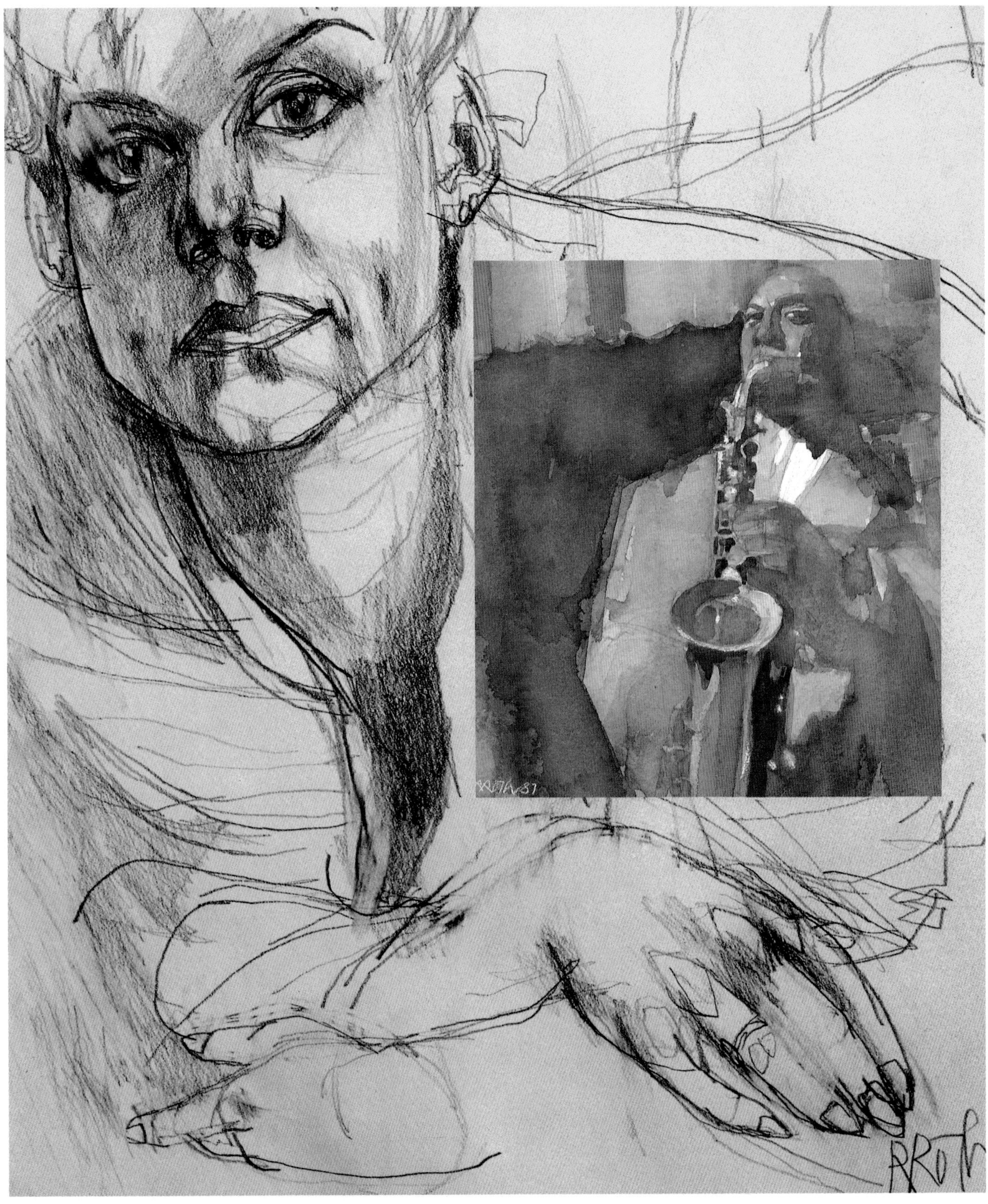

Robert Roth
134 Washington Street, Suite 306
South Norwalk, CT 06854
(203) 838-9755

The New York Times
Grammy Awards

4th ANNUAL SANTA BARBARA CREATIVE SEMINAR SATURDAY MARCH 26th 1988

happy
19
88
JAVIER
DESIGN/ILLUSTRATION
529 W 42 St • 1h NYC 10036
(212) 564 3991
ROMERO

CHEMICAL
CHRONICLE
For the Employees of Chemical Bank, Texas Commerce Bank and their Affiliates
December 1987
CHEMICAL
IN THE BRANCHES: CATERING TO THE CONSUMER

Get in the SPRA sales game—where the odds are in your favor.
It's no trivial matter that the Fifty Plus Market (people aged fifty and older) is the perfect target for SPRA sales. The Fifty Plus generation is wealthy. The 50-64 segment alone makes up 14% of the population, yet has 32% of the disposable income. And they need SPRAs. So they're a group that you should get to know well.
FIFTY PLUS MARKET
One way to get to know them better is to play the new SPRA trivia game in your G.O. This game tests your knowledge of the Fifty Plus Market and SPRAs. After you play the game for a few minutes, you'll see that selling to people fifty and older can substantially (and easily) increase your income. You'll also see how SPRAs can lead to other sales. Take the SPRA Trivia Challenge in your G.O. today. It can help you make the most of the Fifty Plus Market.
SPRA
STAKE YOUR CLAIM IN THE LUCRATIVE FIFTY PLUS MARKET WITH SPRA.

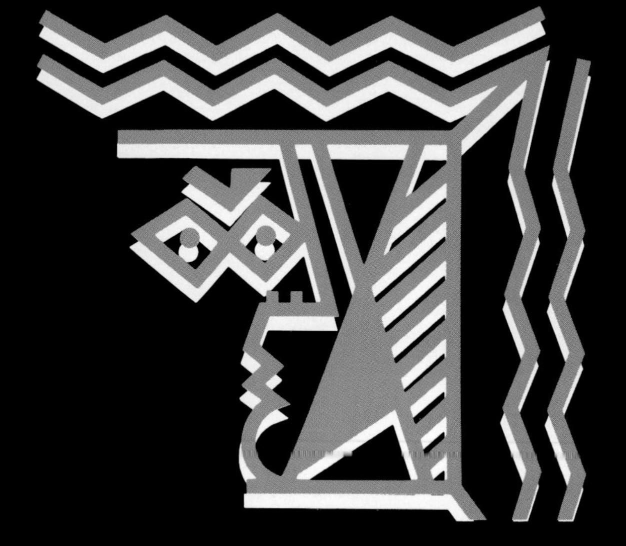

Graphic Design
Illustration
Animation
Advertising
Logotypes
Brochures
Posters
Packaging

JAVIER

D E S

FEBRUARY 14
Like
No Other
Love
In The
World
bloomingdales

SHOWTIME HBO
SHOWTIME &HBO IT'S NOT EITHER/OR ANYMORE

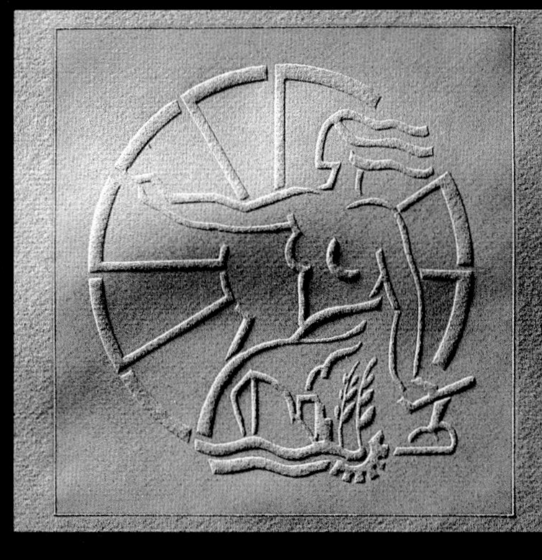

Manhattan Chess Club, Casa de España, American Chess Foundation and José A. Cuchí, present a simultaneous exhibition by World Champion Garri Kasparov
GARRI
KASPAROV
Casa de España

IN PERFORMANCE AT THE WHITE HOUSE
THE SHOWS
A SALUTE TO BROADWAY
AMERITECH

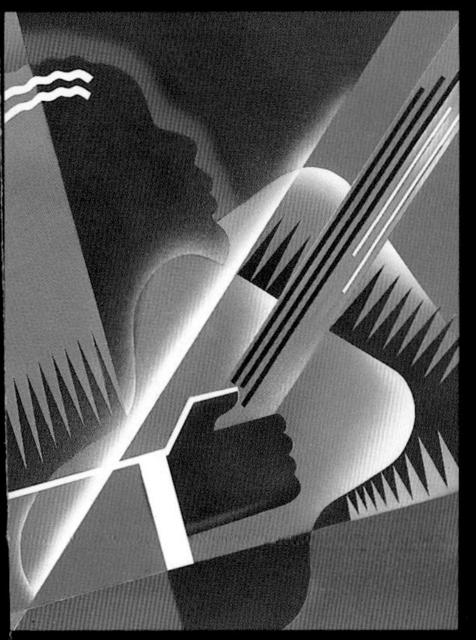

OMERO
I G N

American Express
Phillip Morris
Johnson & Johnson
New York Life
Chase Manhattan Bank
Chemical Bank
Citibank
Bloomingdale's

Benetton
Showtime
Atlantic Records
Business Week
Rolling Stone
Iberia Airlines
Tourism of Spain
Arts & Entertainment

Pentagram
Young & Rubicam
Chiat Day
Burson Marsteller
J. Walter Thompson
AT&T
Clairol
Avon

Fabergé
Macy's
Time Inc.
Fortune
Expo '92
Member Graphic Artists Guild
Member AIGA

Printed in Japan

The Creative Force Inc.

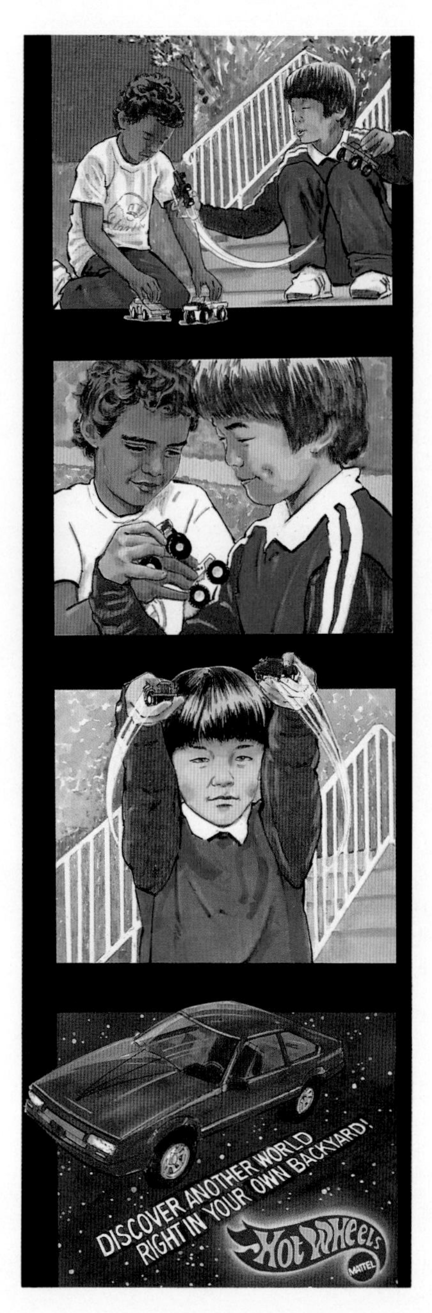

The Creative Force Inc.
84 Monroe Street, 4th Floor
Newark, NJ 07105
(201) 578-8713

We are a full creative service agency committed to turning your design and advertising problems into powerful images. Our services include: art direction for print and TV, illustration, comps, storyboards, logo design and corporate identity programs developed to meet your needs. Sports are our specialty.

Clients include:

Ogilvy & Mather; SSC&B; Dancer Fitzgerald Sample; Bozell, Jacobs, Kenyon & Eckhardt; Metro Creative Services; Glover Advertising; Major Indoor Lacrosse League; The Physical Edge; New Age Muscle; and Marvel Comics, "The Savage Sword of Conan."

Contact Mike Allen.

Claude Martinot

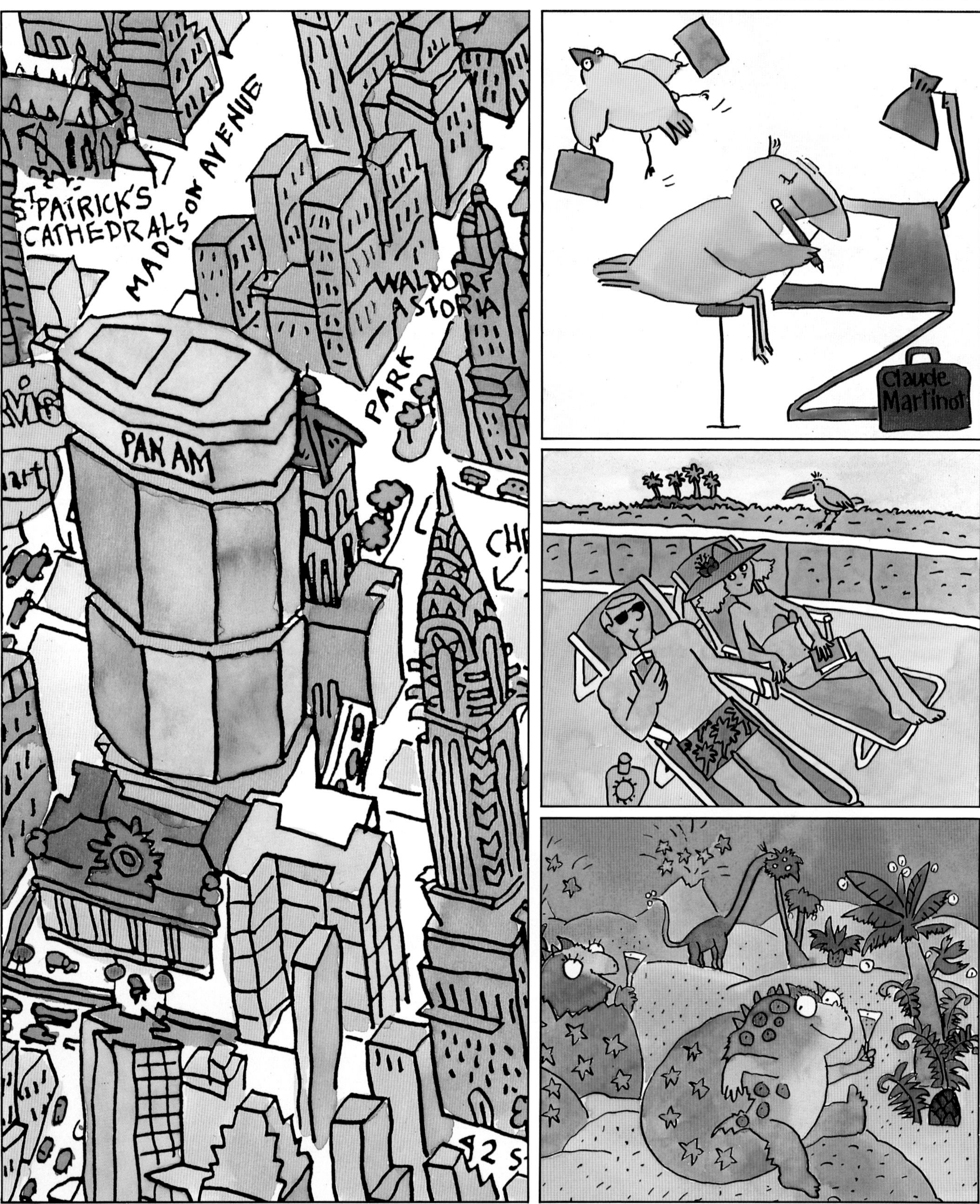

Claude Martinot
145 Second Avenue
New York, NY 10003
(212) 473-3137

Member of the Graphic Artists Guild

Work can also be seen in *American Showcase 6, 7, 8, 9, 11* and in *RSVP 8, 9, 10, 11, 12, 13*

Clients have included:

Burson-Marsteller, Citibank, Cunard Lines, Cunningham & Walsh, Doyle Dane Bernbach, The Bronx Zoo, *Family Circle,* Federal Reserve Bank of New York, Hallmark Cards, HBO, McGraw-Hill, *Mothers Today,* Ogilvy & Mather, *Parents Magazine,* Random House, Rolf Werner Rosenthal, Sudler & Hennessey, Ted Bates, Yale University.

Patrick J. Welsh

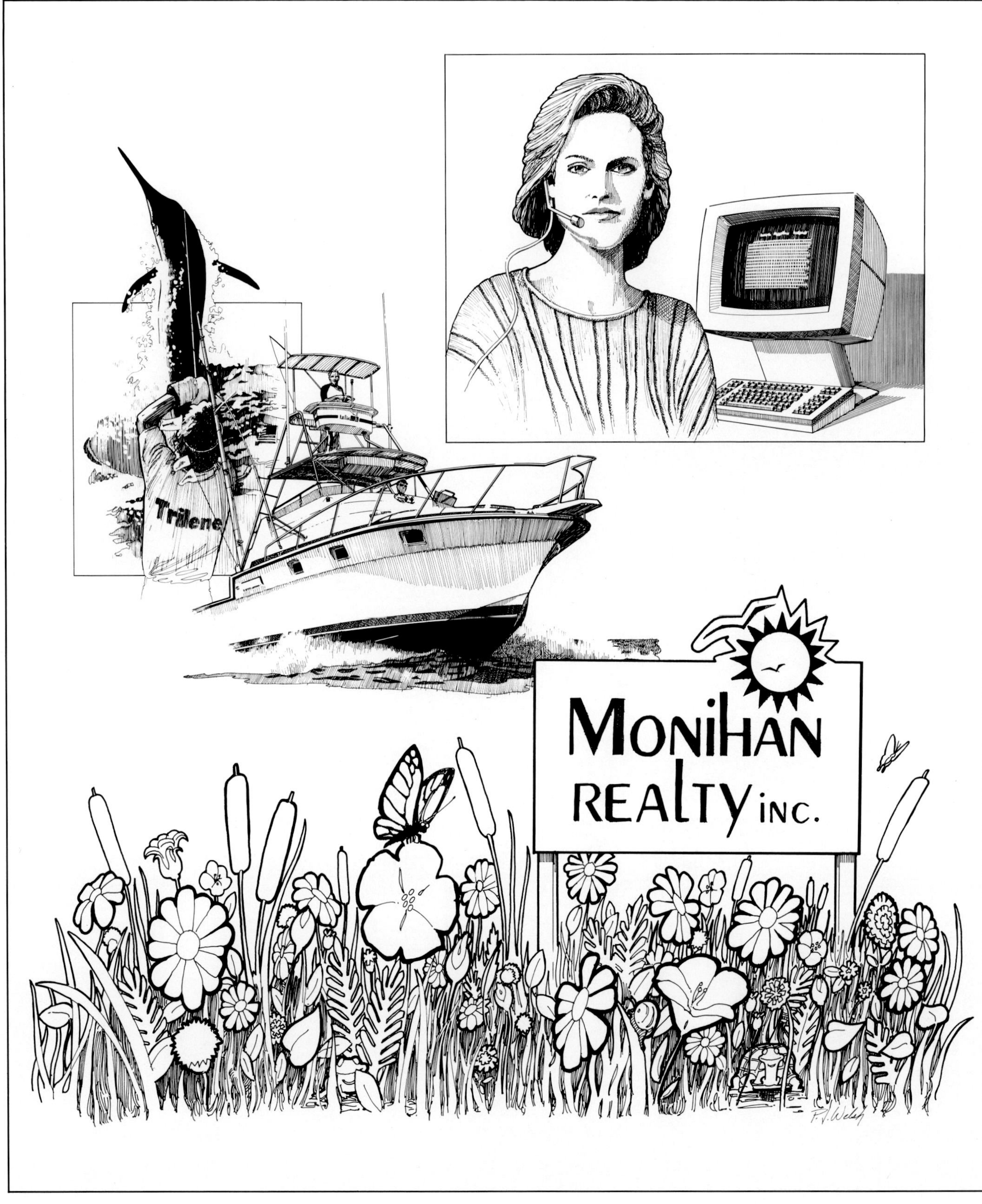

Patrick J. Welsh
P.O. Box 463
Williamstown, NJ 08094
(609) 728-0264

High quality pen and ink illustration that is easy to reproduce at almost any size. No subject matter too diverse, no deadline too tight. Prompt delivery to anywhere using air express courier services.

Andrea Brooks

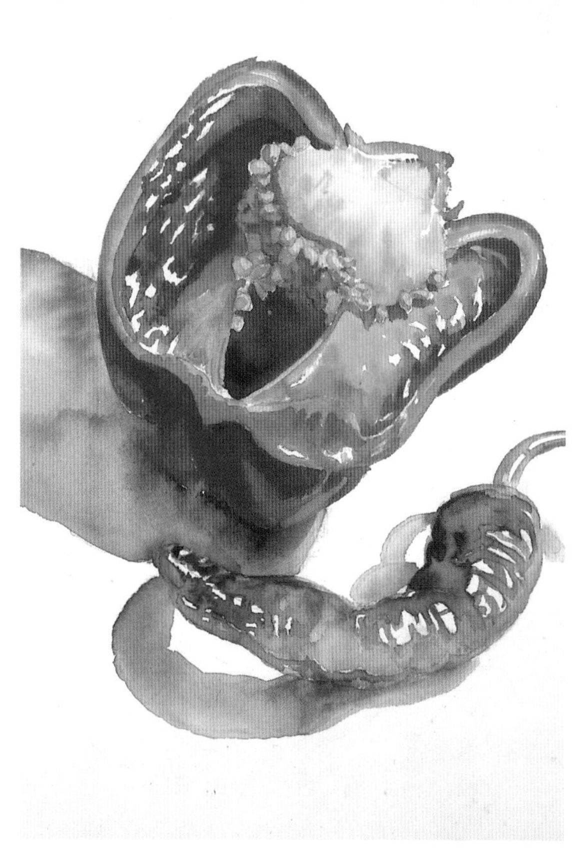

Andrea Brooks
11 West 30th Street, 3rd Floor
New York, NY 10001
(212) 695-0824
(212) 924-3085

Watercolor Illustration

Clients include:
Continental Airlines
Spiedel
Presbyterian Church U.S.A.
Scott Paper Co.
Avon Products Inc.
Charles of the Ritz
Revlon
Coty
Elizabeth Arden
International Wildlife
Redbook
J.P. Stevens & Co.
Little Brown & Co.
Random House
Western Publishing
Putnam Publishing Group
The Scribner Book Companies
W. Atlee Burpee Co.

Also seen in:
Adweek Portfolio of Illustration 1987

Member:
Graphic Artists Guild
Society of Illustrators

Tim Lewis
184 St. Johns Place
Brooklyn, NY 11217
(718) 857-3406

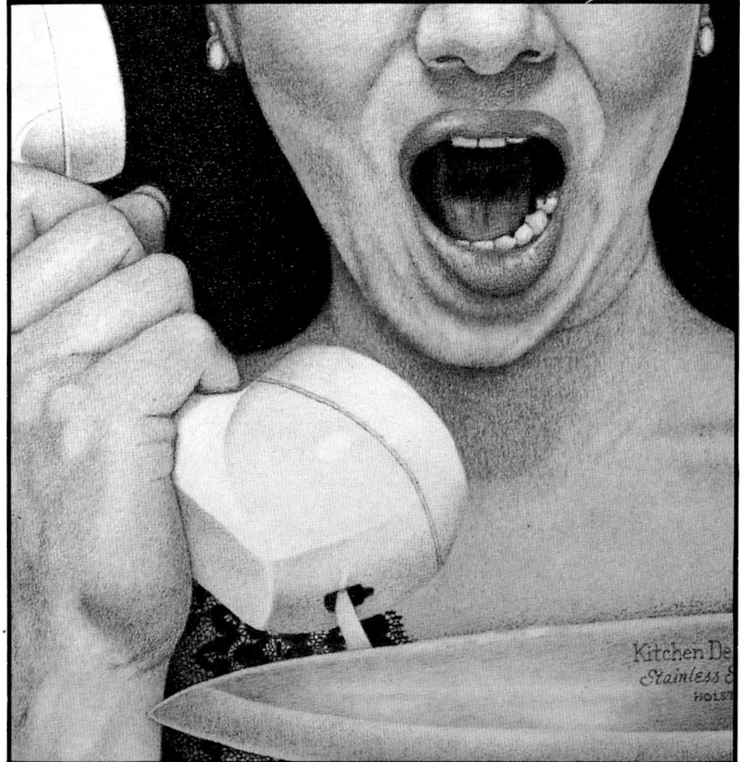

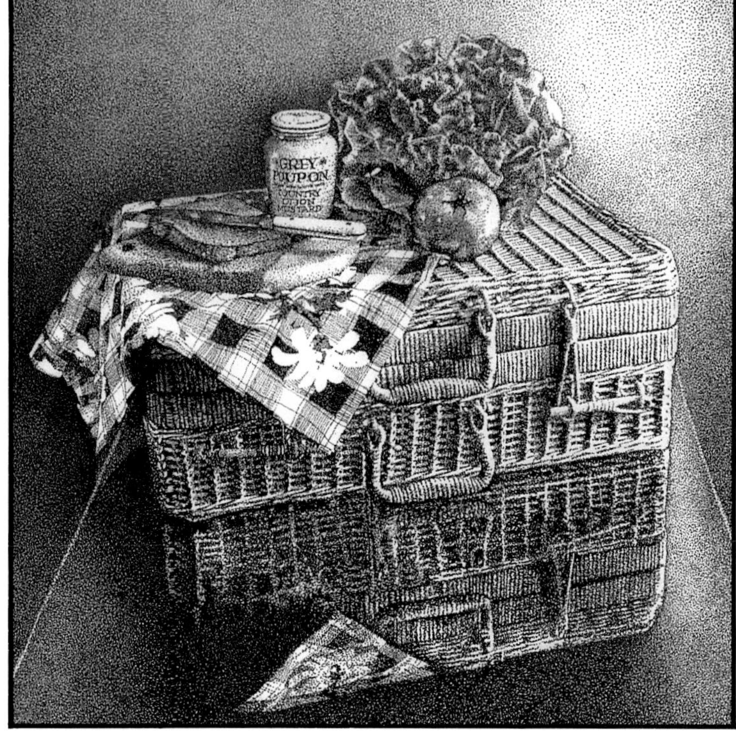

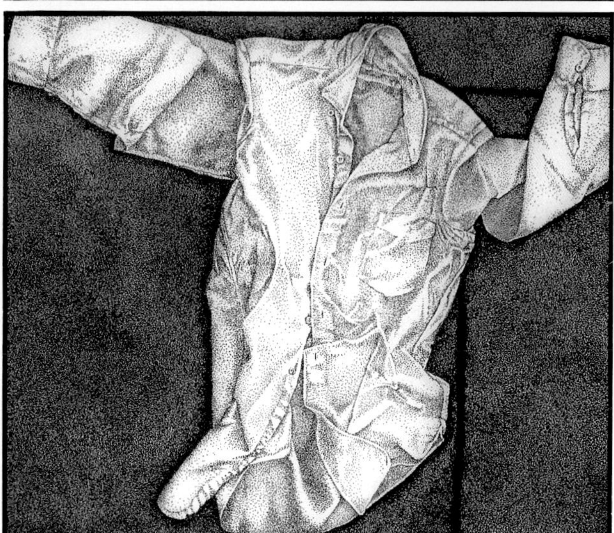

Joni Holst
204 West 20th Street
Suite A-64
New York, NY 10011
(212) 807-4194

Charles McVicker

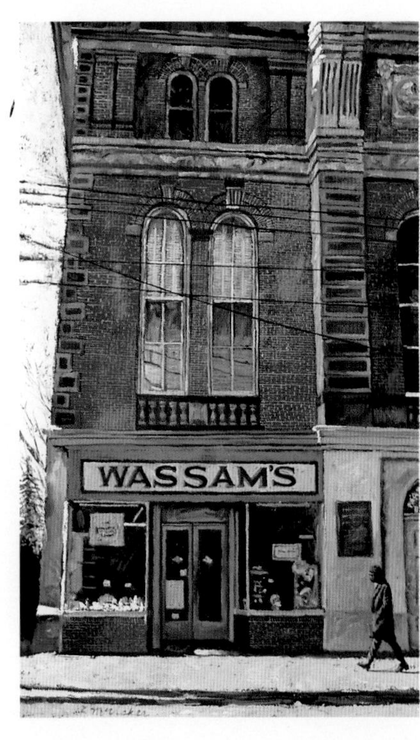

Charles McVicker
P.O. Box 183
Rocky Hill, NJ 08553
(609) 924-2660

An award-winning illustrator and painter, his work has appeared in many national juried exhibitions, including those of the Society of Illustrators, Audubon Artists, The National Arts Club, and the Salmagundi Club.

Clients have included:

Mobil, AT&T, NBC TV, Random House, Macmillan, The Franklin Mint, *Seventeen,* The Book-of-the-Month Club, and *National Wildlife*.

His work is included in the permanent collections of Dupont Corporation, Johnson & Johnson, Princeton University, the White House and National Capitol, Home Life Insurance Company, Mercer County, and Zimmerli Art Museum.

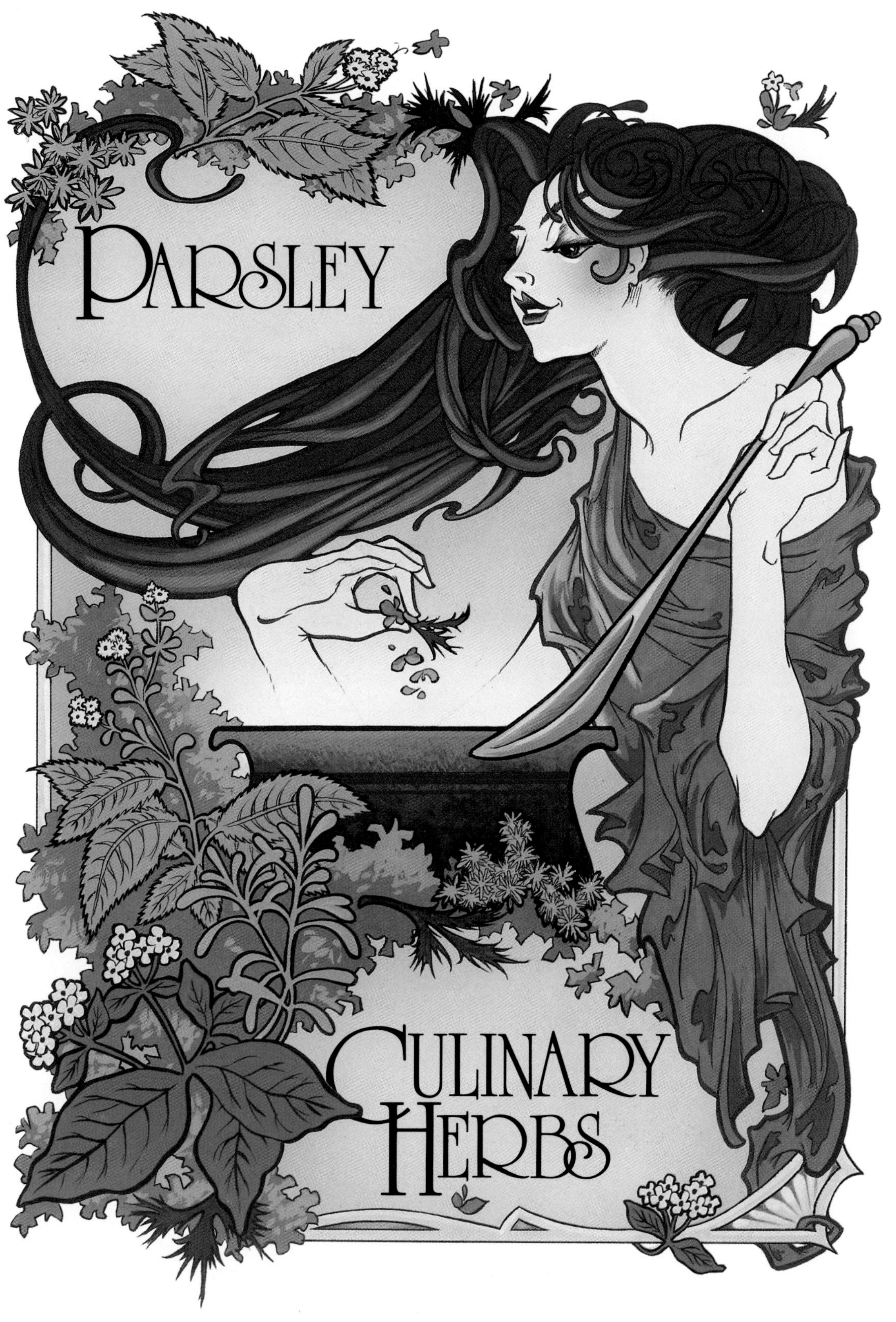

Richard A. Olson
85 Grand Street
New York, NY 10013
(212) 925-1820

Clients include:
Abingdon Press, Automatic Data Processing, Deutsch Shea & Evans, Health Insurance Association of America, International Paper, Macy's, National Gallery of Art (*Washington, DC*), The National Kidney Foundation, Seattle Opera Association, Wm. H. Sadlier, Inc.

Bob Zuba

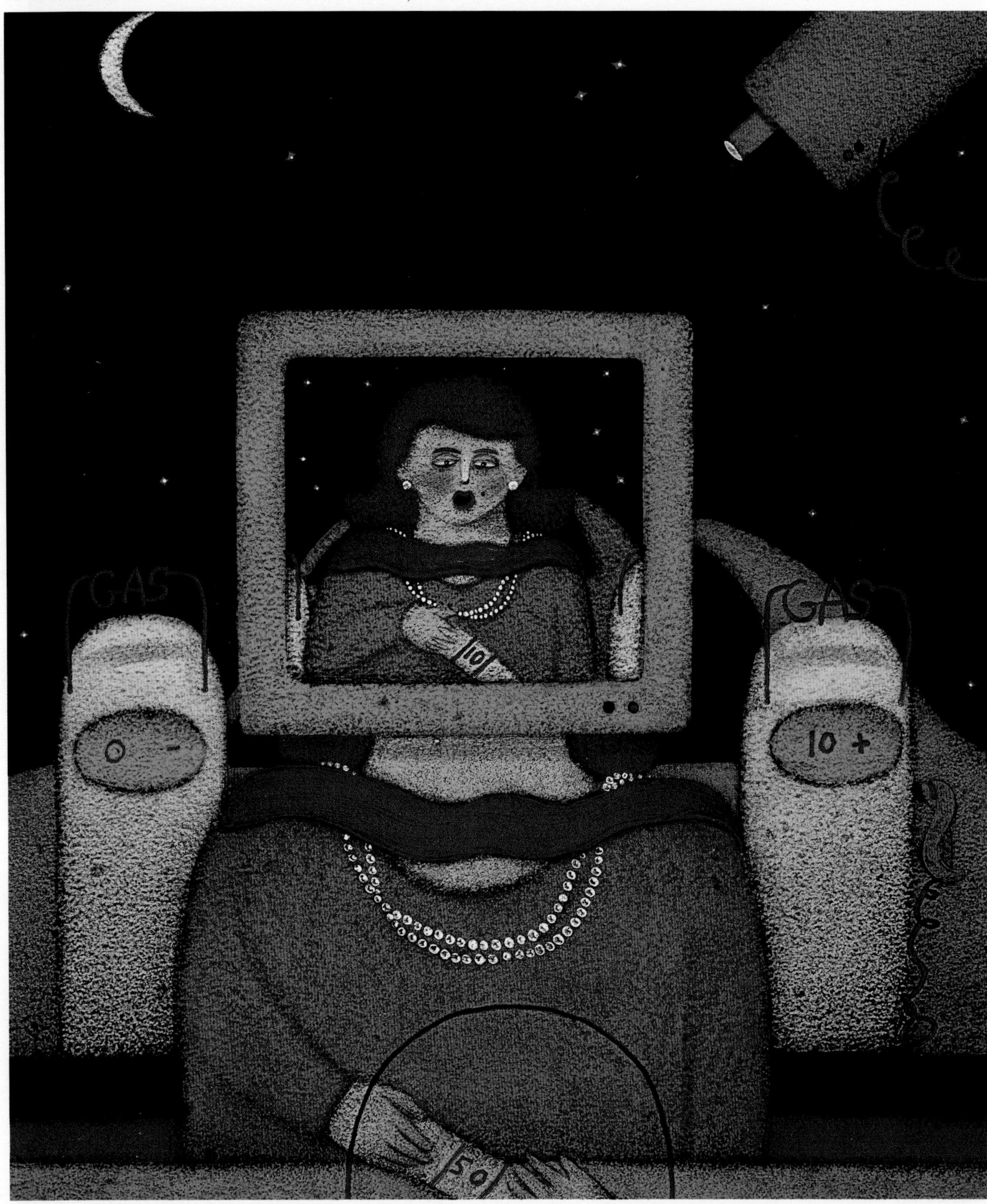

Bob Zuba
103 West Saylor Avenue
Plains, Pennsylvania 18702
(717) 824-5665
FAX 717-824-7399

Rosemary Webber
229 West 78th Street
New York, NY 10024
(212) 724-6529

Experienced in meeting publication deadlines, including major dailies.

High-quality drawings with *low-cost* reproduction.

Selected Client List:
Wall Street Journal, Journal of Commerce, IBM, Westinghouse, Heinz, Security Pacific, Manufacturers Hanover, Mobil, Citibank, American Can, General Electric, Circus Circus, *Writer's Digest, Cosmopolitan, Ski, Success* magazine, Fairchild Publications, *Financial World.*

Society of Newspaper Design Awards of Excellence in Illustration, 2 successive years.

Society of Publication Design Portfolio Show 1984.

Drawings and paintings have been the subject of articles written in *Communication Arts Magazine*, Feb. '87; *Washington Journalism Review*, Mar. '87; *Advertising Age*, Aug. 1, 1985; *Manhattan inc.*, Sept. '84; *Inc. Magazine*, Oct. '82.

Julian Allen

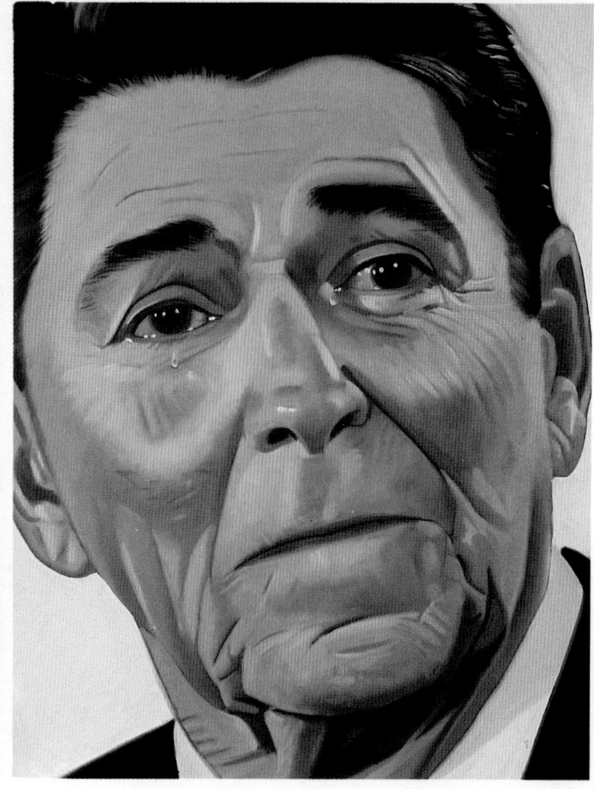

Julian Allen
31 Walker Street
New York, NY 10013
(212) 925-6550

Professional associations:
Committee member of American Illustration
Society of Illustrators Silver Medalist
Teaches at Parsons School of Design

Clients include:
Koppel & Scher, *Bunte*, Capitol Records Inc., Corporate Graphics Inc., *Der Spiegel*, *Esquire*, *European Travel & Life*, *Forbes*, *Fortune*, *Il Giornale Dell'Arte*, Banana Republic, *Ladies' Home Journal*, *LA Style*, *Life*, *London Observer*, *Manhattan inc.*, Mobil Corp., *Money*, *Mother Jones*, *New York*, *Newsweek*, *Paris Match*, *GQ*, *Psychology Today*, *Rolling Stone*, *Sports Illustrated*, *Stern*, *Texas Monthly*, *The Boston Globe*, *The London Times* Sunday magazine, *The New York Times* Sunday magazine, *Parenting*, *The Progressive*, *Regardie's*, *Tatler*, *Time*, *Traveler*, *US News & World Report*, *Vanity Fair*, *The Wall Street Journal*, *Working Woman*.

Step into a different world...

Tom Leigh
Rote Hill
Sheffield, MA 01257
(413) 229-8258
(413) 229-3353

Clients include:

CBS; American Airlines; Random House; Muppets; Children's Television Workshop; Hallmark; Fisher-Price; Milton-Bradley; Hasbro; Kansas City Royals; *Rolling Stone* Interviews; City National Bank; *Kansas City Magazine;* Holt, Rinehart & Winston; Western Publishing; Scholastic.

Awards from:

- Kansas City Art Directors Club
- AIGA

Robert Pasternak

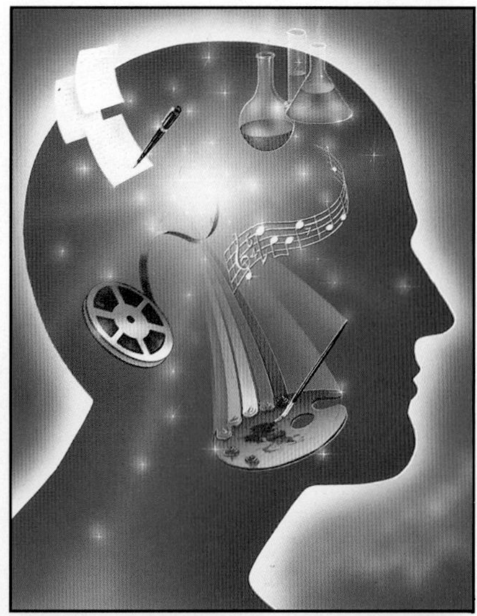

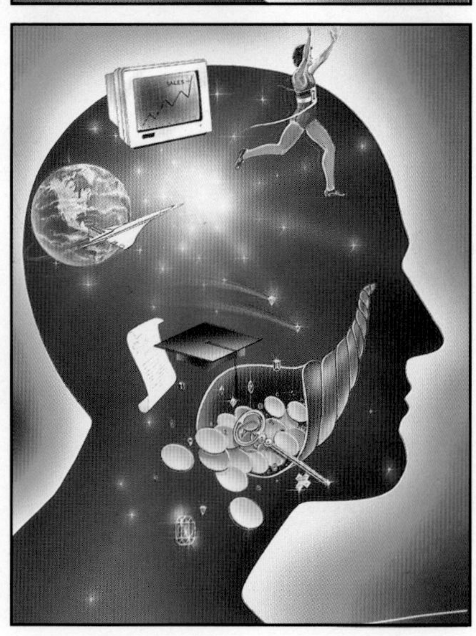

Robert Pasternak
114 West 27th Street
New York, NY 10001
(212) 675-0002

Illustration for advertising, editorial, and corporate communications. Specializing in airbrush and conceptual design.

Member: Graphic Artists Guild

Anders Wenngren
450 Sixth Avenue
New York, NY 10011
(212) 353-1248

Clients include:
New York Times, Vogue, GQ, Vanity Fair, Mademoiselle, Rolling Stone, New York, Fortune, Newsweek, Marie Claire, Bloomingdale's, Henri Bendel.

Nick Gaetano

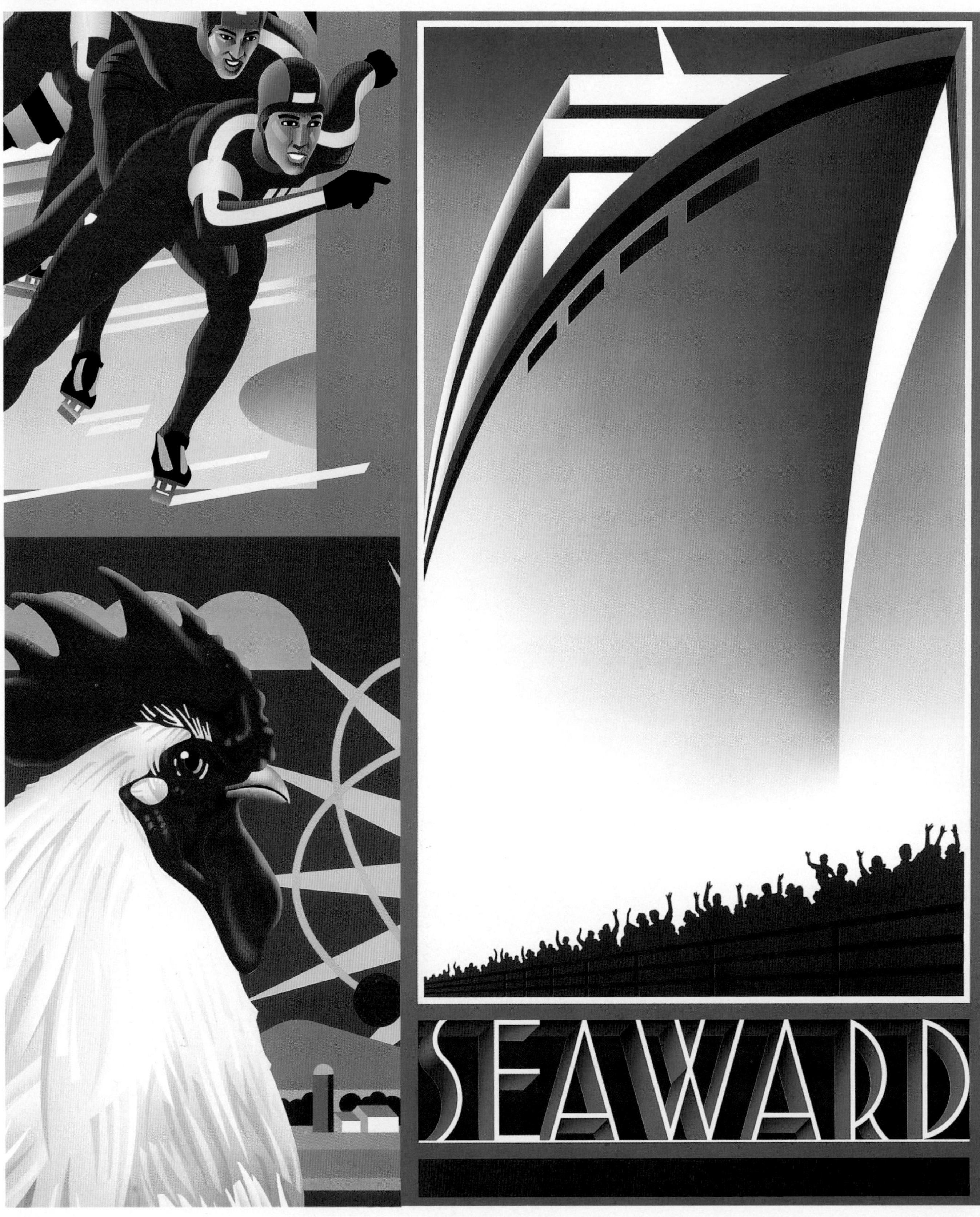

 Nick Gaetano

Represented by
Harvey Kahn
50 East 50th Street
New York, NY 10022
(212) 752-8490

Clients include:
IBM, AT&T, Sony, Ciba-Geigy, Metropolitan Life, N.Y. Telephone, American Express, Federal Express, Atlantic Records, American Greetings, Merrill Lynch, Mountain Bell, Western Airlines, Holland America, G.E., Jell-O, Clairol, Chase Manhattan, ABC, Citicorp, Avis, Bank of America, Disney, Barclay's Bank, Playtex, Sanka, Bantam Books, Vintage Books, Frito-Lay, *Time, Business Week, Fortune,* Atari, Old Grand Dad, General Mills, Dentyne, U.S. Postal Service, N.Y.U., Faberge, Trina, Tropicana, Owens-Corning, Jose Cuervo, Fortunoff, Six-Flags, Hyatt Regency.

Gene Czebiniak
Artistic Pursuits
NY PENN Trade Center
435 Main Street
Johnson City, NY 13790
(607) 729-1984

Advertising and editorial illustration in a variety of media; surface pattern design for home furnishing industry.

Miriam Troop

Miriam Troop
1148 Fifth Avenue
New York, NY 10128
(212) 427-1927

Portrait drawings for editorial, corporate, and advertising use.

(Shown above) Bernard Berenson, Alexander Calder, Helena Rubenstein, pencil on Cameo paper, 14 x 11" (35.5 x 27.9 cm.)

(Not shown) Henry Luce, Norman Thomas, Earl Warren, Richard Wright. Collection: National Portrait Gallery, Washington, D.C.

Clients: *Fortune Magazine, The New York Times,* others.
Portfolios of portraits are available from artist.

Margery Mintz
63 Nottinghill Road
Boston, MA 02135
(617) 783-1691

Included here:

Drawing of house on cover of sales book for Fletcher Granite Company, Massachusetts.

Drawing of book for book cover commissioned by Godine Publishing in Boston.

Other recent clients include:
Stull & Lee Architects
John Hancock
State St. Bank
MCI Telecommunications
Sheraton Corporation
The Traveler's Insurance

Steve Björkman

Steve Björkman
Studio (714) 261-1411
FAX 714-261-7528

New York
Madeline Renard
(212) 490-2450
FAX 212-697-6828

Chicago
Vince Kamin
(312) 787-8834

Los Angeles
Laurie Pribble
(818) 574-0288

San Francisco
David Wiley
(415) 441-1623

Neverne K. Covington
2919 56 Street South
Gulfport, FL 33707
(813) 347-0746

Advertising, Editorial, and Corporate Illustration

Black and white and color work

Jared D. Lee

Jared D. Lee
2942 Hamilton Road
Lebanon, Ohio 45036
(513) 932-2154
Animation reel on request
FAX 513-932-9389

Malcom Karlin, Marshalk, "A terrific talent–always has ideas that you haven't thought of. He made me look good many times."

Brad Pallas, Woman's Day Magazine, "Anyone who can draw women for *Woman's Day* and make the editor, art director, and reader all laugh out loud has got to be great!"

Phil Kimmelman, KCMP Productions Ltd., "Having Jared Lee design for animation has not only produced some of the best animated spots I have worked on, but his contributions beyound the call of duty in continuity and concept have made working with him a unique and delightful experience!"

Alistair Gillett, Young & Rubicam, "Jared is the master of the wiggly line."

Ralph Peter Masiello
14 Woodland Drive
Boylston, MA 01505
(508) 869-2731

"Specializing in the unusual."

Recent clients include:

Viking Penguin Inc., Peachtree Publishing, Irwin Publishing (Canada), Hodder & Stoughton Publishing (England), *Scholastic Magazine,* Scott Foresman and Co., *Computer World Focus Magazine, Micro-market World Magazine, Network-World Magazine, The Boston Review,* Quinlin Press.

Work also appears in *Illustrators 29.*

MUKAI

Dennis Mukai
Chicago (312) 329-1370
Houston (713) 529-0181
Los Angeles (213) 396-1213
New York (212) 391-1830
San Francisco (415) 771-0494

213•452•9060

Dennis Mukai
Chicago (312) 329-1370
Houston (713) 529-0181
Los Angeles (213) 396-1213
New York (212) 391-1830
San Francisco (415) 771-0494

Gene Reynolds

Gene Reynolds
71 Thompson Street
New York, NY 10012
(212) 431-3072

I work in many styles and media. In my opinion, an artist never stops trying to deepen areas of his strengths, or to explore the areas that are new to him. The result of this difficult course is a more varied artist and a more varied person.

Julia Cruz-McLain
c/o Assassins
2011 Greenville Avenue
Dallas, TX 75206
(214) 948-9603
Representatives:
West Coast–Brad Benedict
(213) 470-4037
Chicago–Gordon Kleeber
(312) 341-9764

Clients include:

Atlantic Monthly, Sesame Street, Psychology Today, Changing Times, American Photographer, Sears Corporation, Phillips Petroleum, Zales Corporation, Neiman Marcus, Paper Moon Graphics.

Merle Nacht

The OASIS

By Alice Adams

IN PALM SPRINGS THE POOR are as dry as old brown leaves, blown in from the desert — wispily thin and almost invisible. Perhaps they are embarrassed at finding themselves among so much opulence (indeed, why are they there at all? why not somewhere else?), among such soaring, thick-trunked palms, such gleamingly white, palatial hotels.

And actually, poor people are only seen in the more or less outlying areas, the stretch of North Canyon Drive, for example, where even the stores are full of sleazy, cut-rate goods, and the pastel stucco hotels are small, one-story, and a little seedy, with small, shallow, too-bright, blue pools. The poor are not seen in those stores, though, and certainly not in even the tawdriest motels; they stick to the street; for the most part they keep moving. A hunched-up, rag-bound man with his swollen bundle (of what? impossible to guess) might lean against a sturdy palm tree, so much fatter and stronger than he is — but only for a moment, and he would be looking around, aware of himself as displaced. And on one of the city benches a poor woman with her plastic splintered bag looks perched there, an uneasy, watchful bird, with sharp, fierce, wary eyes.

A visibly rich person would look quite odd there too, in that nebulous, interim area, unless he or she were just hurrying through — maybe running, in smart pale jogging clothes, or briskly stepping along toward the new decorator showrooms, just springing up on the outskirts of town. In any case, rich people, except in cars, are seen in that particular area of Palm Springs quite as infrequently as the very poor are.

However, on a strange day in early April — so cold, such a biting wind, in a place where bad weather is almost unheard of and could be illegal — on that day a woman all wrapped in fine Italian wool and French silk, with fine, perfect champagne hair and an expensive color on her mouth — that woman, whose name is Clara Gibson, sits on a bench in what she knows is the wrong part of Palm Springs (she also knows that it is the wrong day for her to be there), and she wonders what on earth to do.

There are certain huge and quite insoluble problems lying always heavily on her mind (is this true of everyone? she half suspects that it is, but has wondered); these have to do with her husband and her daughter, and with an entity that she vaguely and rather sadly thinks of as herself. But at the moment she can do nothing about any of these three quite problematic people. And so she concentrates on what is immediate, the fact that she has a billfold full of credit cards and almost no cash: a 10, two ones, not even much change. And her cards are not coded for sidewalk cash withdrawal from banks because her husband, Bradley, believes that this is dangerous. Also: Today is Tuesday, and because she confused the dates (or something) she will be here alone until Thursday, when Bradley arrives. The confusion itself is suspicious, so unlike her; was she *Continued on page 64*

ALICE ADAMS IS THE AUTHOR OF *SUPERIOR WOMEN* AND *RETURN TRIPS*, WHICH WAS PUBLISHED IN SEPTEMBER BY ALFRED A. KNOPF. HER FICTION APPEARS FREQUENTLY IN *THE NEW YORKER* AND OTHER MAGAZINES.

Merle Nacht
374 Main Street
Wethersfield, CT 06109
(203) 563-7993

Clients include:
The New Yorker (cover and spot drawings)
Travel & Leisure
New York
Gourmet
Ms.
GQ
Vogue
Lotus Magazine
Technology Review
Harcourt Brace Jovanovich
Houghton Mifflin
The New York Times
The Boston Globe
The Plain Dealer Magazine
THe Hartford Courant
Philadelphia Inquirer
United Technologies
Xerox Corporation
General Electric
Otis Elevator
Georgia-Pacific
Dayton-Hudson Department Stores
Northeast Utilities
The Watergate Hotel Restaurants

Richard Romeo

Richard Romeo
1066 Northwest 96th Avenue
Fort Lauderdale, FL 33322
(305) 472-0072

Member of Graphic Artists Guild
Featured in *Airbrush Action Magazine*
Graduate of Pratt Institute

Illustration For:
Advertising, Publishing, Television, Albums, Packaging, Pharmaceuticals, Etc.

Client list:
American Express, Bendix, Canada Dry, Carrera, Cartier, CBS Records, Clairol, Capital Bank, Cordis Dow, David's Cookies, Del Monte, Elizabeth Arden, Ford, Fontainbleau Hotel, Geoffrey Beene, Godiva, Haggar, Hasbro, Hilton Hotels, Hyatt Hotels, IBM, Intercontinental Hotels, Jamaica Resort Hotels, Lancôme, Marriott Hotels, Mayors Jewelers, Monet, National Distillers, Northeastern Airlines, Panasonic, Penthouse, Pepsi Cola, Personnel Pool, Pierre Cardin, Piper Aircraft, Playboy, Revlon, Royal Caribbean Cruise Line, Ryder Trucks, Salada, Scandinavian Cruise Lines, Sony, Taco Viva, Talon, Van Heusen, Waterford, Yves Saint Laurent.

TAK MURAKAMI

Three-dimensional art is Tak's specialty. His materials include plastics, clay, paper, wood, metal, or whatever a particular job dictates. He works on pieces that range from the very small to the very large, i.e., 10½′ welded stainless steel sculpture. His repertoire also includes two-dimensional art in line and color. Samples on request.

The ArtBunch Inc. 368-877

230 N. MICHIGAN, CHICAGO, IL 60601 312-368-8777 TELECOPIER IN STUDI

COMPS, STORY BOARDS, ANIMATICS, DESIGN, ILLUSTRATION, LETTERING, RETOUCHING, KEYLINE.

PROBLEM SOLVING

We do it every day. Maybe it's the illustration that makes your client's product look good or that extra pair of hands that makes you look good. Your problem is our challenge at The Art Bunch.

Whether you have a month-long project for a new client, or those two last-minute storyboards you can't possibly get done in time, we have a studio full of talented people ready to make your problem no problem.

The Art Bunch Inc. 368-8777

30 N. MICHIGAN, CHICAGO, IL 60601 312-368-8777 TELECOPIER IN STUDIO

Patrick McDarby

Patrick McDarby
17 West 45th Street
New York, NY 10036
(212) 840-8516

224 Naples Terrace
Bronx, NY 10463
(212) 548-2483

Concept • Design • Illustration

John Lytle

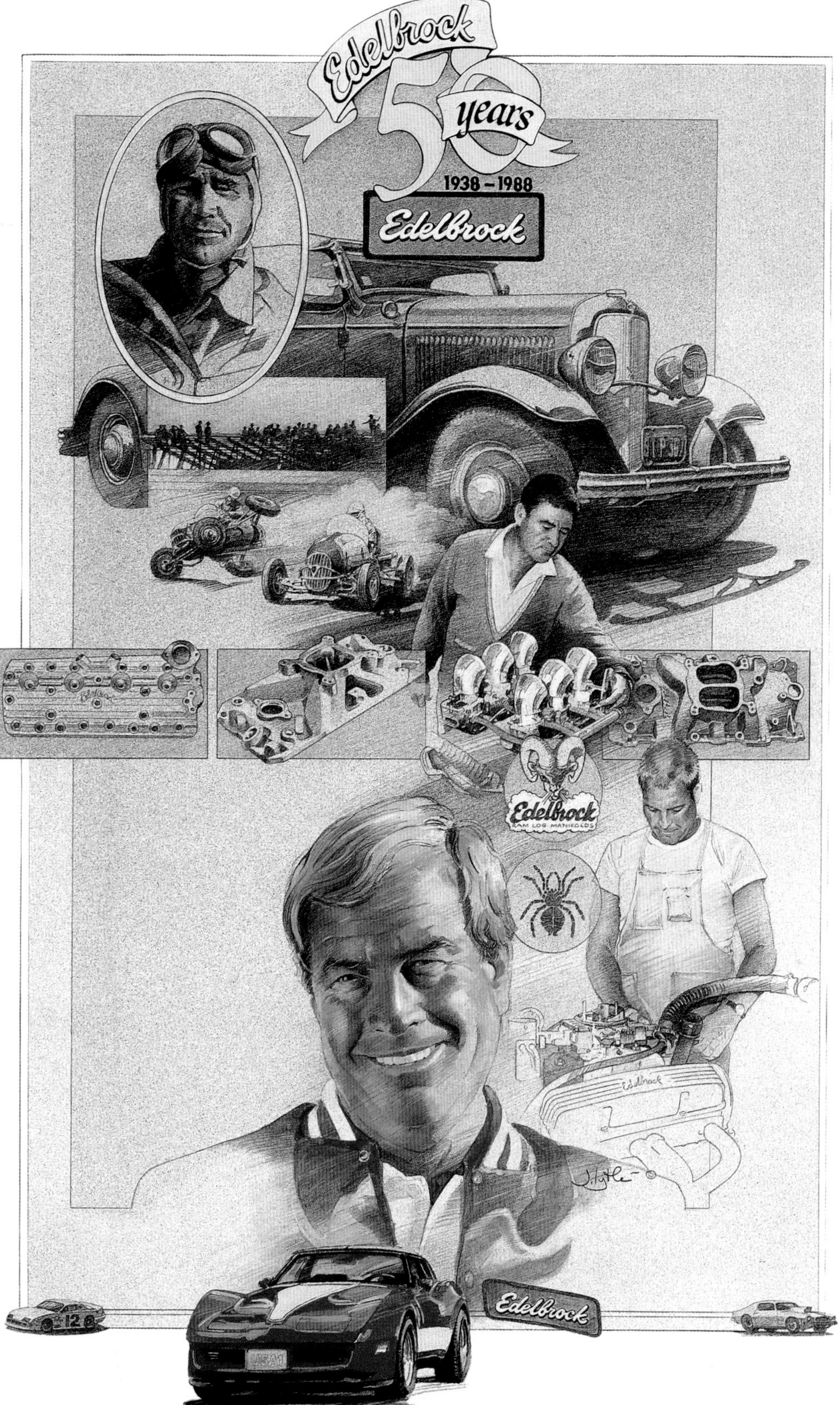

John Lytle
P.O. Box 5155
17130 Yosemite Road
Sonora, CA 95370
(209) 928-4849

Clients Include:

ABC Sports, American Express, Ampex, AT&T, Atari, Bank of America, Boston Gas, Edelbrock, Goodyear, Hewlett-Packard, Jaguar, Levi-Strauss, Massachusetts Mutual, National Advanced Systems, Nike, New York Telephone, NFL Films, PG&E, Raychem, Reebok, R.J. Reynolds, Ryder Trucks, Seagrams, Sheraton, Sperry, Visa, Yamaha Motorcycles.

Additional illustrations may be seen in *American Showcase 5, 6, 7, 10, 11; Art Directors Index 10, 11; Adweek Portfolio of Illustration 1986; Society of Illustrators 24th Annual; San Francisco Society of Illustrators Volume 5.*

Member Society of Illustrators

Emmanuel Amit

Emmanuel Amit
4322 Sunset Avenue
Montrose, CA 91020
(818) 249-1739

Peter Cascio

Peter Cascio
810 Seventh Avenue
41st Floor
New York, NY 10019
(212) 408-2177
(201) 445-3262

Clients include:
Armstrong
AT&T
Black & Decker
Citizen Watch
Dannon
Drexel Burnham
Gabby Gourmet Restaurant Guides
Gillette
Manhattan Cable
NBC
Newsweek
NutraSweet
Orangina
Owens Corning Fiberglas
Peat Marwick
Peugeot
Popular Photography
RCA
Xerox

Linda Holland Rathkopf

Linda Holland Rathkopf
133 Clinton Street
Brooklyn Heights, NY 11201
(718) 875-5990

Bruce Day
8141 Firth Green
Buena Park, CA 90621
(714) 994-0338

Clients include:
Campbell's Soup Company
C.B.S.
Chiat/Day Inc.
Burger King Inc.
N.F.L. Properties
Los Angeles Times
Doyle Dane Bernbach
Focus on the Family
Scholastic Magazines
Morrison/Knudsen Co.
Sullivan Bluth Studios
Horlick Levin Advertising

CINDY SALANS-ROSENHEIM

TERRA MUZICK

Square Moon Productions
21 Lafayette Circle
Lafayette, CA 94549
(415) 283-7793

Art Director:
Diane Goldsmith

Artist Representative:
Deborah Akers

We at SQUARE MOON are expert in matching the unique talents of illustrators to the spirit of the text. For years, as a design studio producing books for children, we have created the moment when all the verbal and graphic elements come together to communicate the special essence of a story.

SQUARE MOON represents: Ellen Beier, Cindy Brodie, Pat Hoggan, Roberta Holmes-Landers, Mas Miyamoto, Terra Muzick, Cindy Salans-Rosenheim, Doug Roy, Jeff Severn, and Stan Tusan.

Clients include: Macmillan, Harcourt Brace Jovanovich, Houghton Mifflin, McGraw-Hill, Ginn, Scribner's, and Dutton.

DOUG ROY

STAN TUSAN

Square Moon Productions
21 Lafayette Circle
Lafayette, CA 94549
(415) 283-7793

Art Director:
Diane Goldsmith

Artist Representative:
Deborah Akers

We at SQUARE MOON are expert in matching the unique talents of illustrators to the spirit of the text. For years, as a design studio producing books for children, we have created the moment when all the verbal and graphic elements come together to communicate the special essence of a story.

SQUARE MOON represents: Ellen Beier, Cindy Brodie, Pat Hoggan, Roberta Holmes-Landers, Mas Miyamoto, Terra Muzick, Cindy Salans-Rosenheim, Doug Roy, Jeff Severn, and Stan Tusan.

Clients include: Macmillan, Harcourt Brace Jovanovich, Houghton Mifflin, McGraw-Hill, Ginn, Scribner's, and Dutton.

PAT HOGGAN

MAS MIYAMOTO

Square Moon Productions
21 Lafayette Circle
Lafayette, CA 94549
(415) 283-7793

Art Director:
Diane Goldsmith

Artist Representative:
Deborah Akers

We at SQUARE MOON are expert in matching the unique talents of illustrators to the spirit of the text. For years, as a design studio producing books for children, we have created the moment when all the verbal and graphic elements come together to communicate the special essence of a story.

SQUARE MOON represents: Ellen Beier, Cindy Brodie, Pat Hoggan, Roberta Holmes-Landers, Mas Miyamoto, Terra Muzick, Cindy Salans-Rosenheim, Doug Roy, Jeff Severn, and Stan Tusan.

Clients include: Macmillan, Harcourt Brace Jovanovich, Houghton Mifflin, McGraw-Hill, Ginn, Scribner's, and Dutton.

CINDY BRODIE

JEFF SEVERN

Square Moon Productions
21 Lafayette Circle
Lafayette, CA 94549
(415) 283-7793

Art Director:
Diane Goldsmith

Artist Representative:
Deborah Akers

We at SQUARE MOON are expert in matching the unique talents of illustrators to the spirit of the text. For years, as a design studio producing books for children, we have created the moment when all the verbal and graphic elements come together to communicate the special essence of a story.

SQUARE MOON represents: Ellen Beier, Cindy Brodie, Pat Hoggan, Roberta Holmes-Landers, Mas Miyamoto, Terra Muzick, Cindy Salans-Rosenheim, Doug Roy, Jeff Severn, and Stan Tusan.

Clients include: Macmillan, Harcourt Brace Jovanovich, Houghton Mifflin, McGraw-Hill, Ginn, Scribner's, and Dutton.

Ed Little

Ed Little
8 Buttonball Drive
Newtown, CT 06482
(203) 270-1098

Member Graphic Artists Guild

I work in combinations of graphite, color pencil, gouache and oil, creating illustrations that are characterized by close attention to detail, strong design and produced on time!

My work has been used on magazine covers, for general editorial, annual reports, food packaging, point of sale displays and advertising.

Some of my clients include American Cyanamid, American Express, BBDO, Best Foods, Control Data, *Golf Digest/ Tennis Inc.*, IBM, Max Factor, MBI, Medical Economics Group, Nabisco, Ogilvy & Mather, Olin, *Reader's Digest*, Scholastic, UPS.

I look forward to working with you and the opportunity to show you my portfolio.

John Monteleone

John Monteleone
127 Hunnewell Avenue
Elmont, NY 11033
(516) 437-1879

Member Graphic Artists Guild

Society of Illustrators 30th Annual Exhibition

Bill Andrews

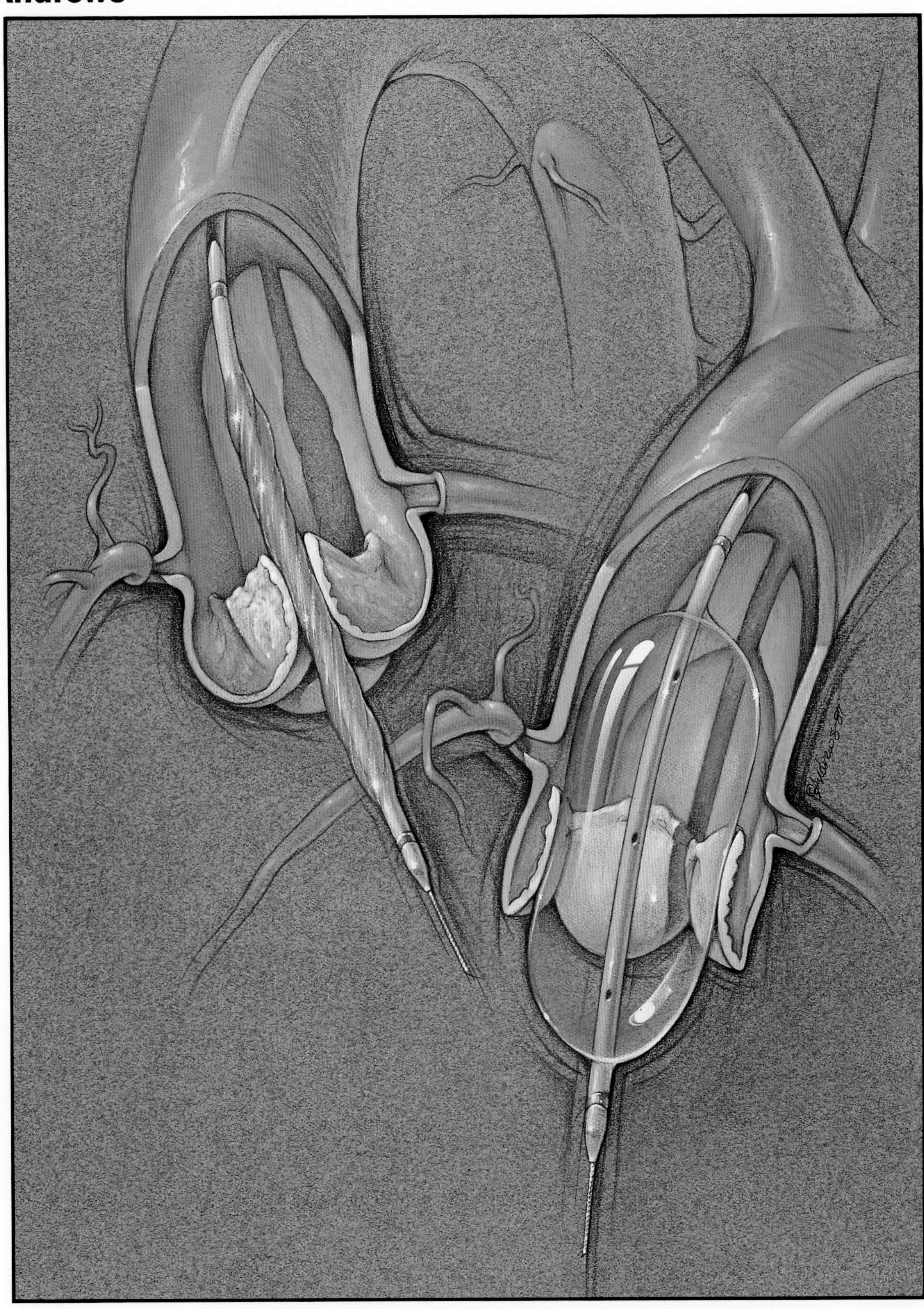

Bill Andrews
Bill Andrews & Associates, Inc.
1709 Dryden Road, Suite 709
Houston, TX 77030
(713) 791-4924

Specializing in high-touch illustrations of high-tech medicine for advertising and editorialuse. Areas of special expertise include the heart, blood vessels, and nervous system.

Eight years of experience as a medical illustrator since receipt of Master of Arts in Biomedical Communications. Studio located in the Texas Medical Center, a world-renowned multi-institutional campus for medical research, education, and healthcare delivery.

Selected Awards: Gold Medal from Society of Illustrators Los Angeles in '87, Silver Medals from the Societies of Illustrators Los Angeles and Houston in '86. Selected Awards from the Association of Medical Illustrators: Russell Drake Award in '83, '84 & '85; Best Illustrated Medical Book Award in '85 & '86; Will Shepard Award in '87; Best of Show in '87.

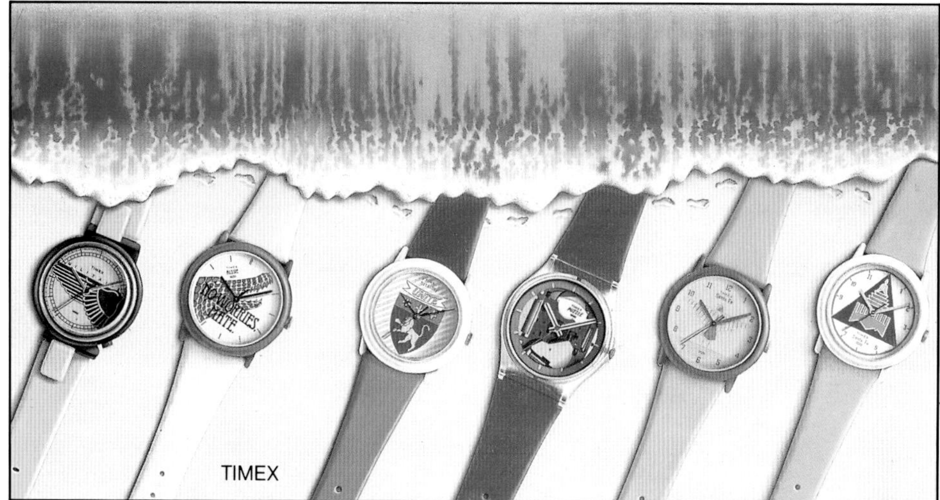

TIMEX

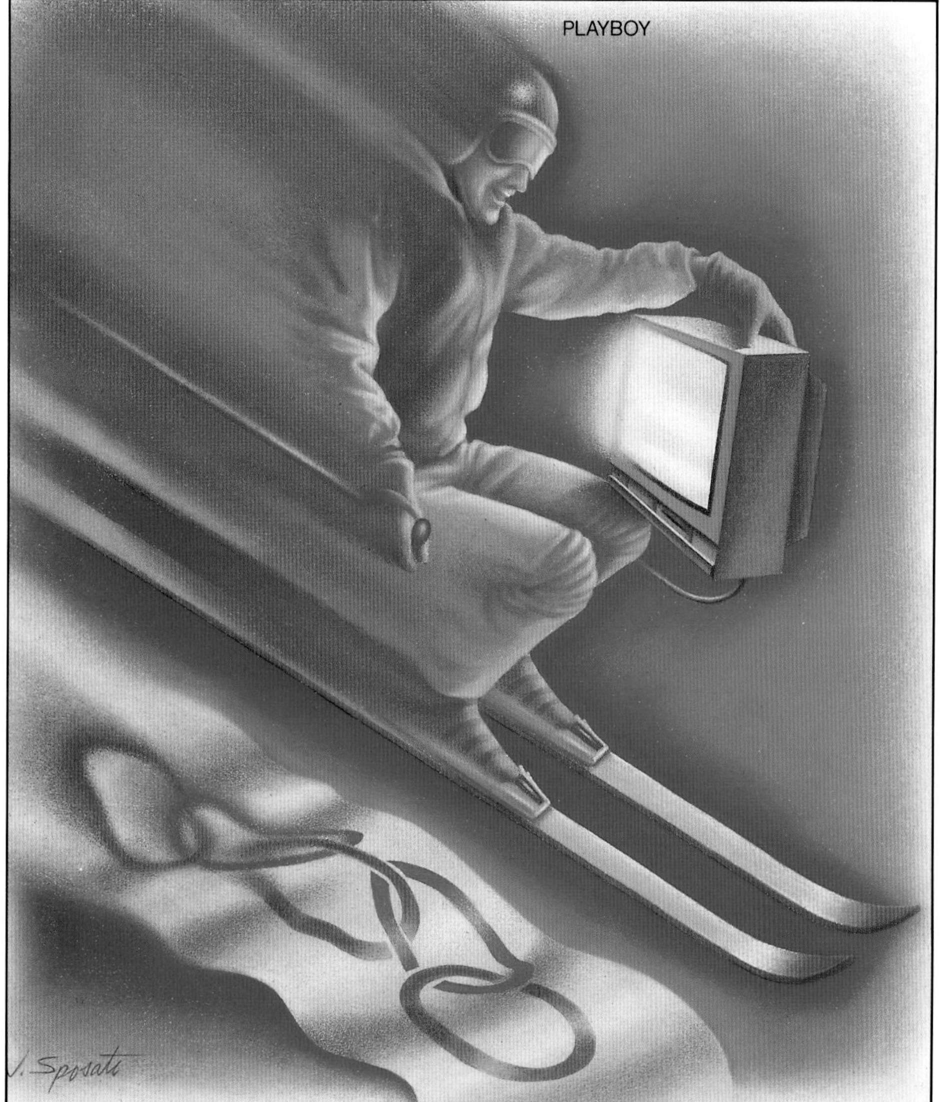

PLAYBOY

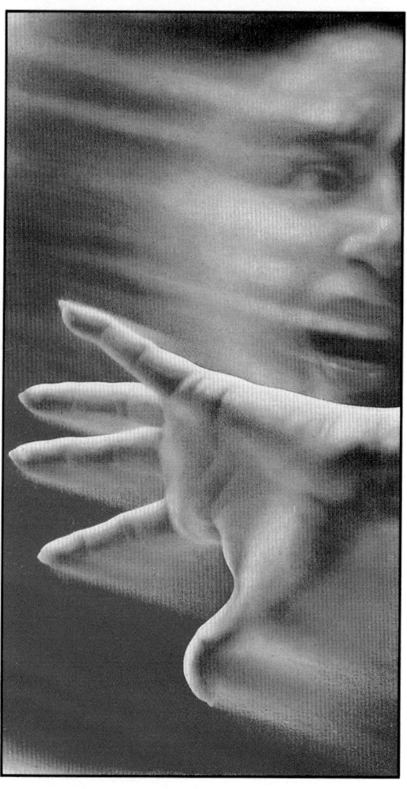

John Sposato
43 East 22nd Street
New York, NY 10010
(212) 477 3909

ILLUSTRATIONS IN OIL PASTEL

Clients:

Coca-Cola, Sony, Gulf + Western, Timex, Nabisco, Calvert Distillers, Strathmore Paper, Winston-Salem, *Playboy, Esquire, Newsweek, New York* magazine, Massachusetts Lottery, Paramount Pictures, HBO, NBC, Random House, Simon & Schuster, Warner Books.

Awards:

Society of Illustrators 18, 19, 21, 26, 29, 30
Art Directors Club Annual '85, '86, '87, '88
Graphis Annual, Graphis Posters, American Institute of Graphic Arts, *CA Annual,* Advertising Club of New York (Andy Awards)

Member:

AIGA, Graphic Artists Guild

Doreen Gayer

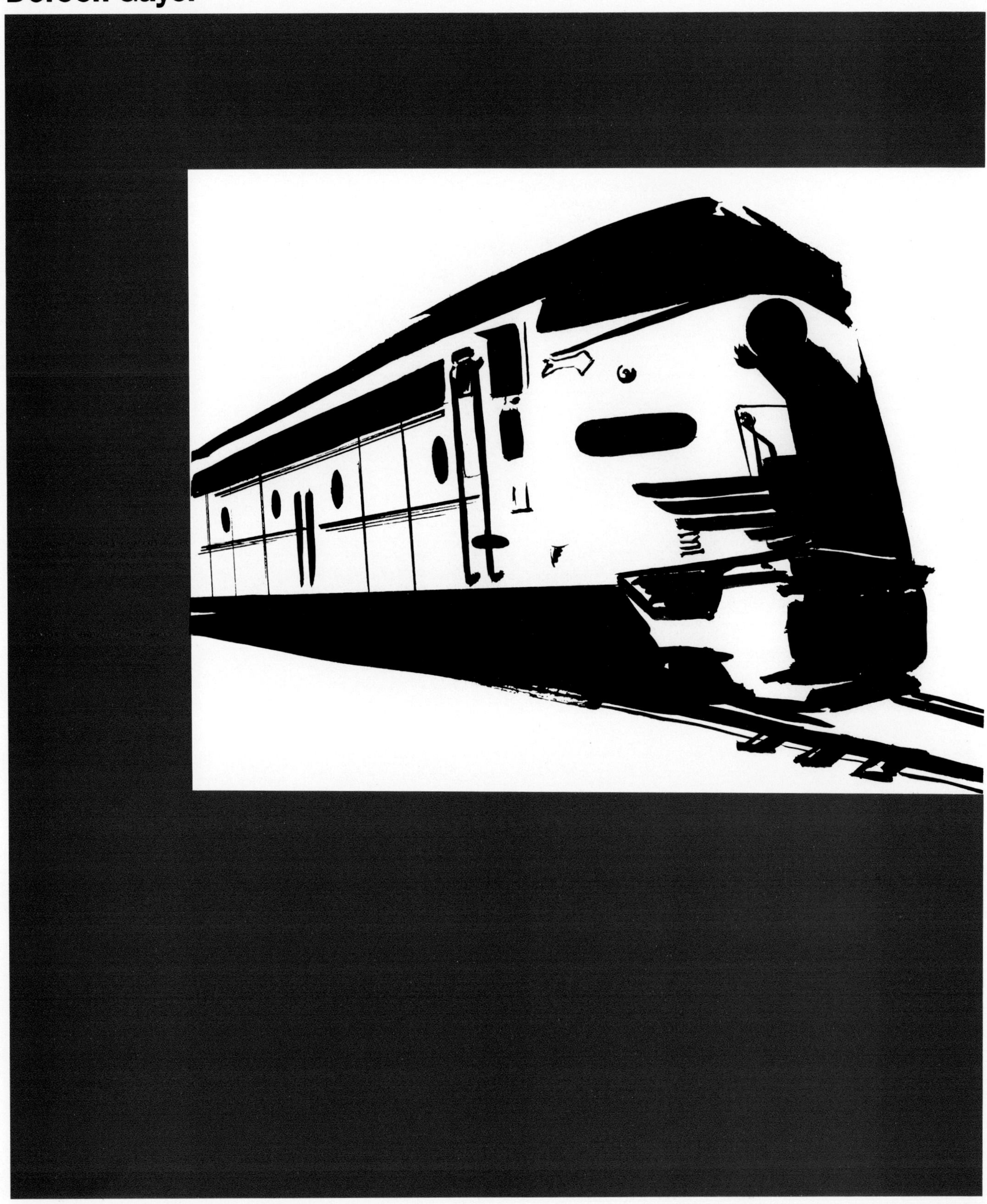

Doreen Gayer
2 Hine Place
New Haven, CT 06511
(203) 562-3716

Clients:
Media Images Greeting Card Company
Incas Records
Theatricide
Studio One
Sero Shirtmakers
Kenny Lloyd Productions
R. Hewlett Incorporated
Bonnie & Clyde
New Haven Advocate

Corporate Advertisers

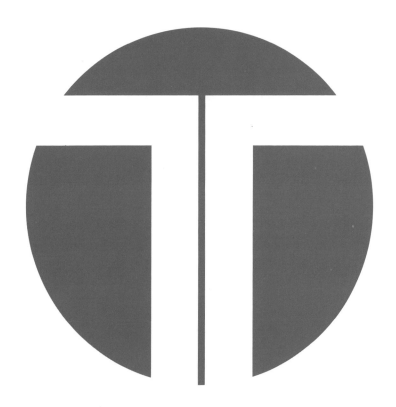

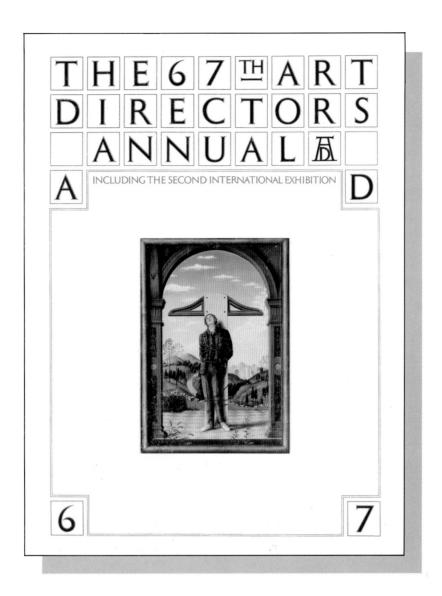

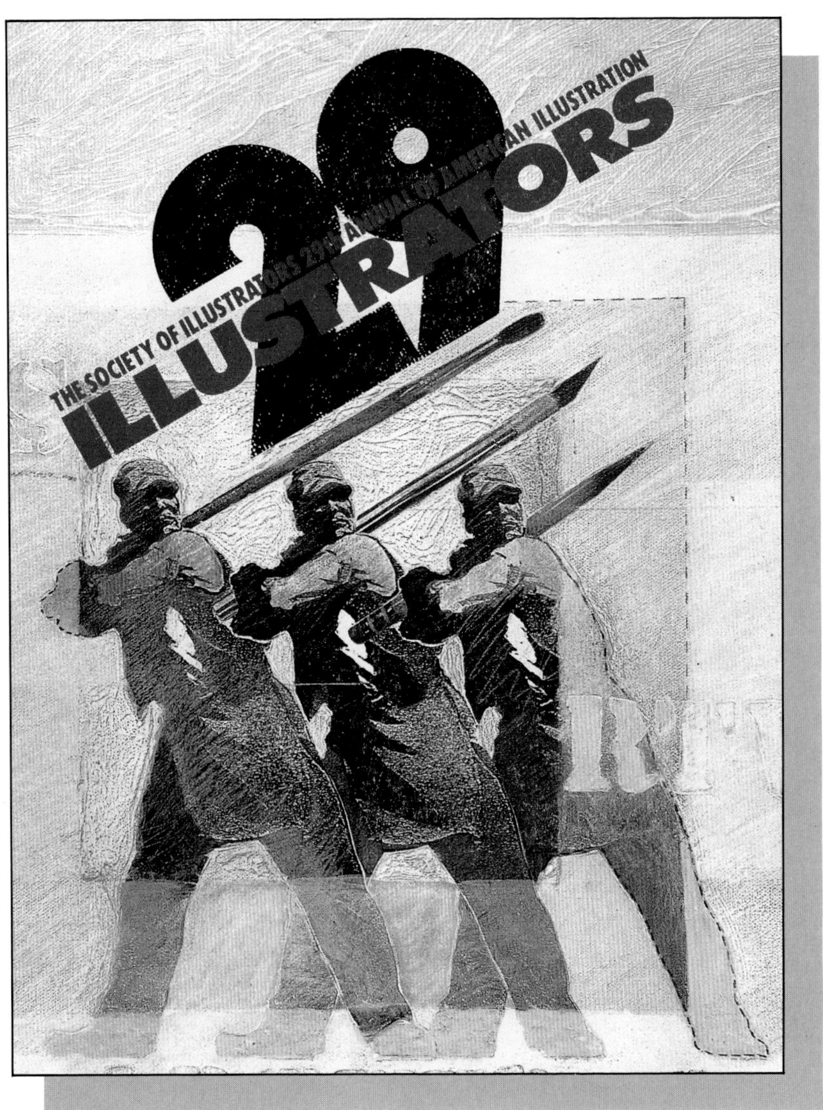
29
THE SOCIETY OF ILLUSTRATORS 29th ANNUAL OF AMERICAN ILLUSTRATION
ILLUSTRATORS

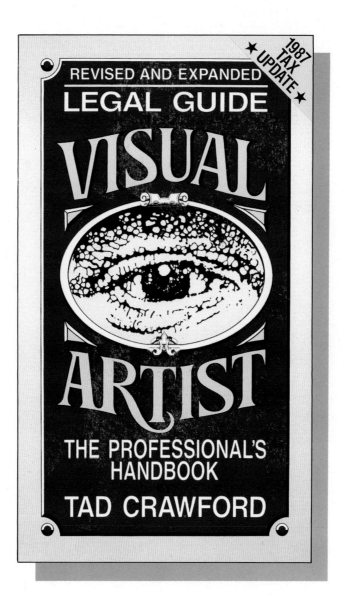

Indexes

Index Of Artists

Index Of Artists

Index Of Artists

Index Of Artists

Index Of Artists

Easy Access Index

All artists in Directory 5 do work which would fall into the Advertising and Editorial categories. The following listings reflect the subjects shown on the artists' pages, and do not necessarily demonstrate the full range of their skills.

Adventure

Animals

Animation

Architectural

Easy Access Index

Easy Access Index

Children's Books and Products

Collage

Fashion and Cosmetics

Food

Graphic Design and Lettering

Easy Access Index

Easy Access Index

Easy Access Index

GRAPHIC ARTISTS GUILD